THE LIFE
AND DEATH
OF THE COLD WAR:

SELECTED STUDIES
IN POSTWAR
STATECRAFT

Morton A. Kaplan

THE LIFE
AND DEATH
OF THE COLD WAR:

SELECTED STUDIES
IN POSTWAR
STATECRAFT

Nelson
Hall
Chicago

Library of Congress in Publication Data

Kaplan, Morton A
  The life and death of the cold war.

  Includes index.
  1. World politics—1945—   I. Title.
D842.5.K36   327′.09′044   76-20539
ISBN 0-88229-335-4

CONTENTS

Preface

During the academic year 1954–55, while preparing the first draft of the Brookings Institution book *United States Foreign Policy: 1945–1955,* I also wrote several more detailed studies of critical episodes in the birth and stabilization of Cold War politics. In 1956, while at the Center for Advanced Studies in the Behavioral Sciences at Palo Alto, I produced, with minor editorial changes, a multilith edition of these studies for use in my foreign policy course at the University of Chicago.

It had been my intention to engage in further research on the period, to footnote these studies more extensively and to publish them. However, other books intervened, including *System and Process in International Politics* (1957) and *The Political Foundations of International Law* (1961). Eventually, although students who used the materials and scholars from other institutions who asked for them on interlibrary loan urged me to publish, I never found the time to do the additional research that seemed necessary.

Recently, however, I reread the manuscript and now see merit in publishing these studies as they were originally written because certain significant observations about foreign policy can be made more easily if I follow this course.

I am at one disadvantage. Had I published this material in 1955, even without additional research, I would have put it through several revisions. Yet, if I revise the original draft now, readers may infer that I have retrospectively changed my interpretations.

Therefore, I will live with some infelicitous judgments that I might have changed even in 1955. But I gain the advantage of showing that contemporary historians have been creating a myth about the views that were held during the height of the Cold War—a myth at least as simplistic as that with which they charge others. However, I have added some identifications my editor has requested.

Two chapters have been added to the original manuscript. Chapter VIII, "United States Foreign Policy in a Revolutionary Age," written in late 1960, was intended for my friends in the Kennedy administration, in the hope that it might influence their foreign policy judgments. Also included is a more recent (1975) manuscript, Chapter IX, entitled "American World Strategy and the Mediterranean Basin," intended as a prospectus for the international system that is now emerging from the death of the Cold War.

Chapter I, "Interpretations of Soviet Policy," surveys American views of the Soviet Union from the prewar to the early Cold War period, and shows—revisionist historians to the contrary notwithstanding—that the American leadership arrived at its Cold War position reluctantly and with reservations. Moreover, although the Marshall Plan was not the focus of any of my studies, it will be clear from evidence in this and Chapter II, "The Great Deterrent," that the main purpose of the Marshall Plan was political and that it was intended to stabilize Western Europe. Revisionists often attempt to justify their economic interpretations of the Marshall Plan by quoting administration spokesmen who asserted its advantages for American business. Such comments are misleading for— apart from the fact that the United States did have some legitimate interests in international commerce—economic arguments used by Marshall Plan supporters were intended primarily to gain the support of a business-oriented, conservative Congress. Even so, they were ineffective, and it was their failure that led the Truman administration to mount the barrage of propaganda about an imminent Soviet attack—a barrage that eventually colored its own perception of the world.

Chapter II is useful for several reasons. It undermines, to some extent at least, the myth that atomic weapons deterred the Soviet Union in the postwar period. It also casts serious doubts on the "realism" of American proposals for controlling atomic weapons, for there likely was no plan that simultaneously satisfied the security interests of the United States and the Soviet Union. Many well-intentioned plans, of which the nuclear nonproliferation treaty is one example, fail to take into account adequately the realities of the world in which they are intended to be implemented.

Chapter III, "The China Debacle," shows the extent to which American policy was immobilized by suspicions aroused by lack of candor on the part of Dean Acheson, an otherwise distinguished statesman. Except for the fact that the intellectual establishment supported the Democratic administration in the case of China, it would be easier to recognize a parallel in the collapse of policy following the Vietnamese War.

The chapter on China should help dispel what I consider the simplistic views of Chiang. Chiang Kai-shek did not lose the civil war because of simple-minded stupidity. He was caught in a trap created by the war and exacerbated by his narrow political and social base and by the political necessity that he establish himself as the leader of a unified China.

The discussion of Yugoslavia in Chapter IV casts significant doubt on Senator J. William Fulbright's thesis that the way to lure countries away from the Soviet bloc is to act in a friendly fashion. One may wonder about the rationality of American policy toward Yugoslavia before it left the Soviet bloc, but there can be no doubt that Yugoslavia broke away at a time when American pressure against it was greater than it was against the Soviet Union.

Chapter V, on the Czechoslovak coup, is presented in its original and less sophisticated form, not in the later version published in 1961. It casts doubt on standard Cold War interpretations of Soviet policy and employs what I regard as a sounder framework of political analysis than that used either by Cold War or revisionist historians.

Chapter VI, "The Korean War," casts further light on the China problem. Neither the Democratic administration nor John Foster Dulles saw the Communist bloc as monolithic, although at one point during the war in Korea, Dean Acheson professed to see Chinese policy as a projection of Russian policy. The myth of a monolithic bloc in its paradigmatic form was a postwar invention by academics. The reader will note that this study mentions the possibility of a split between China and the Soviet Union in 1950. However, this does not justify the views now being spread by self-interested Far East experts that the United States might have reached an accommodation with the Chinese Communists as early as 1949. Surely American policy might have been pursued in a far more sensible manner than it was. It does not do justice to Mao's revolutionary idealism to interpret, as some historians do, his possible willingness to accept loans from the United States as evidence that he would have supported American policy against Russia in 1950.

The more interesting question is why China was unable to respond to the overtures in Richard Nixon's *Foreign Affairs* article, published in October 1967 during the early stages of his campaign for the presidential nomination, until the "ping-pong" diplomacy of 1971 and despite the Soviet nuclear threats of 1969. Democratic Senator Gale McGee of Wyoming has speculated, presumably on the basis of inside information, that the Soviet Union was again considering a nuclear attack on China in 1971. But there is less information to support this hypothesis than there was concerning the far more public Russian nuclear threats against China in 1969, including inquiries to the Nixon administration concerning its possible response to such an attack. One infers, among other reasons, that an accommodation with the United States imposed a severe ideological strain on the Chinese—a strain they were not willing to resolve for a considerable period of time. Indeed, even Yugoslavia, which was under a more serious Soviet threat in 1948, did not make an accommodation with the United States until several months after the formal break with the Soviet Union. The reader will see from Chapter IV, "The Rise of Titoism," that this decision was far from easy for the Yugoslav leadership.

Chapter VI, on Korea, will show how United States policy officials jumped to certain conclusions at the start of the Korean War, how the United States misused the United Nations, and how that misuse made it more difficult to follow a sensible policy there. Third World nations have merely copied us in their misuse of the United Nations, and it might have cleared the air to acknowledge this when we protested these later misuses of that organization. This chapter will also show how public opinion helped to produce, although it fails to explain, the faulty judgments the United States made at the thirty-eighth parallel and at the narrow waist of Korea.

Korea holds an important lesson for us in another respect. Dean Rusk played a crucial part in the miscalculations made during the Korean War. He was among those who were convinced that the Chinese would not intervene if the United States crossed the thirty-eighth parallel. Having been proved wrong in Korea, he "learned" his lesson and was persuaded that China was behind the South Vietnamese War and that it would intervene if the United States moved against the North.

Unfortunately, Dean Rusk must not have read Edgar Snow's 1965 interview with Mao Tse-tung in which he made it clear that if China ever fought the United States, it would only do so after an American attack. Santayana was no doubt correct when he stated that those who do not learn the lessons of history are condemned to repeat them. Unfortunately, people are more likely to learn the wrong lessons from history and to make mistakes that might have been avoided if they had ignored them.

Chapter VII, "The Big Scare," on German rearmament, shows how the United States pursued the right problem at the wrong time and in the wrong way. The chapter was prescient in pointing out that we were misleading the Germans in talking about German unification, but the doubts expressed about an eventual German contribution to NATO read poorly today.

Chapter VIII, "United States Foreign Policy in a Revolutionary Age," the first of the two chapters that are not part of the original manuscript, was written in 1961 and emphasized the need to design a foreign policy that would command sufficient public support, both in this country and abroad, for successful implementation. Despite my strong support for adequate military preparations, it points out the relevance of relinquishing apparent military assets, such as bases in Spain, that committed us to authoritarian regimes, or the bases in Japan, that could not be used if they were needed and that constituted a political liability for the Japanese government.

On the other hand, concessions should be made from strength and not from weakness. It is one thing to retreat from foreign bases while one's world posture is high and another thing to be forced out of them when one's world posture is low. We would have been far better off, for instance, if we had agreed with the Thai government to the eventual withdrawal of American bases before the loss of South Vietnam.

Despite my many friends in the Kennedy administration, they rejected both my public and my private advice, particularly with respect to Vietnam. It was essential, as I urged them privately, either to get out while the commitment was small or to do the job right, but never to engage in a series of small escalations that could only produce a debacle.

I have one further comment on the Kennedy administration. It marked the wholesale introduction of intellectuals into government. Although they shared many of the defects of the Truman foreign policy team, they shared few of its virtues. Acheson was arrogant, narrow of vision, and unresponsive to changed features in the world. However, Dean Acheson, Will Clayton, Paul Nitze, General George Marshall, and others did design a program for implementing foreign policy that shored up the West politically and economically and minimized Communist expansion elsewhere.

The Kennedy and the Nixon teams neither consolidated nor expanded that structure. They proved incapable of responding to important changes in the character of world affairs. That is the topic of the last chapter, "American World Strategy and the Mediterranean Basin." With the end of the Cold War, we need to design, with the help of other nations, a new type of international system. If we do not engage in this task effectively, others will engage in it, and to our disadvantage.

I

Interpretations
of Soviet Policy
(1954)

War Interpretations of Soviet Policy

Although Immanuel Kant proclaimed that his reading of David Hume awakened him from his "dogmatic slumber," very few individuals are able to reverse their attitudes and opinions suddenly. People resist change. And, unfortunately, most individuals can hold inconsistent opinions simultaneously. The same is true with government policies. There seems to be a law of inertia that states that it takes more energy to change policy than to continue it. Over a period of time different ideas eventually provoke a changed policy, but this is neither an easy process to formulate nor to describe.

With hindsight fortified by the experience of the last decade, it is clear that the conduct of American foreign policy has hinged upon American interpretations of Russian intentions, motivations, and capabilities. In 1945, there seemed to be one rather than two worlds. In reinterpreting what happened and how it happened, we have to examine the behavior of individuals, not all of whom saw the problem as we now see it; and, of those who saw the problem as we now see it, few worked out the premises of their reasoning, and even fewer related their prescriptions for action consistently to their premises.

Politicians are practical rather than theoretical people, and as such they seek practical solutions to problems. If politics is the art of compromise—as some claim—it is little wonder that politicians tend to reject rigorous and schematic interpretations of the international situation.

1

Interpretations During the Nazi-Soviet Pact

During the period of the Nazi-Soviet pact (August 1939–June 1941), the Soviet Union was quite unpopular in the United States. Since no objective of American policy seemed to require cooperation with the Soviets, the Soviet attack upon Finland could safely be viewed as an example of totalitarian treachery and oriental cunning. No American politician of the stature of David Lloyd George had the subtlety or felt the political need to relate that attack to Soviet political objectives and security needs or to see that it was directed against the potential German threat.

Later Interpretations

When Germany attacked the Soviet Union in 1941, the Soviet Union became a bulwark of Western defense. Since Americans have generally been too moralistic in their foreign policy to accept the dictum of Winston Churchill—that one should cooperate with the devil if it is to his advantage—there was a strong compulsion to reassess Soviet intentions. However, the United States was not yet in the war, and opinion toward the Soviets still was not generally favorable. The Roosevelt Administration was fearful that Catholic, right wing, and pro-fascist elements would prevent a program of aid to the Soviets. The necessity of overcoming this hostility also facilitated a reassessment of Soviet intentions.

After the United States entered the war, it was only natural that the heroic Soviet defense against Adolph Hitler's legions would inspire sympathy and admiration. The Soviet refusal to permit American or British observers on their war fronts and their refusal to allow American planes to fly over Russian territory, even to deliver Lend-Lease supplies, were regarded as remnants of defensive attitudes that had developed when the West aided the counterrevolutionary White Russian armies against the Communists in the period from 1918 to 1920.

Rather blunt demands for more U.S. aid were ascribed to the difficult military situation in Russia and the tremendous Russian losses in men, materiel, and territory at a time when the Western powers were engaging in limited combat only.

In governmental circles, which considered the problems of building a postwar order that required Soviet cooperation, interpretations of this order were psychologically even more compelling. Moreover, the conduct of the war required some degree of Allied unity. The experiences arising from the practical necessities of cooperation with the Soviets facilitated habits of thought and action that were based upon it.

Events in the Soviet Union Affecting Interpretations

In order to rally the people behind the Soviet military effort, Josef Stalin had resurrected the bourgeois "virtues." His public statements contained references to God; considerably greater freedom was given to religious practice in the Soviet Union. Atheistic propaganda was soft-pedaled. Peter the Great and Alexander Nevsky suddenly were regarded as heroes. The term "Russia" came back into official use. The war was referred to as "The Great Patriotic War." The Comintern was abolished, and the Communist parties abroad entered United Front movements in which they played down radical and revolutionary aims.

Range of Interpretation

Many Americans began to distinguish between Trotsky's brand of Communism and Stalin's. Leon Trotsky was a violent revolutionary with whom one could reach no agreements; but Stalin was primarily a Russian nationalist, not an overly dedicated Communist. At worst, he was interested in Communism "in one country." Stalin was a conservative at heart and, if his appetite was a bit large, it could still be satisfied.

Others began to assert that Russia was an economic democracy but was authoritarian politically. The United States, on the other hand, was a political democracy, but its economic system was authoritarian. Under pressure of war, however, Russia's political system was becoming more democratic and the economic system of the United States was becoming more democratic. The two countries really had systems which were converging.[1]

Still others saw signs of emerging capitalism in the Soviet Union. If Nikolai Lenin was able to adopt the New Economic Policy, in which capitalistic measures temporarily were encouraged, Stalin would eventually come to a more reasonable position also.

General Douglas MacArthur publicly stated that the "extraordinary achievements of the Red Army represent . . . the most magnificent war efforts the world has yet seen." He prayed to God for Russian victory. Many others of conservative bent were equally enthusiastic.

This viewpoint was not unanimous. Many Republicans and Democrats retained suspicions of the Bolsheviks. This skepticism, however, did not have important consequences during the war period. It was generally not asserted loudly and it had little effect upon the conduct of foreign policy. Moreover, a suspicious attitude tended to be unpopular at that time.

Many of those who were suspicious of the Soviet Union were considered part of the lunatic fringe. Some asserted that President Franklin Roosevelt deliberately allowed the American navy to be sunk at Pearl Harbor in order to force the United States into war. Many others had connections with native fascist movements or were notoriously sympathetic to the Axis powers. Gerald L. K. Smith asserted that the war was nothing but a Jewish-Bolshevik conspiracy to dilute the purity of the white race.

The Socialists—both those who favored and opposed American participation in the war—were skeptical concerning Soviet intentions and warned of "tactical shifts in Soviet policy." However, the Socialist movement in the United States was weak and had few organs of communication. Many ex-Communists also took this position, but they were not a significant political force either.

Toward the close of the war, doubts also began to develop in administration quarters. By May of 1945, U.S. State Department Joseph Grew stated in a memo he read to Charles E. "Chip" Bohlen and Averill Harriman, "A future war with the Soviet Union is as certain as anything in this world can be certain." Later he added "unless we recognize the danger and take steps to meet it in time."[2]

As 1945 progressed, more figures in the administration began to entertain doubts about Russian objectives and policies. Yet few were ready to challenge the objective of Allied unity. And at no time did official American policy give the public any reason to believe the Russians were not proper democrats, who would cooperate in building a sound postwar order. Toward the end of 1945, American policy seemed to be searching for ways to obtain unity and also to protect American interests in the event of a failure

Immediate Postwar Interpretation

Soviet political maneuvers in Eastern Europe after the war were still being interpreted as possible security moves, but this interpretation was no longer invested with much confidence. Secretary of State James Byrnes' offer of a twenty-five-year security treaty against renewed German aggression was an attempt to test this hypothesis by offering the Soviet Union a "guarantee" of American aid in case Germany should again engage in aggression. Of course, the Byrnes' offer tested this hypothesis only on the assumption that the Soviet Union would place as much reliance in a treaty as it did in physical possession of territory, manpower, and productive capacity.[3]

Coincidentally, the American occupation of Japan was a hedge against the breakdown of cooperation. The United States was protecting itself in the event that a hostile Communist empire would gain control of the Asian mainland. In these circumstances, control of South Korea, the Japanese islands, Okinawa, the Marianas, the Jimas, the Philippines, and possibly Formosa, would act as a counterweight to Chinese power and seal it off from the sea routes of communication.

The Postwar Soviet Pattern

Late in 1945 and early 1946, a series of Soviet and Communist actions demonstrated the seriousness of the situation for the Western powers. In December 1945, "democratic" elements in Azerbaijan Province, Iran, rose in revolt against the authority of the central government. Soviet troops prevented new government forces from entering the area and quelling the revolt. Early in 1946, the matter came before the United Nations, and the Soviet obstruction was a bitter issue. The United States was concerned for two reasons. The Soviet Union was apparently using its army to sponsor a revolution in a friendly country, and it was doing this at a time when Allied agreements specified that occupation forces should be removed from Iran. This was a serious violation of the principles of the United Nations, and it could not be justified on security grounds since the Soviet Union had never been invaded from the south.[4]

The second reason was strategic. If the Iranian government were denied Western support in this crisis, it might easily be taken over by the Soviet Union. One could then expect the Arab countries in that area to go over like a row of tenpins. In the process, Turkey's military position would become untenable, the Soviets would gain control of the largest oil reserves in the world, and the entire military and strategic situation in the Near East, Africa, and the Mediterranean would be changed to the disadvantage of the West.[5]

Greece, which was flanked on three sides by Communist regimes, was undergoing a civil war, with veterans of the Communist guerrilla forces (ELAS) infiltrating back into the country from havens in Yugoslavia, Bulgaria, and Albania. It seemed as though the Soviet Union was reneging on the Greek agreement. The accession of Greece to the Soviet sphere would turn the Eastern Mediterranean into a Soviet lake.

Albania was interfering with British naval vessels in the straits off Corfu. Yugoslavia was behaving in a quite belligerent fashion. It charged that American army transport planes had violated Yugoslav territory 176 times and demanded an end to these incidents. On August 9, an army transport was forced down by Yugoslav planes. On August 19th, another army plane was shot down and five Americans were killed.

Friction between the West and the Soviet bloc was apparent in United Nations meetings, meetings of the Council of Foreign Ministers, and the Paris Peace Conference. Andrei Gromyko staged a walk-out on Security Council meetings during the Iranian dispute. At Paris, Molotov accused the West of forming a bloc against the Soviet Union.

It was clear that the West and the Soviet Union had been pursuing divergent objectives, but that the divergence had escaped notice because of the war effort. Whatever the ultimate objectives of the Soviets and the West might have been, winning the war was necessary and took precedence over longer-range objectives. Evidently, the Soviets and the Western nations desired quite different postwar worlds, and these differences were revealed as their respective postwar policies unfolded.

The Moderate Interpretation

The West, however, still believed that Soviet objectives were limited. Top policy-makers, on the whole, were not yet citing the statements of Bolshevik leaders in the early 1920s, of which the following is an example:

> We should make it plain in our programme that every proletarian state has the right of Red intervention.... In the *Communist Manifesto* we were told that the proletariat should conquer the whole world. Now this could not be done with bare hands. [laughter] This has to be done with bayonets and rifles.[6]

Western leaders continued to view the Soviet Union as an expansionistic and nationalistic, rather than as a revolutionary state. In a speech of February 27, 1946, Senator Arthur Vandenberg, the distinguished leader of the Republicans in the field of foreign policy, asked, "What is Russia up to now? We ask it in Manchuria. We ask it in Eastern Europe and the Dardanelles.... We ask it in Iran ... in Tripolitania ... in the Baltic and the Balkans ... in Poland ... in the capital of Canada ... in Japan ... and sometimes even in connection with events in our own United States.... It would be entirely futile to blink the fact that two great rival ideologies ... find themselves face to face with the desperate need for mutual understanding in finding common ground to strive for peace for both."

Vandenberg did not consider Russia's ideology to be militantly revolutionary, however, for he asserted his "own belief that we can live together in reasonable harmony if the United States speaks as plainly upon all occasions..." as the Soviet Union. He associated himself with the statement of General Walter Bedell Smith, the new Ambassador to the Soviet Union, "It is imperative that our national temperatures remain at normal...; both nations want nothing so much as peace and security."

Senator J. William Fulbright, Arkansas Democrat, echoed President Truman's statement that the United States must make the United Nations the cornerstone of its policy. In a speech on March 5, 1946, Fulbright viewed Vandenberg's speech to the Senate as a "tactful but firm warning not to go too far in the expansion of her [Russian] power over neighboring states." Nevertheless, he continued to view the present system of power relationships as a necessary one. According to Fulbright,

> These power relationships cannot be substantially altered by the unilateral action of any one great state without profoundly disturbing the whole structure of the United Nations.... I am in agreement with Senator Vandenberg and Secretary Byrnes that the world's best hope is in making the UNO work.

Although Senator Fulbright thought that the Soviet Union was endangering the balanced structure of the great powers, his solution was to restore that structure in concert with the Soviet Union. Byrnes, Vandenberg, and Fulbright were in agreement that Russia must be induced to play the game the American way; apparently they never thought that the United States should begin to play a different game.

Churchill at Fulton, Missouri

On the very same day that Senator Fulbright spoke, Winston Churchill, ex–Prime Minister of Great Britain, delivered the commencement address at Westminster College in Fulton, Missouri. President Harry Truman was a conspicuous figure on the platform. Churchill proclaimed, "The old doctrine of the balance of power is unsound. We cannot afford ... to work on narrow margins, offering temptations to a trial of strength."

"Our supreme objective," he said, "is to guard the homes of the common people from another war.... It is nothing less than the safety and the welfare, the freedom and the progress of all the homes and families of all the men and women in all the lands." This safety and welfare were in danger then from war and from Russian tyranny. "Nobody knows what Soviet Russia and its Communist International intend to do... what are the limits, if any, to their expansive and proselytizing tactics. ...We welcome Russia to her rightful place among the nations of the world.... But it is my duty... to place before you certain facts about the present position in Europe. . . . From Stettin in the Baltic to Trieste in the Adriatic, an *iron curtain* [italics supplied] has descended across the continent. . . . Athens alone . . . is free to decide its future at an election under British, American, and French observation." The Russian Communist party had been placed in controlling positions in the satellite countries. They were attempting to build up the Communist party in their zone of Germany. "Turkey and Persia are both profoundly alarmed . . . at the claims which are made upon them and at the pressure being exerted by the Moscow government."

The Communist parties were strong threats to democratic governments in France and Italy. This "is not the liberated Europe we sought to build up. Nor is it one which contains the essentials of permanent peace. The safety of the world . . . requires a new unity in Europe from which no nation should be permanently outcast." Churchill, at this point, was appealing both to the Americans who would be appalled by remarks critical of the Soviet Union and to the Russians who were being assured that there was a place for them in the new Europe if only they would take it.

"I do not believe that Soviet Russia desires war. What they desire is the fruits of war and the indefinite expansion of their power and doctrines. . . . Our difficulties and dangers will not be removed by shutting our eyes to them. . . . From what I have seen of our Russian friends and allies during the war, I am convinced that there is nothing they admire so much as strength, and nothing for which they have less respect than for military weakness." The situation can be saved, he said, but if we "become divided or falter in our duty, and if these all-important years are allowed to slip away, then indeed catastrophe may overwhelm us all."

To save the situation, Churchill proposed an Anglo-American bloc within and without the United Nations, which would be related to the principles and goals of that organization. "Neither the sure prevention of war, nor the continuous rise of world organization will be gained without . . . a special relationship between the British Commonwealth and Empire and the United States . . . including the continuance of the intimate relationships between our military advisers, leading to common study of potential dangers, similarity of weapons and manuals of instruction, and interchange of officers and cadets at colleges. It should carry with it the continuance of the present facilities for mutual security by the joint use of all naval and air force bases in the possession of either country all over the world."

In retrospect, Churchill's analysis and proposals seem mild. At the time, he was challenging the central thesis that the United Nations must operate within the unity of the great powers. Although the United States was willing to challenge this policy on single issues, as in the case of Iran, the public at large and most members of the Congress were not willing to challenge it in general. Churchill had stirred a hornet's nest. Press comment was largely unfavorable.

Reaction to Churchill

Few went to the lengths of *New York Daily News* analyst John O'Donnell, who wrote: "...so,—hold your hats boys—we're off again, hell-bent for a nice rough and tumble with all the 1938–1939 build-up by which Roosevelt and Churchill suckered their nations into war against Germany for strictly economic and cash ends...while dishing out the tawdry...argument about a crusade for humanity...."[7]

Lowell Mellett wrote in the *Washington Star*, "No surer way of bringing ourselves—and the British—into a head-on clash with Russia could be devised." The *New York Herald Tribune* editorialized that the speech miscarried. The *Chicago Daily News*[8] proclaimed that alliances were not the American way, that we needed to allay the fears besetting the United States and the Soviet Union, that we should not feed those fears. In her column in the *New York World Telegram*, Eleanor Roosevelt protested that Churchill was asking for a return to power politics. The noted columnist, Max Lerner, stated that Russian aims were limited and that Churchill's proposal was out of proportion to the need.

Veteran Democratic Congressman Sabath of Illinois complained that Churchill's proposals would demolish the new foundations of the United Nations, destroy the unity of the great powers, and lead Americans to repudiate the advice of George Washington who so strongly warned against entangling alliances. "It is gratifying to all honest-to-God Americans that American newspapers were not misled by the shrewd efforts of...Churchill...to inveigle America into saving England's tottering empire...."

Democratic Representative Ellis Patterson of California shouted that it "is incredible to me that the Tory representative from Great Britain used the heart of the United States as a platform for the reactionary proposal to set up one power with another, with only one possible objective: creating a bloc against a third power. History has proved the insanity of this."

Democratic Representative Thad F. Wasielewski of Wisconsin defended Churchill, but he represented the Polish bloc that had been disaffected by the Yalta agreements on Poland. One hundred and two members of the British Parliament signed a petition criticizing Churchill's speech as inimical to world peace. Democratic Representative Louis Ludlow of Indiana wrote to Prime Minister Clement Attlee to discover whether or not Churchill's effort represented the policy of Great Britain. Attlee, cognizant of tempers in both countries and of the adverse effects the speech might have on a proposed American loan to Great Britain, accurately replied that Churchill spoke as a private citizen and that he did so without the consent or approval of the government.

On March 15, the Hearst newspapers syndicated correspondent, H. R. Knickerbocker, concluded: "Mr. Churchill's speech was called a 'trial balloon.' It was, and the result has been everything that Stalin could hope for. The reaction of Washington—the reaction of Congress to Mr. Churchill's speech was so negative that we may take it as almost certain that this played an important role in the orders Stalin gave to his Red Army to march on Iran."[9]

The Practical Approach

Although such important public figures as Republican Governor Thomas Dewey of New York supported an Anglo-American alliance, the project did not generate much support at that time. Such a conservative figure as Republican Representative (later Senator) Karl Mundt from South Dakota thought that negotiations between the Americans and Russians would proceed much better if the United States did not act in concert with the British. "... we should ... arrange soon a conference between the Big Two. Why ... ? Because ... we have three of them sitting around a conference table—Churchill, Roosevelt, Stalin—now Stalin, Attlee and Truman perhaps. On the way over Roosevelt and Churchill conferred together, and on the way back ... ; and Joe Stalin being a realistic cuss was more interested in knowing what Churchill said to Roosevelt ... than what was said when they were all three together. I don't blame him. ...

"We don't make progress in a conference like that. ... Stalin feels that he is being taken for a ride. Let's meet them once man to man as equals across the table ... ; say, 'Joe ... you have a great country over there. ... We want to be friends with you ... we need your help on certain matters. ... Joe ... we are going to let you write the ticket for dealings between Russia and the United States. ... If you think it is a good idea to have newspapers and visitors from your country visit ours, that will be all right; that is, provided we can have the same. ...' If the United States lets the Russians know it is not afraid of them and cuts out appeasement, things will work out. God has been good to the United States.... I am convinced that only stupidity or cupidity on our part can so mismanage our foreign and domestic affairs that a war with Russia becomes inevitable." A realistic policy "will reject appeasement of Russia and renounce opposition to Russia in the same breath...."

Certainly Secretary of State James M. Byrnes had not given up on the hope of coming to terms with the Russians. Despite his friction with Molotov, he recorded in his book, *Speaking Frankly*, "When Mr. Molotov decides the time has come to agree, he does it in a big way.[10]... With the close of the United Nations Assembly on December 16, 1946, ...we had passed one important milestone on the long road to peace. ...The treaties...represented an important step in the restoration of stability."

The most serious debate in this period was not between the advocates of an alliance with Britain and the partisans of Allied unity, but between those who thought the United States could get along with the Soviet Union by acting as tough as it did and those who favored a more conciliatory policy.

Henry Wallace's Sanguine Interpretation

In an important speech on September 12, 1946, Secretary of Commerce Henry Wallace presented his reaction to Churchill's speech:

> Throughout the world there are numerous reactionary elements which had hoped for Axis victory—and now profess great friendship for the United States. Yet, these enemies of yesterday and false friends of today continually try to provoke war between the United States and Russia.... They long for the day when the United States and Russia will destroy each other. We must not let our Russian policy be guided... by those...who want war with Russia. This does not mean appeasement.... We want cooperation [from Russia].... The real peace treaty we need now is between the United States and Russia. On our part, we should recognize that we have no more business in the *political* affairs of Eastern Europe than Russia has in the *political* affairs of Latin America, Western Europe, and the United States [although] we may not like what Russia does in Eastern Europe. Her type of land reform, industrial expropriation, and suppression of basic liberties offends the great majority of the people of the United States...; the Russians should stop teaching that their form of Communism must, by force if necessary, ultimately triumph over democratic capitalism— while the United States must close its ears to those who say the two systems cannot coexist.
>
> Under friendly competition the Russian world and the American

world will gradually become more alike. The Russians will be forced to grant more and more of the personal freedoms; and we shall become more and more absorbed with the problems of socio-economic justice. Russia must be convinced that we are not planning for war against her, and we must be certain that Russia is not carrying on territorial expansion or world domination through native communists faithfully following every twist and turn in the Moscow party line.

President Truman announced to the press that he agreed with the speech, although there appeared to be some conflict between Wallace's opinions and the conduct of American foreign policy. Secretary of State Byrnes, who was at the Paris Peace Conference, frantically informed the president that this evident lack of agreement within the administration concerning the conduct of American foreign policy was severely impeding the efforts of the American delegation in Paris and undermining bipartisan support for American foreign policy. Truman, in response, forced Wallace's resignation.

The interesting thing about the Wallace speech is that, while the conciliatory aspects of the speech were well received by the C.I.O. and in liberal circles, his reference to a division of the world into spheres of influence—the proposal was very similar to Churchill's argument of 1944 with Stalin and was presumably based upon a similar set of assumptions —was so unpopular in this same circle that he was forced to disavow it.

In his letter of July 23 to Truman, which was not released publicly until he had been dismissed from the Cabinet, Wallace presented a more systematic treatment of the assumptions underlying his position. After expressing his recognition of the irritations accumulating from the bargaining tactics of the Russians, Wallace asked the president to consider how American actions must appear to others. Although the 1938 appropriation for the armed services was only $1 billion, the projected appropriation for 1947 was $13 billion in a budget of $36 billion. Since another $5 billion would go for war-liquidation activity and $10 billion for veterans' activities and debt service—largely the cost of past wars—roughly 80 percent of the budget was being applied to activities connected with war. The Bikini atom bomb tests were being interpreted as a demonstration of American armed might.[11] Non-Americans would interpret American actions to mean either that the United States was preparing for war or that it intended to intimidate the rest of the world by armed might.

Wallace continued by pointing to what he considered flaws in both objectives. Technology was revolutionizing the nature of war. Atomic weapons and the new biological weapons would be relatively cheap to produce. The destructiveness of the weapons would be so great that the size of opposing stockpiles would be relatively unimportant. All major nations would soon have them. An armaments race of this type, in which vast and long-range preparations were not necessary, would constitute a temptation to use those weapons. He said that these facts were already recognized in certain American military circles and that these circles were advocating a "preventive war" as a consequence. However, Wallace said, this solution was unsound. American moral scruples would prevent it unless a dictatorship were established at home. Moreover, the Red Army, as a countermeasure, would occupy all of Europe. Wallace questioned the practical or moral desirability of this consequence and again contended that some form of friendly agreement was the only answer to the problems that confronted the United States.[12]

The response to Wallace's position was quite favorable in liberal circles. Within six days of his resignation as Secretary of Commerce, he had received 6,700 messages pledging support for his position, while hundreds of messages—the great majority of them supporting his position—were pouring daily into the vacated Department of Commerce offices.

Major Positions Restated

During 1946, there were three major positions in the United States with respect to the Soviet Union. The most important of the positions was represented by Byrnes and Vandenberg. Followers of this position agreed that, in general, appeasement of the Soviet Union had prevented the realization of our war aims and had permitted the Soviet Union to expand at the expense of the West. The Soviet Union had definite expansionistic tendencies, and it was necessary to deny expression to these tendencies. For this purpose, a "tough" policy *vis-à-vis* the Soviet Union was called for.

The object of this "tough" policy was to stop the Soviet Union in its aggressive foreign policy, however, not to remove it from the inner circles of the victorious coalition. Thus, the policy of toughness was confined to specific issues as they arose. There was no thought—or not much thought—of forming an organized grouping of states hostile in general to Soviet policy. The United Nations organization continued to represent, in this school of thought, the place where policy should be implemented. Therefore, mere tactical use of the United Nations in pursuance of strategic objectives of American foreign policy would have been frowned upon. The amorphous group that adhered to this thesis[13] felt, with varying degrees of optimism, that a "tough" policy would work and that the Soviet Union would eventually reach an acceptable agreement with the United States. Throughout the next two years, this optimism diminished considerably.

The liberal, left position for which Wallace was spokesman—except for its Communist fringe—was in agreement that difficulties in the international situation stemmed from the rather blunt conduct of the Soviet Union. Those who took this position agreed with the Byrnes-Vandenberg thesis that the Soviet actions were in response to what the Soviet Union considered its "security" needs.

However, this group assigned some of the blame to the United States, asserting that the high military budget and the opposition to the Soviet Union with respect to its access to Iranian oil could only appear hostile to Moscow. It was felt that the United States should take a stronger stand toward British imperialism, thus convincing the Soviets of American impartiality. The United States should stop supporting reactionary elements abroad. Moscow would respond favorably, not to "toughness," but only under circumstances that broke the circle of suspicion.

In April, Democratic Senator Claude Pepper of Florida, a leading advocate of this position, called for a top-level meeting between Eisenhowever, Montgomery, and Zhukov for this purpose. This group was optimistic that the United States and the Soviet Union could come to agreement once an atmosphere of confidence was recreated. They felt that there was no major divergence between the national objectives of the United States and the Soviet Union. The Byrnes–Vandenberg position, on the other hand, implied some divergence but indicated that the divergence could be compromised if the costs to the Soviet Union of pursuing her objectives were raised.

In his speech at the opening of the United Nations General Assembly on October 23, 1946, President Truman stated the position most Americans accepted:

> The war has left many parts of the world in turmoil. Differences have arisen among the allies. It will not help us to pretend that this is not the case. But it is not necessary to exaggerate the differences.
>
> For my part, I believe that there is no difference of interest that need stand in the way of settling these problems and of settling them in accordance with the United Nations Charter. Above all, we must not permit differences in economic and social systems to stand in the way of peace either now or in the future. To permit the United Na-

tions to be broken into irreconcilable parts by different political phi-
losophies would bring disaster to the world.

In his State of the Union message on January 6, 1947, Truman declared, "Whatever differences there may have been between us and the
Soviet Union, however, [they] should not be allowed to obscure the
fact that the basic interests of both nations lie in the early making of a
peace under which the peoples of all countries may return ... to the essential tasks of production and reconstruction.... Our policy toward
the Soviet Union is guided by the same principles which determine our
policy toward all nations."

Truman, in these messages, had summarized the position generally
taken by the American public and by Congress. Still, there were difficulties. Americans were no longer so confident concerning Russian intentions.
But, whatever revision the United States would make in its policy, it was
still committed to the unity of the victorious coalition and believed that
the coalition could be maintained. American policy, at this stage, did not
seriously contemplate the organization of rival blocs of states.

The radical position was that enunciated by Winston Churchill and
endorsed by Governor Dewey. Churchill's position was that the major
objectives of the United States and the Soviet Union differed so greatly
that no compromise was possible unless the West systematically organized
itself to erect a barrier against Russian expansion. For this purpose the
objectives of the United Nations organization must be relegated to a less
urgent present priority—although not to a less urgent priority in the
future—and that organization must be mobilized by an Anglo-American
partnership as an instrument of their national policies and objectives.

This stand constituted a radical break with previous policy inasmuch as its consequence would be the organization of states internationally into two opposed blocs. By contending that the balance of power
no longer applied, Churchill was stating that the cleavages between the
Communist and non-Communist worlds were of such an order that a
non-Communist nation could not afford to cooperate with Russia.

Since a similar flexibility did not exist within the Soviet bloc,
such a policy would gradually result in the deterioration of the non-
Communist position. Therefore, non-Communist countries must organize
their efforts collectively. The maintenance of this organized effort must
assume greater immediate importance than any particular and immediate
advantage that an individual country might achieve by disrupting the
alliance or by pursuing immediate objectives directly.

In effect, Churchill was advocating a revolution in the statecraft of the West. Although the proponents of the "tough" and "soft" policies differed in their interpretation of Soviet intentions and motivations, they proposed no alteration in the system of national relations. Churchill insisted that the coming revolution in statecraft must have an organizational base. In this sense, he was the "Lenin" of that revolution.

Since the United States was the only center of power around which the anti-Soviet coalition could be built, Churchill attempted to arouse the American nation to this task. He informed the United States that the Soviet power center, using the Communist parties abroad or the Red or satellite armies, would expand until halted by a force capable of matching it. If not halted by force, it would acquire world hegemony. But no sentimental or ideological concerns would halt it short of the point at which it had to pay too high a price for the gain achieved.[14] Moreover, the West must act soon. Possession of atomic weapons still could raise the costs of expansion so high the Soviet Union might possibly be deterred. But if the United States failed to act, the Soviet Union would be able to blackmail individual nations into capitulation while the United States would be forced to remain inactive and would be unable to halt the process. Thus, the free world would undergo a "chemical dissolution."[15]

FACTORS AFFECTING AMERICAN POLICY

Economic Factors

While the United States was becoming concerned with the Russian problem and while the public was taking a less favorable view of Russian intentions than it had in the past, the country had a major concern in the problems of reconversion to a peacetime economy. Moreover, the public was war-weary and simply unwilling to face up to any stern measures. In his State of the Union message in 1946, President Truman pointed out that the "$275-billion debt poses a problem that requires careful consideration in the determination of financial and economic policies."

While Truman had no doubt that this problem could be solved, he remarked, "It is good to move toward a balanced budget and a start on the retirement of the debt at a time when demand for goods is strong and the business outlook is strong.... This is not the time for tax reduction." Under these circumstances, a strong foreign policy that undercut a balanced budget and required even heavier taxes was unlikely to evoke an enthusiastic response from a public longing for "normal" times.

Political Factors

With the end of the war, the president and the executive branch of the government were no longer so free to make policy decisions as had earlier been the case; nor was it easy to secure funds for their policies. The Senate was eager to resume its traditional watchdog role over the conduct of foreign policy. Thus, domestic considerations began to play an increasingly important role in our foreign policy. The president and his subordinates were no longer able to think of foreign policy primarily in terms of the external relationships of the United States with foreign states. Their conception of the possible policy decisions they might make, and of the objectives they might pursue, was modified by the adjustments they had to make according to the mood of the public and the Congress.

Military Factors

While the Soviet Union could mobilize its army from the existing population, dependent only on its conception of the most advantageous use of that manpower, the United States could not mobilize its manpower nor organize it into combat units unless Congress authorized an army of sufficient size, approved a draft, if necessary, and appropriated the funds to maintain the armed forces.

Relationship Between Factors

One aspect of the shift in focus was the American evaluation of Soviet intentions and capabilities. What was the Soviet trying to accomplish and did it have the necessary resources to accomplish it? Since American foreign policy—beginning in 1946—could no longer be made primarily by the Chief Executive, attention must also be paid to the viewpoints held by the public and members of Congress.

In his State of the Union message in 1947, Truman advised the nation:

> We live in a world in which strength on the part of peace-loving nations is still the greatest deterrent to aggression. World stability can be destroyed when nations with great responsibilities neglect to maintain the means of discharging those responsibilities.
>
> This is an age when unforeseen attack could come with unprecedented speed. We must be strong enough to defeat, and thus to fore-

stall, any such attack. . . . When a system of collective security under
the United Nations has been established, we shall be willing to lead
in collective disarmament, but until such a system becomes a reality,
we must not again allow ourselves to become weak and invite attack.

The potential aggressor, against whom a strong defensive and retaliatory force was necessary, could be only the Soviet Union. Although
the Truman administration thought it advisable to attempt to succeed
in a policy of cooperation, it was not prepared to see the United States
in a weak military position should that policy fail.

But these are words. We cannot discover what they mean until we
compare the Soviet and American military positions. Whether the state
of the armed forces in 1946 and 1947 represented the administration's
conception of what was necessary or whether it represented its conception of what was advisable to request from Congress, such a comparison
will reveal much about the American state of mind.

In 1946, the Soviet Union had approximately 6,000,000 men in its
army. Of this total, 1,500,000 had been drafted during the preceding
year.[16] The Soviet Union had a policy of compulsory military service.
It is reasonable to assume that Russian demobilization did not interfere
excessively with the efficiency of these military units, inasmuch as the
Kremlin has not ordinarily permitted principles of abstract justice or
consideration for human emotions to interfere with its policy requirements. In 1946 and 1947, the Soviet aircraft industry underwent an extensive retooling designed to modernize it.

In May 1946, Congress extended the Selective Service Act for six
weeks. In June, it was extended for an additional nine months. However, Congress specified that on July 1, 1946, the number of men in the
army "shall not exceed 1,550,000 . . . this number shall be reduced consistently month by month so that the army's strength shall not exceed
1,070,000 on July 1, 1947."

In January 1947, a new Congress convened. Since the Congress had
a Republican majority, it was anticipated that the budget recommendations of the president would undergo the closest scrutiny. With this consideration in mind, and after a state department and war department
conference with the president, it was decided not to ask for an increase
in the 1,070,000-man figure or an extension of selective service.

How effective was the army? As of June 30, 1946, General MacArthur
estimated that the combat effectiveness of all army units (ground and
air) in his command was approximately 25 percent.[17] This estimate
may be taken as indicative of the readiness of the army generally. Of

218 effective combat air groups that existed on V-J Day, only fifty-five groups remained sixteen months later, and only two of these groups were effective. Some progress was made in the air force in the first six months of 1947. By the end of that period, there were eleven effective groups in a total of seventy, although some had little more tangible existence than a headquarters record. Turnover of personnel resulted in inefficiency and inexperience. As a result, equipment deteriorated and became useless. Air Force General Spaatz asserted that ". . . one prefers not to speculate on what might have happened only one year after V-J Day, when the combat readiness of AAF first-line planes had dropped very low, if our air force had been called upon to resist a new aggression or to suppress a recurrence of combat activity from an uncontrolled element in one of the occupied countries."[18] The naval situation was also serious.

When Secretary of State Byrnes was informed while in attendance at the Paris Peace Conference that American troops in Europe were to be reduced even further, he became alarmed at the effect of this reduction on the political position of the United States. According to General George C. Marshall, the relationship between the two factors was impressive. He recounts:

> I remember, when I was Secretary of State, I was being pressed constantly, particularly when in Moscow March-April 1947, by radio message after radio message to give the Russians hell. . . . When I got back, I was getting the same appeal in relation to the Far East and China. At that time, facilities for giving them hell—and I am a soldier and know something about the ability to give hell—was $1\frac{1}{3}$ divisions over the entire United States. That is quite a proposition when you deal with somebody with over 260, and you have $1\frac{1}{3}$. We had nothing in Alaska. We did not have enough to defend the air strip up at Fairbanks. . . .

Except for the atom bomb, the United States was impotent militarily.

Throughout 1946 and 1947, the United States lacked a sufficient military establishment to pursue a bold diplomatic policy. Many who advocated such a policy were unwilling to pay the monetary and human consequences of their position. Balancing the budget and reducing taxes was popular and the draft was not. It would not be until March 1948—after the Communist seizure of power in Czechoslovakia—that the administration found itself in a position to approach these problems with some hope of success. Even so, full-scale rearmament would have to await the Korean War.

During 1946 and 1947, public opinion concerning the Soviet Union was undergoing reorientation. There was minimal consistency between thought and action, between conception and policy. Objectives were not related to capabilities.

Finally, one may question the urgency with which some regarded the Russians as a menace. If the Soviet Union would respond to mere verbal toughness by adopting a more conciliatory policy—as many evidently thought it would—its intentions could not be quite so forbidding as they were made to sound. But the focus of American opinion was beginning to shift.

II

The Great
Deterrent
(1954)

American explosion of secret atomic weapons on Hiroshima and Nagasaki, Japan, revolutionized world history. The fact of the bomb's existence changed the entire course, not only of military strategy, but also of diplomatic strategy. The ramifications of this new state of affairs constitute too specialized a topic for the present volume. However, the impact of this situation on the concrete alternatives open to the United States in determining its policy objectives, with specific reference to the problem presented by the Soviet Union, is of direct concern.

Strategic Possibilities of Atomic Weapons

Consideration of U.S. policy objectives *vis-à-vis* the Soviet Union with regard to the bomb logically entails examination of the military potential of the new weapon. The bomb dropped at Hiroshima produced total destruction within an area circumscribed by a radius of one and one-fourth miles originating at the center of the explosion, or within an area of approximately four square miles. The area of overall damage was twenty-one square miles. The bomb dropped at Nagasaki was more powerful and would have produced total destruction within an area of ten square miles had not the physical characteristics of the area limited the targets subject to destruction.

A single atomic bomb, at that time, contained the concentrated destructiveness of 20,000 tons of TNT, although it must be noted that the effect of its explosion would not have been equal to that caused by the explosion of 20,000 bombs, each containing one ton of TNT. Nevertheless, 500 separate bomber sorties, carrying the largest conventional bombs, would have been required to produce the effect caused by the explosion of a single atomic bomb. Any city in the world could have been destroyed effectively by the explosion of one to ten atomic bombs.

No defense adequate to meet the threat posed by the bomb could be envisaged in the 1945–1947 period, provided the stockpile of bombs was sufficiently great and means of delivery available. The bomb could be carried in a B-29. Presumably its size would be diminished and its effectiveness increased over a period of time. Even assuming the unavailability of air bases outside the United States and the Soviet Union, it was to be noted that the distance between Moscow and New York over the great circle route was only approximately 4,800 miles. No major city in either country was much beyond 6,000 miles from an air base in the other country, if the great circle route over the arctic regions were utilized. Bombers capable of flying such distances were already past the blueprint stages; and, of course, each country had bases somewhat closer than assumed in the examples given.

The fact that so much destructiveness could be carried in one plane had vast consequences. It was relatively unimportant for the air bases to be close enough to permit round trips. Sacrifice of bomber and pilot to deliver the explosive would be economical, if only a military calculus were used. Moreover, control of the air would no longer be important as it was in the past. The rate of attrition would be unimportant, for only a given number of planes needed to get through to their targets to cripple the enemy. Production of enough bombs to enable a sufficient number to get through to cripple either the United States or the Soviet Union was clearly within the range of possibility.

The fission of the atom permitted an unprecedented concentration of violence in a single package. The bomb concentrated violence in terms of time. It greatly reduced the number of airplanes and sorties required to inflict an enormous amount of death and destruction. It brought within the range of the possible an intercontinental surprise knockout attack. Such an attack would provide victory if the ability of the other side to retaliate with atomic weapons could be destroyed at the same time. Even if the latter condition did not hold, the result would include the effective destruction of the state attacked. But the aggressor would also be effectively crippled by the retaliatory counterattack. Diplomatic miscalculation, producing atomic war, held possibilities for destruction so great that civilized human beings did not care or dare to think much about it. The possible gains of treachery and cunning were magnified.

The possible damage to both sides resulting from the gambles of an insane or reckless adventurer was, in a word, horrifying.

However, these possibilities were dependent upon the possession of large stockpiles of atomic weapons by the United States and the Soviet Union. For the time being, at least, the United States had an effective monopoly of atomic weapons. On the other hand, the most important information the Soviet Union could possess, the knowledge that the bomb had been produced and that it worked, was public property. The knowledge of theoretical physics required for the production of the bomb was already known by Soviet physicists. The remaining engineering secrets were largely concerned with the "triggering" mechanism of the bomb. According to the best informed estimates at the time, the Soviet Union would be able to solve this problem and marshal the economic resources to begin quantity construction of the bomb within five to ten years.

When that time came, it was thought the United States no longer would be able to balance Soviet manpower and logistical advantages by monopolistic possession of the atomic bomb. For the first time, the United States would become vulnerable to air attack. Moreover, there would be the recurrent danger of a sneak, knockout attack. Therefore, the United States had to consider the measures it would take to maximize the advantages it held then and also to minimize the future dangers arising from multilateral possession of the bomb. At the same time, it had to attempt to relate its possession of the bomb to the measures it was taking to contain the expansionism of the Soviet Union.

The first alternative open to the United States—and there is reason to believe that it was not seriously considered either feasible or desirable except in isolated and relatively subordinate levels in the military establishment—was preventive war. If the Soviet Union were as determined and dangerous a foe as the containment thesis implied, the risks involved in permitting the Soviet Union to gain the atomic bomb were possibly too great to be permitted. Apart from the moral revulsion the public would have felt for measures of so brutal a character and the inability of a democracy to strike in this fashion without public debate, there were other reasons to question this alternative.

It is extremely doubtful that the United States had a sufficiently large stockpile of bombs during 1947 to incapacitate the Soviet Union, a vast country with great recuperative capacity. Several thousand bombs, each striking its target, would have been required to incapacitate the Soviet Union. A stockpile that large—let alone a stockpile large enough to permit a margin for error or loss—did not exist. Moreover, a strategic air force, large and modern enough to deliver the bombs, was not in existence.

However, even if the bombs and the strategic air force had existed to accomplish the task of incapacitating the Soviet Union, it would not have been possible to prevent the Red Army from occupying the rest of Europe. In this event, the Soviet Union would have regained most of the industrial capacity lost as a result of the bombings, and it would have accomplished one of the primary objectives preventive war was designed to forestall.

The United States, then, would have been required to wait until it had accumulated another stockpile of atomic arms. In the meantime, Asia, as well as Europe, would have been conquered. The Near East and North Africa would also have come within the Soviet orbit.

When the new stockpile of bombs was built, the United States would have been faced with the agonizing need to atomize its former allies in Western Europe, for Western European industrial potential under Communist control would have constituted the most potent threat to the United States.

Assuming this were accomplished, the United States would have been unable to occupy Europe against the resistance of a superior Red Army and the hostility of the European populations, whose lives would have been so rudely shattered by America's preventive war. The rest of the Communist world would have been too large for atomic raids against any but its most densely populated centers. In the meantime, it is at least possible that the Communists would have produced the atomic bomb, under great handicaps, in subsurface installations immune to atomic attack. The United States would then have been faced with the prospect of indefinite intercontinental atomic warfare, in which great portions of its industrialized centers would have been atomized.

Even assuming the best, that the use of American atomic weapons would have prevented the Communists from developing their own atomic weapons, to prevent this situation from changing, the United States would have been forced constantly to send air missions from this country to destroy any efforts to repair the industry of Europe. The United States would have been reduced to hemispheric isolation and the maintenance of a permanent strategic air force dedicated to the task of destroying any signs of reemerging civilization in the other hemisphere. The economic costs of the program, the permanent militarization of American society it would have entailed, and the brutalization of American morality required by this policy alternative were sufficient to deny it serious official consideration.

A long-range alternative that was considered by the United States—and which became part of its official policy—was the international control of atomic power. Since atomic power was so destructive and deadly, the United States hoped to deny its use to all other nations. For this purpose, it proposed an international authority, which would own and control the production of atomic materials from the raw material stage to finished product.

So intent was the United States on accomplishing this objective that it was apparently willing to forego the only weapon likely to permit it to balance the Soviet Union's superiority in manpower. Indeed, there are indications that the representatives of the United States were not even thinking in these terms; otherwise they could not have opposed the Soviet Union's highly rational proposal to link conventional and atomic armaments. Although the Soviet Union may have been interested in a percentage reduction of conventional armaments that would have further increased its advantage, the United States could hope to maintain parity only by linking the two classifications of armaments and insisting upon large Soviet reductions in conventional armaments as a *quid pro quo* for American relinquishment of the atomic weapon.[1]

In any case, there was little reason to believe that the alternative plans offered by the United States and the Soviet Union could meet the security needs of the other party sufficiently to permit adoption of atomic controls, although this point was obscured by official propaganda from both sides that presented the issues in legalistic or moralistic terms. The United States was not prepared to relinquish its stockpile of bombs or its production secrets without the safeguards it considered sufficient. These safeguards, which were included in the plan special adviser Bernard Baruch presented to the United Nations, included international ownership and inspection rights inconsistent with, and dangerous to, the requirements of a totalitarian regime. The United States would retain its atomic monopoly until this regime was in operation.

If the Soviet Union made these concessions, there could be no tangible guarantee, other than good faith, that the United States would perform its end of the bargain, including turning over its weapons secrets. The United States could hardly be coerced by states not possessing the atomic bomb. In the meantime, acceptance of the first stages of the Baruch proposals would have interfered with Soviet efforts to produce the atomic bomb.

There were, however, even more serious difficulties in the proposals. There was no reason to believe that either the American or the Russian proposal would prevent the launching of an atomic war. If a stockpile of weapons were retained for an international police force (as envisaged by some), it would be necessary to maintain part of the stockpile in areas accessible to each of the major powers. It would then be possible for one of the major powers to seize a supply of bombs by force.

If all bombs were destroyed (and this would be difficult to determine, for there is no way of detecting the existence of an unexploded bomb), atomic facilities would be subject to seizure. At most, control would insure a warning period preceding atomic attack; namely, the warning provided by seizure of the bombs or of atomic facilities. Control was not an absolute safeguard against atomic war.

Ultimate considerations were relatively unimportant, however. The specific proposals put forward by each of the two major powers were unacceptable to the other. The American plan put the Soviet Union at a disadvantage. In addition, the proposal to eliminate the veto in punishing states that broke the agreement provoked needless Soviet opposition. Punishment of a major power implied world war; therefore, legal considerations were inconsequential. The Soviet proposal, on the other hand, would have forced the United States to dispose of its existing stockpile of atomic weapons without any satisfactory assurances that the Soviet Union would not secretly produce atomic weapons.

The question, therefore, became clear. In what way could the United States utilize its atomic strength in implementing its foreign policy? The atomic bomb was not useful for purposes of preventive war. It was apparently not even useful for purposes of establishing an international authority for the production and control of atomic power. Would it have been useful in case of Soviet aggression? This question is much more difficult to answer.

As later proved in Korea, atomic weapons probably would not have been used in the case of aggression by a satellite. There would have been less drastic measures available to the United States to repel satellite aggression, even given the relative disarmament of the American nation at that time. Whether or not atomic weapons would have been used against direct Soviet aggression would probably have depended on the strategic importance of the area in question and the consequences, in terms of morale and diplomatic considerations, of American inaction.

In case of direct Soviet aggression, the atomic bomb would not have produced victory for the United States, particularly with the low level of military preparedness in the United States at that time. Moreover, despite use of the atomic bomb, the Soviet Union would have been capable of occupying all of Europe (with the possible exception of England) and most of Asia.

Therefore, the atomic bomb did not have a deterrent effect of insuring, or even making likely, American victory. However, it could have been used to disrupt, or possibly destroy, the Soviet economy. If the Communist goal was oriented toward the creation of a Communist order of society, rather than mere domination over a large area of the earth, this was possibly a price the men in the Kremlin would be unwilling to pay. It would probably have made impossible their hopes of seeing the Communist system become a worldwide one.

If the Soviet Union could not lose a war under these conditions, it could certainly not win it. Moreover, the longer the war lasted—and an intercontinental war of this type might last indefinitely—the more disruption would take place in the areas under their control and the harder it would be for them to impose their chosen pattern of society.

Thus, it may be said that the bomb did exercise a deterrent effect. However, it is necessary not to exaggerate even this effect. It was quite doubtful, in the period under discussion, that the Soviet Union would have been willing to engage in a major war even had the United States not possessed the atomic bomb. The exchange of letters between the Yugoslavs and the Soviet Union preceding the break in 1948 and later published by the Yugoslavs contains the following interesting passage:

> As is well known, after a series of territorial concessions for the benefit of Yugoslavia which the Soviet Union extracted from the Anglo-Americans the latter, together with the French, rejected the Soviet proposal to hand Trieste over to Yugoslavia and occupied Trieste with their own forces, which were then in Italy. Since all other means were exhausted, the Soviet Union had only one other method left for gaining Trieste for Yugoslavia—to start war with the Anglo-Americans over Trieste and take it by force. The Yugoslav comrades could not fail to realize that after such a hard war the USSR could not enter another.

The Soviet Union was more concerned with internal reconstruction, consolidating its war and postwar gains, and in reducing internal tensions than it was with external conquests. The strain of fighting a war and undergoing strategic aerial bombing attacks would have inhibited any reckless Soviet actions, even were the Kremlin's policy not a traditionally cautious one.

Rather than preventing Soviet action, the United States possession of the atomic bomb may have been viewed as a goad to action by the Soviet Union. It was, of course, possible to argue that the Soviet Union ought to wait until it possessed the atomic bomb before risking war with the United States.

But the opposite contention may have had equal or even greater weight with the Soviet leaders. The United States stockpile of atomic weapons in 1946 and 1947 was extremely small. The aircraft to deliver the weapons were nonexistent. The ground forces to fight land warfare were not in existence. The organizational alliances with Western Europe were only in the opening stages. The industrial production of Western Germany was just beginning to be restored.

If the Soviet Union waited, its possession of the bomb might not counterbalance the losses on the other side of the ledger. Moreover, there is a traditional suspicion of the capitalistic powers in the Soviet Union. Waiting might merely give the United States the opportunity to choose the time to strike. It is possible that only the internal unreadiness of the Soviet Union for war, plus the hope of capturing Italy and France by the electoral process, were sufficient to rule out an argument for an immediate war, which derived from exclusive American possession of the atomic bomb.

Thus, while the existence of the atomic bomb revolutionized strategy, inasmuch as the possibility of unrestricted atomic warfare introduced a new calculation of costs and probabilities, its consequences for American policy at that time were quite debatable. Its effect as a deterrent conceivably would not be felt completely until the Soviet Union had a stockpile of bombs.

At that time, Soviet retaliatory power would deter American attack, according to the possible reasoning of the men in the Kremlin. This element of security would, then, deter them from a reckless venture. Thus, except for the possibility of a surprise knockout attack in which the retaliatory forces were also destroyed, possession of the stockpile might deter both sides from actions likely to bring about world war. In this sense, possession of the bomb stockpile might compensate the United States for the growing population and logistical strength of the Soviet Union. In this case, rather than being a curse, the invention of the bomb may have been the only factor permitting the United States effectively to promote world peace and the independence of the free nations. As such, it would enable the United States to limit the territorial expansion of the Soviet Union and to contain its power.

American Attitudes on Atomic Weapons

Whether or not exclusive American possession of atomic weapons deterred the Soviet Union from war in the period following 1946, official American estimates of the deterring effects of the bomb were decisive for the determination of American policy in that period. The view expressed by Winston Churchill in 1950—that the atom bomb deterred the Soviet Union from military aggression in Europe during the period in which it had a preponderance of conventional military force on that continent—has now been accepted generally. Nevertheless, it is questionable whether this view had gained complete official American acceptance in the early postwar period.

Initially, in 1945, there were efforts to deflate the effectiveness of atomic weapons. United States Air Force officers stated that the destructiveness of the Hiroshima bombing could have been reproduced by two days of conventional bombing, a contention which, though true, neglected the investment in manpower, planes, and logistical elements involved in two days of conventional bombing.

Canadian General A. G. L. McNaughton was reported to have stated in October 1945, that the means to counter the atomic bomb were "clearly in sight." In his third report to the Secretary of War in November, General H. H. Arnold took the position that the atomic bomb could be delivered only by heavy bomber until long-range guided missiles were developed. Their use could be successful, he said, only if air superiority were achieved. Moreover, according to General Arnold's report, "The great unit cost of the [atomic] bomb means that as nearly as possible every one must be delivered to its intended target." The opinion of General Arnold may be challenged on technical grounds, and it is not certain that this viewpoint received official acceptance in this period. On the other hand, there is no convincing evidence to the contrary.

Some facts are pertinent to this inquiry. Throughout the period in question, no official decision had been made as to whether the bomb would be dropped in the event of war. No decision had been made as to which branch of the government or armed forces was to have custody of the bomb. President Truman had decided that the bomb would not be dropped except by his direct order.

Thus, official opinion, with respect to the deterrent power of the bomb, could not be based on an express or implied decision or willingness to use it in war. The Russians could not be sure of this, however. The ambiguity of the American position, therefore, was not decisive for

Soviet response or for American estimates of their response. Clearly, the bomb was a deterrent in the sense that any military capability will deter a potential enemy or at least make him check his calculations before he strikes. The question, however, is whether or not American leaders believed that the bomb would deter the Soviet Union in the absence of strong conventional capabilities.

In a memo to Republican Senator Charles Gurney of Florida on December 8, 1947, Secretary of Defense James Forrestal listed four facts that he regarded as important in the struggle between the United States and the Soviet Union. The first was the predominance of Russian land power in Europe and Asia. The second was the predominance of American sea power. The third was exclusive American possession of the atomic bomb. The fourth was America's great industrial capacity.

According to Forrestal, the last three facts permitted the United States to assume risks it could not otherwise take to restore the international balance of power. Thus, for instance, Forrestal was willing to risk cutting other American forms of military power in order to finance European economic and political recovery. In his view, therefore, the possession of the bomb balanced to some extent American weakness in conventional military power. If it did not absolutely deter the Soviet Union, it nevertheless made rational the assumption of military risks that could not be taken in its absence.

During July of the following year, however, Forrestal took issue with the contention of General Hoyt Vandenberg that the available military funds should largely be funneled into the Strategic Air Command. Forrestal contended that this implied a decision to rely solely on the use of the atomic bomb; he regarded this as an unsound position. Even Forrestal's view of the usefulness of the bomb, however, was probably stronger than that of the Canadian Cabinet Defense Committee and Chiefs of Staff, who regarded it as formidable but not decisive.

Opinions were also divided on American ability to withstand a Russian attack in Europe. In June of 1947 General Dwight Eisenhower reported that, in the event of Soviet attack, American troops in Europe could be safely withdrawn to Hamburg at which point they could embark. Admiral William D. Leahy, however, did not believe that a withdrawal could be carried out safely.

By July of the following year, General George Marshall felt that a stand in Europe could possibly be made by American, French, and British forces. Forrestal disagreed and pointed out that the army had only two and one-third reserve divisions. General Lucius Clay felt that there was only about one chance in four of war breaking out, and his estimate was based to some extent upon American possession of atomic bombs. On the other hand, the greater the ease of Soviet occupation of Europe, the less the deterrent power of the atomic bomb.

There was still apparently much high level vagueness as to the possible deterrence of the bomb. In the fall of 1948, Churchill warned that America's minimizing of the destructive power of the bomb encouraged the Russians dangerously. General Vandenberg took the most sanguine view of the matter and reported that the bomb could be dropped when, how, and wherever wanted. Whether he thought the Russians believed this and were thereby deterred is not clear. Moreover, his optimism was at least questionable.

In September, the American Ambassador to the Soviet Union, General Bedell Smith, reported that the Russians would not be able to produce an atomic bomb for another five to ten years. He recognized that the Russians might have the know-how, but doubted that their industrial facilities were adequate for the task. Nevertheless, he did not believe that this fact would deter the Russians from making war. He stated that the Soviet leaders placed great reliance upon their "diversification and vast spaces."

By implication, General George Marshall endorsed the view that the Russians, at least until that fall, were not greatly deterred by exclusive American possession of atomic weapons. On October 10, 1948, General Marshall, in a conference with Forrestal and the three service Chiefs of Staff said, "The Soviets are beginning to realize for the first time that the United States would really use the atomic bomb against them in the event of war."

Later that month as his biographer, Walter Millis, reveals, Secretary Forrestal entered among his notes the following analysis of the military situation:[2]

> I do not believe that air power alone can win a war any more than an army or naval power can win a war, and I do not believe in the theory that an atomic offensive will extinguish in a week the will to fight. I believe air power will have to be employed massively in order to really destroy the industrial complex of any nation and, in terms of present capabilities, that means air power within fifteen hundred miles of the targets—that means an army has to be transported to the areas where the airfields exist—that means, in turn, there has to be

security of the sea lanes provided by the naval forces to get the Army there. Then, and only then, can the tremendous striking power of air be applied in a decisive—and I repeat decisive—manner.

After the Czechoslovakian coup in February 1948 and the beginning of the Berlin blockade in April 1948, public opinion hardened toward the Soviet Union. The dangers of overt military conflict seemed more real, and the pressures to use the atomic bomb in that eventuality mounted. Forrestal, who wanted to use the weapon in the event of war, sounded out influential opinion and found it "unanimous" (at least in the circles he polled) by the fall of 1948. Even so, no decision had been made officially to use the bomb. Nevertheless, the fact of its probable use in the event of war, according to General Marshall, was beginning to impress the Russians.

During this period, the sinews of the Brussels Pact and the projected North Atlantic Treaty Organization were beginning to take recognizable shape. The Western powers were beginning to establish interallied commands, bases, supply depots, and logistic support. Air bases were established and protected. The American military draft was reestablished. Despite difficulties over a small defense budget, the striking power of the strategic air command was being refurbished. This development apparently took place throughout the remainder of 1948, 1949, and 1950. Official opinion came generally to accept the thesis of the atomic bomb's deterring power.

In a sense, all this is paradoxical for, in 1949, the Soviet Union exploded its first atomic bomb. Nevertheless, there are reasons for these estimates. In the first place, the American stockpile of atomic weapons had grown to a point at which a crippling attack against the Soviet Union became feasible. The bases and air striking power to carry out the attack were brought into being. Sufficient strength on the continent of Europe was built to delay and make more costly Soviet attack and occupation.

The Soviet Union, as yet, had no stockpile of atomic weapons and, therefore, lacked the ability to retaliate decisively against the United States. On the other hand, the fact that it had produced the bomb worked against a preventive Soviet war. A stockpile was within reach, and, therefore, the advantages of waiting increased. On the other hand, while the Soviet Union was utilizing time to build its stockpile of atomic weapons, the Western powers could use the same period of time to make their conventional military power in Europe more effective.

Thus, official Washington apparently came to accept the thesis that, in this period, its atomic capabilities offset its growing but deficient conventional military capabilities. According to this view, therefore, a balance of military power was achieved and the Soviet Union was deterred from waging war.

It is doubtful, however, that this view of the matter would have been accepted so generally had not American conventional capabilities been increased and the Western powers organized defensively. It is also probable that the ouster of the Communists from the governments of France and Italy and the more favorable economic and political prognoses for those countries also contributed somewhat to this point of view by increasing the strength and cohesiveness of the Western powers.

III

The China
Debacle
(1955)

Historic American Policy

Toward the close of the nineteenth century, the European powers and Japan began to scramble for exclusive possessions and spheres of influence in China. At the height of this activity, Secretary of State John Hay sent his circular letter to the major powers involved in the contest for China and secured their acceptance of principles that came to be known as the Open Door Doctrine. His efforts had some success in mitigating the continuing dismemberment of China, and his policy became the traditional American policy toward China. The objectives of the American policy of the Open Door were epitomized in Article I of the Nine Power Treaty of 1922, the provisions of which read as follows:

The Contracting Powers, other than China, agree:

(1) To respect the sovereignty, the independence, and the territorial and administrative integrity of China;

(2) To provide the fullest and most unembarrassed opportunity to China to develop and to maintain for herself an effective and stable government;

(3) To use their influence for the purpose of effectually establishing and maintaining the principle of equal opportunity for the commerce and industry of all nations throughout the territory of China;

(4) To refrain from taking advantage of conditions in China in order to seek special rights or privileges which would abridge the rights

of citizens or subjects of friendly states, and from countenancing action inimical to the security of such states.

Background Events in China

From 1919 until Communist victory in 1949, the Kuomintang, founded by Dr. Sun Yat-sen, was a powerful political force in China. For much of that period, however, the Kuomintang was able to establish itself only in the south of China rather than as a national government. Many warlords in the north were able to maintain effective independence, and a more powerful government existed there throughout much of the 1920s.

In 1924, Dr. Sun appealed for recognition of the Canton government of which he was president. He was turned down by all governments including those of Great Britain and the United States. The Soviet Union, however, had already sent to the aid of Dr. Sun an advisory group headed by Comintern agent Michael Borodin.

As a result of Borodin's activity, Communist Party members joined the Kuomintang. Further, the Kuomintang was reorganized according to Leninist principles of democratic centralism.[1] The Kuomintang armies were reorganized by Russian military advisers.

Dr. Sun soon died, and the Kuomintang split into warring factions. Borodin maneuvered to take advantage of this situation. His intrigues in favor of Chiang Kai-shek[2] led to Chiang's appointment as commander of the Kuomintang military forces. Wang Ching-wei was appointed political head of the Comintern as a consequence of Borodin's efforts.

Having used the Communists to achieve military power, Chiang found other pastures greener. Chiang wanted to replace Wang as political head of the Kuomintang, but he could not depend on Communist support for this goal. The only way to achieve this, therefore, was to use his military position in collaboration with right-wing elements within the Kuomintang.[3]

Chiang's maneuvers succeeded. He consolidated his position within the Kuomintang and took steps against his most serious political opposition—the Chinese Communists. For a time, he continued to cooperate with Russian Communists, who kept advising their Chinese comrades to cooperate with Chiang despite the measures he was taking against them.

Chiang was not able to dispense with Soviet government aid until 1927. Nevertheless, the dominant Comintern faction, headed by Stalin, continued to support a pro-Chiang policy even after he openly took anti-

Communist actions. As late as 1928, the Communists in Shanghai were ordered to bury their arms when Chiang's armies approached that city. As a consequence, Chiang was able to execute many leaders of the Communist Party and effectively to destroy their urban apparatus. In this period, Chiang gained recognition from the European powers.

In the meantime, Mao Tse-tung was building his not inconsiderable power in the Chinese hinterlands. Other surviving leaders of the Communist Party were hiding in Shanghai, without party organization and without funds.[4] Mao invited these leaders to his strongholds and in this period displaced the Moscow favorites, Li Li-san and Wang Ming. Mao adopted a policy oriented toward the peasant class. Under Kuomintang harassment, Mao and Chu Teh organized a resistance movement and in 1934 carried out the Long March to the northwest, where a new base of operations was established.

In 1931, the Manchurian incident occurred. It may have been engineered by Japanese hawks or by the Chinese Communist Party. The threat of continuing Japanese conquest led to increasing pressure for a united Chinese front against the Japanese. The kidnapping in 1936 of Chiang by the warlord Chang was to induce Chiang to agree to a united front against the Japanese. This agreement was reached just before the next Japanese attack on China in 1937. This agreement was broken in 1941 when the Nationalists established an armed blockade of the area in North China controlled by the Communists. In December of that year, Japan attacked the United States at Pearl Harbor and, for the Western Allies, the European and Pacific wars were merged into one global war.

United States War Aims

In order to prosecute the war successfully, the United States attempted to close the breach between the Chinese Nationalists and the Communists. Pressure for coalition mounted through 1943. It was not successful in its positive purpose, but it did have the negative success of preventing the Kuomintang from engaging in war with the Communists in September 1943.

The Far Eastern operation was of secondary concern to the United States. The Chinese were rarely consulted on major decisions. Support that was promised was often withdrawn without so much as a by-your-leave for reasons that the Joint Chiefs considered sufficient.

On the other hand, General Stilwell had his own problems with Chiang and the Chinese military. From the vantage point of 1955, we know that the military grand strategy of the Joint Chiefs succeeded namely, to win the war in China by defeating Japan in its homeland. Nevertheless, the poor military situation in China was dispiriting to the Kuomintang leadership and was not designed to create the greatest possible harmony between the Nationalists and the United States.

The Department of State made occasional efforts to satisfy Nationalist demands for more military aid, but it usually ran into military objections from the Joint Chiefs. In cooperation with the British, however, the United States did renounce the extraterritorial rights that had long been a thorn to all Chinese. China was also given sufficient aid to keep her in the war.

The American government had the intention of restoring China to the lists of the great powers. It also intended to help China regain the territories it had lost to the Japanese. Although the British government had little hesitation about the latter objectives, it was dubious about granting great power status to China. The Soviets also were not especially eager to give China great power status.

At the 1943 Quebec meeting between Roosevelt and Churchill, the British, for whom the China issue was unimportant, accepted the American position. Molotov later had objections but these were modified at the Moscow meeting of the foreign ministers. Although China was not present at that meeting, she was permitted to sign the Moscow Declaration, as one of the issuing powers, thus giving her status as one of the Big Four. Article 6 of the Moscow Declaration was much to Chinese liking. It read, "That after the termination of hostilities the Big Four will not employ their military forces within the territories of other states except for the purposes envisaged in this declaration and after joint consultation."

The Soviets Enter

At Moscow, the Soviet Union promised to enter the Far Eastern War. Because of the well-known Chinese inability to keep secrets, they could not be informed of this offer. However, the Chinese Ambassador to Moscow, after asking Hull what position the Russians might take toward China, stated that China would be willing to enter any kind of alliance with the Soviet Union.

At Cairo in November, Roosevelt told Generalissimo Chiang that Manchuria, Formosa, and the Pescadores were to be returned to China. Roosevelt went on to Teheran to seek Stalin's approval. After some hesitation, Stalin agreed, but added that China should be made to fight. The United States agreed that China should be forced to make greater efforts in the war. When Roosevelt attempted to press the Soviet Union, however, on its entry into the Pacific war, Stalin was evasive. When Roosevelt returned to Cairo, he issued the Cairo Declaration, which stated Allied aims in the Pacific war and embodied the promises to China.

Roosevelt returned to Washington and summed up the agreements for the Pacific War Council. Japan was to be stripped of her island possessions. He reported that Stalin agreed that Manchuria, Formosa, and the Pescadores should be returned to China and that Korea was to undergo a forty-year tutlelage.[5] He added that Russia was interested in Dairen and passage rights on the Manchurian railway. The Soviet Union wanted all of Sakhalin Island and the Kuriles. China's ambassador, Dr. Wei Tao-ming, was present at this meeting of the Pacific War Council and raised no objections to Russia's ambitions.

The Wallace Mission

Vice-President Wallace was sent to China in June 1944 to attempt to get united action against the Japanese. Chiang complained to him that the Americans were being taken in by Communist propaganda and that the American military were taking a short-sighted point of view toward the Communist problem. Chiang requested that the United States take the lead in securing better relations between China and the Soviet Union.

Wallace said that the United States might act as a middleman in bringing the parties together, but that it could not attempt to arbitrate matters. The one firm agreement reached was that the United States military observers could go to the Communist districts in Yenan.

Wallace came away from the meeting convinced that Chiang was sincere, but he was puzzled over the inability of the Kuomintang and the Communists to get together. This inability distressed the American government, which feared that great power unity and the American plan for organizing the world for peace would be undermined if civil war broke out in China and the United States felt compelled to support one side while the Soviet Union felt compelled to support the other.

Attempts at Uniting China

By late summer of 1944, the United States was increasing its pressure to bring the Communist army under a unified China command and to arm it with American supplies. General Stilwell, according to this plan, was to be given the unified command of the theater, although he was to be responsible to Chiang Kai-shek as chief of state. Chiang bitterly resisted efforts to bring Communist forces within the command, claiming that these efforts weakened him and encouraged the Communists to be more stubborn in their opposition. The Communists evidently agreed. Mao Tse-tung remarked to John Service of the State Department that the chief benefit to the Communists of having American military observers attached to their command was political rather than military.

Meanwhile, a crisis developed between Chiang and General Stilwell, the most active proponent of unification and a severe critic of the Generalissimo. While the bickering continued, the military situation in China deteriorated. It became so bad for the Nationalists that General Chennault, who generally opposed Stilwell and took Chiang's point of view, reported that an agreement between Chiang and the Commuinsts in Yenan was mandatory; the Nationalists were so weak, he reported, that the Communists would be able to defeat them even without Russian aid.

Chiang, however, held out against collaboration and insisted that Stilwell be removed. The United States eventually resolved this impasse by removing Stilwell on the advice of Wallace. While no one of comparable authority was appointed to take his place, General Wedemeyer was appointed Chiang's Chief-of-Staff in October, 1945. In December, the new ambassador to China, Patrick J. Hurley, stated that the purposes of his China mission were to prevent the collapse of the Nationalist government and to sustain Chiang Kai-shek as president of the Republic and generalissimo of the armies.

American Conceptions of Chinese Politics

In this atmosphere, Hurley continued his efforts to secure a coalition. But the terms the Nationalists proposed would have given the Communists a tenuous status within a one-party Kuomintang dictatorship. Democratic reforms would be postponed to the indefinite future. In the meantime, the Communist armies would have lost their identity, and the Communist political leadership would have been at the mercy of Chiang's political police.

The terms the Communists proposed would have permitted them to carry on revolutionary activity while denying the Nationalists the right to interfere.

Ambassador Patrick Hurley regarded the Communists as a party with democratic aims. He remained sanguine about the chances for agreement. In accordance with American objectives, he refused to sanction aid to the Communists unless they subordinated themselves to Nationalist leadership.

A somewhat different view was taken by a group of China experts in the State Department, chiefly John Stewart Service, John Carter Vincent, and John Paton Davies. As did Hurley, they doubted that the Chinese Communists were genuine Marxists. However, they regarded them as the most viable political force in China and viewed the Nationalists as corrupt, hopeless, and doomed to eventual defeat.

This group of experts urged support for the Communists and warned that the Communists would look to the Soviet Union for leadership unless the United States seized the opportunity to back them. They also believed that political, social, and economic reform in the Nationalist areas of China was urgent if any kind of coalition were to be achieved, whereas Hurley had more faith in the vigor of the Nationalists and felt that reform could be postponed safely to the end of the war.

Yalta

In the midst of this struggle over United States policy in China, the Yalta Conference took place. China was not present. The Agreement Regarding Japan was formulated in bilateral Russian-American meetings. The British were not informed until agreement had been reached. Churchill gave his assent against Foreign Secretary Eden's advice in order that Britain might remain a power in the Far East.

The terms of the secret agreement were as follows:

> The leaders of the three Great Powers—the Soviet Union, the United States of America and Great Britain—have agreed that in two or three months after Germany has surrendered and the war in Europe has terminated the Soviet Union shall enter into the war against Japan on the side of the Allies on condition that:
>
> 1. The status quo in Outer-Mongolia (The Mongolian People's Republic) shall be preserved;
>
> 2. The former rights of Russia violated by the treacherous attack of Japan in 1904 shall be restored, viz:
>
>> (a) the southern part of Sakhalin as well as all the islands adjacent to it shall be returned to the Soviet Union,
>>
>> (b) the commercial port of Dairen shall be internationalized, the preeminent interests of the Soviet Union in this port being safeguarded and the lease of Port Arthur as a naval base of the USSR restored,
>>
>> (c) the Chinese-Eastern Railroad and the South-Manchurian Railroad which provided an outlet to Dairen shall be jointly operated by the establishment of a joint Soviet-Chinese Company, it being understood that the preeminent interests of the Soviet Union

shall be safeguarded and that China shall retain full sovereignty in Manchuria;

3. The Kurile Islands shall be handed over to the Soviet Union.

It is understood, that the agreement concerning Outer-Mongolia and the ports and railroads referred to above will require concurrence of Generalissimo Chiang Kai-shek. The President will take measures in order to obtain this concurrence on advice from Marshal Stalin.

The Heads of the three Great Powers have agreed that these claims of the Soviet Union shall be unquestionably fulfilled after Japan has been defeated.

For its part the Soviet Union expresses its readiness to conclude with the National Government of China a pact of friendship and alliance between the USSR and China in order to render assistance to China with its armed forces for the purpose of liberating China from the Japanese yoke.

Many points of protocol were left unclarified, including those concerning the Soviet Union's "preeminent interests." Although the terms of the agreement required Chiang's concurrence, Roosevelt promised that "these claims of the Soviet Union shall be unquestionably fulfilled. . . ." Evidently, there were no doubts that Chiang would concur.

American leaders were pleasantly surprised by the Soviet demands, which were less drastic than anticipated. It had been expected that the Soviet Union, in return for its aid in the war against Japan, would demand: (1) control of a belt of territory extending to the Persian Gulf; (2) control of and access to the Dardanelles, with definite rights to adjacent territory; and (3) commercial and military rights in Dairen and Port Arthur, with commanding control of those ports and the land approaches to them, including the Manchurian Railway. If the Soviet Union did not insist upon all these demands, it was expected that their order of importance coincided with the order of the listing.

Thus, Soviet demands were viewed as tolerable. At the same time, the Joint Chiefs agreed with the estimate of General MacArthur that a land invasion of Japan would be necessary to conclude the war successfully in the Pacific. Moreover, General MacArthur had stated that sixty Soviet divisions were necessary to pin down Japanese forces in Manchuria while he struck at the Japanese home islands.

Beyond this, General MacArthur warned against American involvement on the mainland of China. He feared that the Russians might in fact entice the United States to do this.[6] Only Admiral Leahy had confidence that Japan could be subdued without invasion of the home islands.

Therefore, in this period, Soviet cooperation was viewed as necessary in order to end the war quickly.

According to Averill Harriman, then ambassador to Russia, Roosevelt thought he had obtained his principal objectives. The Soviet Union had agreed to enter the war against Japan. Stalin had pledged support for Chiang Kai-shek and recognition of the sovereignty of the Nationalist government over Manchuria.

The agreement was reached in a period when the policy of unity was viewed as the indispensable means of achieving American world objectives. Russian intentions were viewed through rosy glasses. The pact seemed, indeed, to limit Soviet objectives in Asia and to strengthen the Nationalist regime.

Moreover, American means were not available to protect the Manchurian rights of the Nationalists if the Russians had the intention of aiding the Communists. Even the Pacific strategy proposed during the war by Admiral Nimitz—which MacArthur successfully opposed—would only have placed American troops on Formosa and on the mainland below the Great Wall, where they would not have been useful to Chiang for the reconquest of Manchuria.

Although Roosevelt believed wholeheartedly that the Russians would cooperate, a less optimistic interpreter of Russian aims might well have justified the agreement as a last ditch gamble to safeguard American objectives in Asia.

After he returned from Yalta, President Roosevelt reaffirmed his support of Ambassador Hurley's position, as opposed to that of the career officers of the State Department. The Chinese Communists would not receive supplies except through the Nationalist government. The United States would not waver in its support for the official regime.

Events in China

In March, Chiang announced that a People's Congress would be called in November to prepare for the introduction of constitutional government. Acting Secretary of State Joseph C. Grew praised this initiative. Mao, however, denounced the move as a fraud. Service reported from Yenan that the Communists were becoming increasingly self-confident and were less likely than ever to compromise. Hurley rejected this reasoning. He thought Chiang's action reasonable, and he thought that the Communists would find it expedient finally to cooperate in the Congress. He may have been influenced in this opinion by his knowledge of the secret Yalta accord and the belief that an agreement between China and the Soviet Union would affect the balance of the parties in China.[7]

Opposite Views of Soviet Intentions

Hurley went on a mission to Moscow to confer with the Soviet Union concerning China. He arrived on April 15, 1945, shortly after Roosevelt's death. During his stay, he informed Stalin that both the Kuomintang and the Chinese Communists had democratic aims, but that the United States was committed to the Nationalist cause. He told the marshal that the United States was training and equipping thirty-six Nationalist divisions and that, if the Communists would consolidate themselves under Chiang's command, the United States would train and equip them also. Stalin thought the arrangement a good one and agreed to support it.

Hurley cabled to Washington that Stalin was in complete agreement with American policy for China. Harriman—who flew back to Washington—was of the opposite opinion. He felt that Stalin would not cooperate with Chiang and would support the Communists. However, he agreed with Hurley's policy recommendation, although for the opposite reason. It was, he felt, most important for Chiang to conciliate Moscow and to strive for unification. Counselor George F. Kennan, in Moscow, was even less sanguine concerning Soviet aims. He thought they intended to control all of North China. However, Secretary of State Edward Stettinius leaned toward Hurley's view of the matter.

American Policy Reconsidered

In late April, Mao broadcast that the Communists had liberated areas containing ninety-five million people. He formulated plans for a coalition government under Communist leadership. However, the Department of State reaffirmed its intention to push for a unified government that was "broadly representative." In the interim, it continued to support Chiang Kai-shek.

A SWNCC[8] paper on military policy reaffirmed the policy of giving military support to the Nationalists to enable them to prosecute the war. At the same time, the paper stated that the United States would not assume any obligations to aid the Nationalist government in developing a postwar military force. This matter would be reconsidered when internal political unity and stability were achieved in China, when the government had the support of the people, and when the Chinese economy, with some American assistance, could support a modern army and air force.

General Albert C. Wedemeyer acted to carry out American policy, although he had to fight great Chinese inefficiency in organization and inability in strategy and tactics. He solved this problem by placing American advisers in key positions at the division level. Meanwhile, inflation was causing great difficulty in China. The United States was reluctant to act because the Treasury felt that aid was misused for the benefit of speculators.

In May 1945, persistent doubts were arising concerning the secret Yalta accords on China. When the question of maintaining them was put at a high level, Stimson and Marshall responded that (1) the Soviet Union would make its own decision about entering the war against Japan; (2) the United States could not influence that decision at a political level; (3) Soviet entry would shorten the war and save American lives; (4) the Soviets would have the military power to take what had been granted at Yalta unless we went to war to stop them; (5) unless there was some agreement between the Nationalists and the Communists, American military problems in China would become very complicated as the Soviet forces made contact with the Chinese Communists, and (6) the Yalta agreement was a necessity if there were to be a Sino-Soviet accord.

Sino-Soviet Negotiations

In late May, Stalin reaffirmed his support of Chiang to presidential advisor Harry Hopkins and promised that he would ask Chiang Kai-shek to organize the civil administration within the areas of occupation if Soviet troops entered Manchuria. In late June, the Nationalists were informed officially of the details of the Yalta accord on the Far East.[9] T. V. Soong, the Nationalist finance minister and brother-in-law of Chiang, asked that the United States be a party to the projected Sino-Soviet treaty and that the United States also use Port Arthur as a naval base. The United States doubted that Stalin would approve and refused to raise the issues. Meanwhile, clashes between the Chinese Communists and the Nationalists were increasing in scope, and General Wedemeyer feared that full-scale civil war would break out when the Japanese were forced to withdraw.

In July, Soong went to Moscow to negotiate the Sino-Soviet treaty. The Soviet asking price was high. Stalin wanted extensive concessions in Manchuria that seemed to go well beyond the Yalta agreement. Harriman encouraged Soong to resist these demands and secured a promise from Stalin that Soviet troops would begin to withdraw from Manchuria three weeks after the war with Japan ended and would complete the withdrawal in two or three months. This concession was quite welcome to the Americans, and Stalin offered to put it in writing.

In the midst of negotiations, Stalin had to leave for Potsdam. At Potsdam, China was made a member of the proposed Council of Foreign Ministers and participated in its meetings when Asiatic matters were discussed. This participation, together with China's permanent membership in the Security Council of the United Nations, was intended to strengthen the international role of China.

The American Military in China

On August 10, instructions were sent to Wedemeyer to take command of American forces that would land at key ports and communications points in the China theater. Wedemeyer was to assist Nationalist troops in key areas, and with Chiang's approval, he was to accept local surrenders. He was to deal only with Nationalist forces. On the other hand, he was not to permit American forces to become involved in a mainland campaign or civil war. Wedemeyer advocated speedy dispatch of American forces because the Chinese Communists were attempting to persuade the Japanese to surrender to them. The Joint Chiefs, however, could not give the China theater priority as General MacArthur was unwilling to release troops from his command for the venture.

Sino-Soviet Negotiations Resumed

Meanwhile, negotiations concerning the Sino-Soviet accord went on in Moscow. Harriman, disturbed by the Soviet demands, asked Stalin to subscribe to the Open Door doctrine and Stalin agreed. Harriman succeeded in moderating the Soviet demands with respect to Dairen and Port Arthur. Nevertheless, Soong conceded more to Stalin than the Department of State desired. However, the United States did not promise China military help, and Soong felt impelled to come to terms. Stalin failed to issue a public statement affirming support for the Open Door. He did, however, issue an unequivocal pledge of support to the Nationalist regime.

More American Efforts to Effect a Compromise

The Chinese Communists refused to accept the role that had been offered them. They demanded to be treated as a governmental force, competent to accept the surrender of the Japanese. The American observer, Colonel Yeaton, submitted a military report to Wedemeyer in which he stated that the Communists were too weak to oppose the Nationalists in position warfare, but over a long period of time, the Nationalists could not hold out as an occupying force in Communist areas, even with American help.

General Wedemeyer saw no alternative to civil war and ordered American forces to withdraw whenever trouble was brewing. The War Department approved the order. Hurley remained calm, believing that the Communists eventually would see that they could serve their own cause better by reaching an agreement with the Nationalists.

Under American pressure, talks between the Nationalists and Communists were held throughout August in an attempt to find a basis for agreement. Chiang was informed that he could not have unqualified American backing unless agreement was reached; the Communists were told that they could not hope for any support unless an agreement was reached. Meanwhile the Communists captured much in the way of arms from the Japanese, although the large Japanese garrisons, in accordance with MacArthur's General Order Number 1, refused to surrender to them.

The Americans aided the transportation of government troops northward to accept the Japanese surrender. The Chinese Communists bitterly denounced this activity. The marines were to land in Chefoo in August, but Chu Teh protested strongly, pointing out that there were no Japanese in the area and that it was in the control of the 8th Route Army. To land, he said, would be to interfere in Chinese internal politics. The Americans decided that the facts were as stated and refrained from the coastal landing.

As the task of the marines in China was nearing completion anyway, and as the Soviets might use the presence of the marines as an excuse to delay their own departure, on October 20 the Joint Chiefs asked American military headquarters in China to prepare for consideration a departure schedule.

Developments in American Policy

In the same period, a SWNCC report outlined American objectives in China. According to the report, American objectives required a friendly, unified, independent nation with a stable government resting, where possible, on the freely expressed will of the people. Nationalist armed forces should be equipped and supported only for these objectives, not to engage in fratricidal war. Economic assistance needs would also be filled to the extent Nationalist actions furthered these objectives.

Since the armistice, the situation had rapidly deteriorated for the Nationalists. There had been trouble, not only with the Communists but also with dissident groups in Turkestan and other outlying provinces. The Soviets had given the Chinese Communists at least negative assistance. They permitted them to infiltrate Manchuria and to capture stores of arms. They refused to permit Nationalist troops to use the port of Dairen on the pretext that it was an open commercial port. In addition, the promised American airlift to the north was so slow in materializing that Chiang agreed to extend the deadline for Soviet troop withdrawal from Manchuria until January lest the Chinese Communists have the area entirely to themselves.

The marines had been sent into China to help accept the Japanese surrender. By November, the American government instead saw the problem as one of holding the liberated areas for the Nationalists and began to debate whether or not the marines should be kept in China.

Wedemeyer reported to Washington that Chiang could not bring stability and democracy to China because he was surrounded by selfish and unscrupulous men and that he could not clear the Japanese out of North China without American aid. Nor could he beat the Communists in that area. If the marines remained in China, they would inevitably be involved in the fighting.

The Russians were establishing a line of influence in the North, but Wedemeyer regarded it as a defensive line and did not think they would use it as a "jumping off" point for further expansion. He concluded that if the marines were to interfere and aid the Nationalists, it would take forces and shipping "far beyond those now available or contemplated in the area." The War and Navy departments tossed the problem back to State, which decided to temporize and keep the marines in China a while longer.

The Marshall Mission

In November, Chiang's Political Consultative Conference failed to meet as scheduled, and the Communists refused to name any delegates. Hurley resigned with a critical blast at American policy. At the end of November, President Truman asked General Marshall, who had just retired as Chief of Staff, to investigate the situation in China.

At the beginning of December, the Communists reversed their position and agreed to send delegates to the Political Consultative Conference that Chiang had now called for December 16, 1945. They also stated that they were not opposed to the entry of Nationalist troops into

Manchuria and declared their friendship for the United States. The Communists did permit the Nationalists to advance to Mukden without opposition. According to a cable from MacArthur, Wedemeyer, and Spruance, American assistance should be used to effect a compromise "between the major opposing groups in China."[10] The situation was improved, and prospects for a compromise seemed strongly to be picking up.

The situation seemed ripe for a new conciliation effort. In this improved situation, President Truman, Byrnes, and Admiral Leahy instructed Marshall that he was to tell Chiang that the United States would transport the Nationalist troops northward by air if they were reasonable. However, the United States desired a unified China, and, if Chiang still refused to be reasonable, the United States would aid him and move his troops anyway. Marshall was ordered to employ his discretionary power to facilitate a compromise between the contending groups.

Marshall as Mediator

Early in January 1946, before the Political Consultative Conference met, the Nationalists proposed a cease-fire, with a committee composed of a representative of the Nationalist government, a representative of the Communist Party, and General Marshall as chairman, to discuss the cease-fire and related matters. This committee, afterwards known as the Committee of Three, met formally for the first time on January 7.

The Communists agreed, as an exception to the cease-fire, to permit the movement of Nationalist troops northward to Manchuria to reestablish Chinese sovereignty in that area. This concession was incorporated in the cease-fire of January 10, 1946. An Executive Headquarters—or the Committee of Three at a lower echelon—was to be established at Peiping to carry out the agreement, and it would send out field teams to observe on-the-spot compliance.

The Political Consultative Conference

The Political Consultative Conference (PCC) convened on January 10 and remained in session to the end of the month. Although its decisions were not legally binding, the resolutions of this all-party conference were expected to guide postwar political developments in China. At the opening session of the PCC, Chiang announced his agreement to freedom of speech and assembly, equal legal status for all political parties, the holding of elections, and the release of political prisoners.

PCC resolutions proposed a revision of the 1936 constitution and recommended that the Kuomintang establish the State Council as the supreme organ of the government pending the convening of the National Assembly. The proposed State Council was to consist of forty members, who would be chosen by Chiang, half from the Kuomintang and half from non-Kuomintang sources. The president could veto any Council resolution and could be overridden by a three-fifths vote. Otherwise, simple majorities would suffice, except where changes in administrative policy were to be decided. However, a majority vote could determine whether administrative policy was involved. The Communists began to press for fourteen seats, or more than the third necessary to block administrative changes. However, in a country which, in its republican era, had not been noted for legality of procedure, these proposals did not begin to touch the real question: who was to control the means of enforcing compliance?

Reorganization of Kuomintang and Communist Armies

On January 10, 1946, the Nationalists raised the question of the reorganization of the Kuomintang and Communist armies. This was the crux of the problem for it touched on the issues of power and control. Regardless of the governmental ornamentation the two groups might agree upon, the Kuomintang armies, for the most part, would remain loyal to Chiang and the Communist armies would obey Mao.[11]

A Military Subcommittee was established to handle this question.[12] At the end of February, it announced agreement to a program that was to be carried out over the next eighteen months. At the end of a year, the Nationalist military forces were to be reduced to ninety divisions and the Communist forces to eighteen; at the end of the full period, the Nationalists and Communists were to have fifty and ten divisions respectively, of not more than 14,000 men per division, to be organized into twenty armies of three divisions each.

At end of the period, the remaining divisions would be deployed in the following manner: Northeast China (Manchuria), fourteen Nationalist and one Communist; Northwest China, nine Nationalist; North China, eleven Nationalist and seven Communist divisions; Central China, ten Nationalist and two Communist; and South China (including Formosa), six Nationalist divisions.

While the divisional structure permitted the Communist command to work at an effective level, the distribution of divisions was such that the Nationalist units would easily have been able to surround and destroy the Communist units should they desire, except in North China.

North China was the area in which the Communists had their greatest strength in 1946. Despite Marshall's attempts to turn the Chinese army into a nonpolitical agency, these were the realities of Chinese politics.

Although the agreements were quite favorable to the Kuomintang, elements within it were apparently dissatisfied and began to use violence against the supporters of the agreements. Moreover, the Central Executive Committee (CEC) of the Kuomintang approved the proposals with reservations that it did not make public. Thereupon, the Communist party refused to participate in the PCC until these reservations were announced and found agreeable. During this crisis, Marshall left on March 11 for consultations in Washington.

Deterioration of Truce—Nationalist Recalcitrance

Meanwhile there was a deterioration of the truce. Although there had been no stipulation that Manchuria was exempted from the truce—except for Nationalist troop movements to that area—fighting had broken out at Yingkow. On January 24, Marshall proposed that an Executive Headquarters field team be sent to the area to prevent additional incidents of that character.

The Communists agreed, but the Kuomintang refused, apparently with the object of crushing all Communist groups in that area. Finally on March 11, the Kuomintang, after additional pressure from Marshall, did agree. But it imposed stipulations that prevented the field teams from bringing about a cease-fire. In addition, the Kuomintang commander at Canton refused to recognize the authority of Executive Headquarters, and the Nanking command frustrated Executive Headquarters operations by failing to report the movements of its troops according to agreement. In the North Hupeh-South Honan area, the Kuomintang had surrounded 60,000 Communist troops and prevented supplies from reaching them.

Communist Advance in Manchuria

The Chinese Communists took advantage of the breakdown in the operation of the truce teams to infiltrate additional troops into Manchuria. Delayed Russian withdrawal enabled them to take over stores abandoned by the Japanese armies.

In this fashion, suspicions were aroused on both sides. The suspicions were augmented when the Nationalists began removing the civil administrations in the Manchurian areas they had just occupied and

replacing them with the most anti-Communist elements of the Kuomintang. Afterwards, the Communists refused to submit a complete list of
their troops pursuant to the agreement.

In the meantime the PCC steering committee indefinitely postponed
the meeting of the National Assembly. Subsequently, the Russians refused
to permit the Nationalists to use the rail line to Changchun, alleging
that it was prohibited by the terms of the Sino-Soviet treaty of 1945. The
Chinese Communists also attacked the American government for trans-
porting more Chinese Nationalist troops to Manchuria than the agreement called for, although the United States pointed out that it was a
year before the reduction envisaged by the agreement was to be effective.

Changchun—Communist Truce Violation

On April 15, 1946, the Chinese Communists attacked Changchun;
they occupied it on April 18. This was a clear violation of the truce. On
the same day, Marshall returned to China from his short trip to the
United States for consultation with Truman. He found the impasse complete, although the Communists were willing to submit future troop dis-
positions to negotiation if the fighting were terminated.

The Nationalist position deteriorated so much in the next six weeks
that Chiang was willing to accept the terms the Communists had offered,
except that he wanted the Communists to evacuate Changchun. However, the military circle around Chiang was still advocating a policy of
force that it would not be able to carry out even with American logistical
support. As Wedemeyer had predicted, the effort to extend the Nationalist line of communication and control through Manchuria only served
to weaken them while the Communists gained in relative strength.

Marshall Chastizes Both Sides

Marshall lectured Chiang, telling him that Kuomintang actions had
given the Communists reason to be suspicious; he accused him of breaking the truce without gaining any military benefit from these actions.
On the contrary, his position was weaker than it had been. The Communists, feeling their strength, were now demanding a better ratio of Communist to Kuomintang troops in Manchuria.

On the other hand, Marshall told Chou that Chiang was now offering reasonable terms, that it had been agreed that governmental sovereignty should be restored in Manchuria, and that this could not be accomplished unless the government controlled Changchun. He said that
the Communist attack on Changchun had taken the matter out of his

hands and that he could no longer assume the function of mediator, although he would hold separate conversations with each side.

The Communists who had originally cooperated with the field teams were now obstructing their activity. In view of these difficulties, the Committee of Three arrived at an agreement on May 14 providing for more prompt investigation of reported violations of the truce. Marshall now told Chiang what he had told Chou, in this case putting the blame on the Nationalists. Their intransigence, he said, made it impossible for him to continue as a mediator.

Chiang Fails Marshall

Chiang asked Marshall for suggestions. Marshall proposed that the Communists should withdraw from Changchun and that an advance echelon of the Executive Headquarters should be stationed there, preliminary to Nationalist occupation. He urged caution since the Nationalists were weaker than the Communists in Manchuria and argued that Nationalist acceptance of this proposal would bolster the impression that they genuinely desired peace. Moreover, if agreement were not reached quickly, China faced military and economic chaos.

Upon being informed of the American proposals, the Communists expressed the fear that their evacuation of Changchun would serve as a precedent for Kuomintang occupation of other cities, such as Harbin. However, after daily negotiations, agreement was practically completed when a new source of trouble appeared. Chiang told Marshall that he had lost contact with his forces approaching Changchun and that it would be disastrous if the city were occupied by force on the eve of agreement. He then requested and got use of General Marshall's private plane to enable him to establish contact with the Nationalist armies in that area.

Marshall then told Chou En-lai, Mao's representative, of the arrangements and informed him of three new conditions that Chiang had proposed. Chou told Marshall that his conditions were acceptable to the Communists but that Chiang's proposals were new and would have to be studied. However, it was only with respect to the third condition—that in the case of disagreement between the Chinese members of the Committee, the American member of the field team could make the decision—that it was necessary to consult his colleagues in order to reach agreement.

On May 23, 1946, Kuomintang troops entered Changchun. In the meantime, Chiang was making speeches in Mukden that indicated—

contrary to the statements he had made to Marshall—that he welcomed this development. This was quite embarrassing to Marshall inasmuch as his plane had been used to get Chiang to Mukden. Moreover, the Kuomintang armies continued the offensive past Changchun, and Chiang ignored Marshall's protests against this extension of the campaign.

Chiang Extends His Demands

On May 28, Chiang informed Marshall that he would insist on taking over the civil administrations throughout Manchuria, but that he would use no more force than necessary to accomplish this, provided that he had American guarantees of Communist good faith. On June 3, Chiang agreed to a ten-day cease-fire provided that arrangements were made for a detailed cease-fire in Manchuria, the Communists opened communications for him throughout North China, and an agreement was reached for carrying out the military reorganization. Chiang said that lack of coal and communications and starvation in the cities would make an all-out war preferable to a truce if this agreement were not reached.

On the other hand, if the Communists agreed, Chiang would be in a position to build up his supplies without interference for a further attack on the Communists. The Communists agreed to permit the transportation of civilian supplies and to terminate hostilities in Manchuria. The great difficulties to complete agreement centered around the demobilization, reorganization, and redistribution of troops. Marshall, therefore, attempted to solve these technical problems and rejected Third Party attempts to inject political matters. He feared that political discussions would only confuse the issues.

By June 17, it became apparent that Chiang's ambitions had increased. He demanded Communist evacuation of Jehol and Chahar provinces before September 1, the Kuomintang occupation of Chefoo and Weihaiwai in Shantung Province, the reinforcement of Tsingtao with a Nationalist army to permit the withdrawal of American marines, the evacuation of all parts of Shantung occupied by the Communists after June 7, 1946, and Nationalist occupation of Tientsin to permit marine withdrawal, plus Kuomintang occupation of such Communist strongholds in Manchuria as Harbin, Antung, Tunghwa, Mutankiang, and Paicheng. Chou pointed out that, except for the restoration of the status quo in Shantung as of June 7, none of the points could be considered. Chou refused to return to Yenan to discuss these demands with his colleagues, as Marshall requested, because he said there was nothing about which to consult.

Communist Concessions

The truce period was running out as conditions deteriorated. Kuomintang officials were advocating a policy of force, claiming that the Communists could be crushed. Under these handicaps, General Marshall prevailed upon Chiang to extend the truce to June 30, 1946. At the same time, Chiang made fresh demands on the Communists, including Communist evacuation of the Tsinan-Tsingtao Railway. At this point, Marshall resumed his role of mediator and participated in Committee of Three meetings. The Chinese Communists agreed that the Americans were to have the deciding vote at Executive Headquarters and in the field teams. Marshall, however, refused the responsibility of casting the deciding vote in the Committee of Three in matters of great importance that went beyond the interpretation of agreements.

Agreement was quickly reached on the termination of hostilities in Manchuria. However, Chou objected that Kuomintang troops would move into Communist areas under the proposed agreements and would replace Communist civil administration, thus reversing the principle of civilian supremacy. The Communists wanted local self-government to be determined by elections. This unseating of local administration, Chou said, was incompatible with the PCC resolutions. The Communists did agree to withdraw from certain areas to erase Kuomintang fears of a Communist threat, provided that the areas from which they withdrew remained ungarrisoned.

On June 27, Chiang told Marshall that political matters could not be adjusted until after the military adjustments. Chiang then stepped up his military demands and proposed that the Communists should evacuate Kiangsu Province, the Tsinan-Tsingtao Railway, Chengte and Kupeiku, Antung Province, and Harbin within ten days. Within one months, the Communists should have evacuated the other areas Chiang had previously specified. Kuomintang troops would occupy these areas. As a compromise, Chiang proposed that Communist civil administrations in Hsin Heilungchiang, Hsingan, and Nenchiang Provinces in Manchuria and Chahar Province temporarily would be acceptable to the Kuomintang.

Chou protested that garrison troops must not interfere with civil administrations and that, although the Communists would consider readjustments around Harbin and other specified areas, they would not consider the government claims to the Tsinan-Tsingtao Railway, Chengte, Kupeikou, and certain other places. The Communists would be willing to reduce or withdraw entirely their troops in Kiangsu and Shantung, but government troops should not enter these areas. The Communists would withdraw their forces from the Tsinan-Tsingtao Railway if the government would agree not to garrison them. All Communist troops would be withdrawn from the Tsaochuang coal mines, freeing both the railway and coal mines for Kuomintang use. But these withdrawals, Chou specified, were not to prejudice the local administrations. The Kuomintang negotiators, however, found these stipulations unacceptable.

Chiang Creates Difficulties

General Marshall drew up a draft proposal largely following the lines of the concessions that the Communists were willing to make. He showed the draft to Chiang. Although Chiang agreed to allow some of the local administrations to function, he was adamant with regard to others, and insisted that the Communists should withdraw from all the territory he demanded and that this territory should not be left ungarrisoned, but should be occupied by government troops. Chou agreed to Chiang's counterproposals with a few modifications, one of which, concerning the status of local administrations, was, he said, of supreme importance. He also wanted an extension of Chiang's deadline for the evacuation of certain areas.

The Generalissimo refused to allow an extension, whereupon Marshall told him that it was logistically impossible for the Communists to withdraw in the time he specified. Marshall also said that Chiang should compromise on the local government issue and that the Kuomintang had been acting dictatorially in the areas it had been reoccupying. Under Marshall's pressure, both sides continued the truce beyond the specified deadline of June 30.

Anti-Americanism Grows

Both sides, however, unleashed a barrage of anti-American propaganda, the Kuomintang side proclaiming that American economic aid was undermining the Chinese economy and the Communists claiming that American aid without conditions encouraged the Nationalists to follow a war policy. The Kuomintang secret police hospitalized nonparty advocates of compromise in Nanking. During July, hostilities began to spread throughout China proper.

On July 7, the Communist Party issued a manifesto denouncing American policy. Marshall scolded Chou and informed him that such propaganda blasts, which paralleled those coming from Moscow, impeded his activities as an impartial mediator. In late July, the Kuomintang secret police assassinated two Democratic League members and carried out a widespread campaign of intimidation. The Communists ambushed a marine convoy and killed three Americans.

Ambassador Stuart Enters the Picture

The situation had deteriorated to such an extent that Marshall felt he needed the assistance of an American of unquestioned character and integrity with long experience in China. On his recommendation, Dr. J. Leighton Stuart, president of Yenching University at Peiping, was appointed U.S. Ambassador to China. Chou immediately proposed an unconditional cease-fire.

Marshall told a Nationalist leader that Chiang's reputation would deteriorate if he followed his present unyielding policy. Marshall said that Chiang expected conditions to develop favorably for him during this lull but that the opposite would occur, that a financial and military crisis would occur, at which point Chiang would be forced to appeal for aid that would not be forthcoming. Marshall insisted that the Nationalists were creating conditions that would increase the likelihood of a Communist regime in China.

Apparently, American policy in this period was directed to the maintenance of non-Communist power in the bulk of the mainland and was unwilling to risk the loss of this bastion by the pursuance of what it considered an ill-advised venture for the whole of China.

American Pressure on Chiang

Under pressure from the Americans, Chiang agreed on August 5, 1946, to the creation of an informal five-man committee, with Dr. Stuart as chairman, to prepare the organization of the proposed State Council. However, Chiang proposed five conditions for this agreement, and they were more exacting than those he had made at the end of June.

The Communists objected that these proposals made no mention of local government. Marshall and Stuart issued a statement on August 10 indicating that local government, rather than troop redisposition, was the real issue. In conversations with Chiang, they warned him that he was wrong when he thought that his policy of force would compel the Communists to sue for terms. They informed Chiang that his lines of communication were overextended and that disaster threatened. Chiang could not, they said, cope with Communist guerrilla tactics. His ability to capture cities was no indication of his ability to control the surrounding countryside.

Chiang refused to budge from his five conditions, stating that even these conditions involved military danger for his government. On August 13, he issued a statement to the public blaming the Communists for the breakdown in negotiations and offering constitutional rule and a broadened government.

Chou expressed his agreement to participate in the Five-Man Committee. But, when Chiang continued to insist upon his five demands, Chou said that Communist participation in the State Council would only raise false hopes. In the meantime, the fighting widened. Each side accused the other of provoking it. The Kuomintang mounted an offensive in Kiangsu.

On August 10, President Truman had sent a message to Chiang informing him of unfavorable reactions to his policy among the American public, with the possible consequence that American policy toward China would be reexamined. Chiang's reply to Truman contained obvious misstatements of fact. Truman sent another message on August 31 informing Chiang that only the prompt ending of the civil war and the attainment of unity would permit effective American aid for the economic rehabilitation of China.

On August 30, the American government carried out a surplus property transaction with the Kuomintang government. The Chinese Communists unleashed a propaganda barrage against the United States. Marshall patiently pointed out to them that the transaction had been under discussion for some time and that the Communist attitude was quite unhelpful. However, the military aid program did place him in the position of supplying one side with arms while attempting impartial mediation. Marshall, therefore, secured an embargo upon military shipments to China.[13]

The Communists Become Difficult

On September 3, the Five-Man Committee began to meet, but the Communists brought up extraneous matters at the session. Marshall, thereupon, informed the Committee that Dr. Stuart would serve as chairman only when State Council matters were discussed. Chou said that the Communists could participate in the State Council only after a cease-fire was arranged. Otherwise, he said, the Kuomintang-Youth Party majority grouping in the Council would impose any terms it desired.

Chiang agreed that terms for the cessation of hostilities should be determined by the Committee of Three rather than by the State Council. He also said, however, that the question of civil administration in reoccupied areas should be determined by the State Council.

Chou found these terms unacceptable and demanded that the Committee of Three be reconvened to discuss the cease–fire. Marshall considered this a return to the impasse of late June and told the Communists that their proposal would only give the government time to mount an offensive against them.[14] The Communists, however, insisted that they must control sufficient votes in the State Council to veto any revision of PCC resolutions and that there must be an early cease-fire.

Chiang refused to consider a meeting of the Committee of Three until the State Council issue had been disposed of. He was, however, conciliatory with regard to the issues concerning State Council matters that the Committee of Five would discuss.

On September 16, Chou left Nanking for Shanghai, leaving three memoranda for General Marshall. One of these denounced American aid to the Kuomintang as contributory to civil war, the second requested the convening of the Committee of Three, and the third said that Chou would not return from Shanghai until a meeting of the Committee of Three was convened.

Chiang again rejected the demand that the Committee of Three meet. However, he did agree to increase Communist representation upon the State Council so that it would be only one shy of the number required to veto a revision of PCC resolutions. He argued that surely there would be at least one other Councilor who would vote independently.

Chiang Pursues Force

By late September, Kuomintang advances made Chiang's five demands academic. He now advanced new demands, refusing to agree to a cease-fire until the Communist delegates to the National Assembly were named. Chiang indicated that the Executive Yuan, the "cabinet" of the Nationalist government, would not be reorganized until the National Assembly had met. The position of the two sides appeared irreconcilable.

Meanwhile, Communist propaganda attacks on the United States and General Marshall were stepped up. Marshall, incensed, informed the Communists that, if they doubted his impartiality as a mediator, they should inform him and he would immediately withdraw from the negotiations. However, at the same time, Marshall impressed upon the Nationalists the need for caution and warned against putting the Communists in a position where they would seek Russian aid.

Marshall then proposed on September 27 that the Nationalists suggest the convening of the Five-Man Committee and the Committee of Three with the understanding that the tentative agreements of June be carried out, that the Committee of Three determine questions of military reorganization and integration, that the PCC steering committee confirm the decisions of the Committee of Five, that local government issues be settled by the State Council, and that, concurrently with the cessation of hostilities, the Communists publish their list of delegates to the National Assembly. Marshall also recommended that the Kuomintang, at the same time, should take action to secure the cessation of hostilities.

Chiang informed Marshall that he could not agree to a cease-fire until there was complete agreement on the redisposition of troops in the Committee of Three and agreement in the Five-Man Committee concerning the constitution of the State Council. Marshall protested that this would vitiate the entire purpose of his suggestion.

During this period, the Kuomintang forces began to advance toward Kalgan. The Communists, who had been besieging Tatung since late August, lifted the siege of that city to deprive the Nationalists of the pretext that the drive on Kalgan was a reprisal. However, on September 30, the Kuomintang announced plans for the capture of Kalgan, whereupon the Communists refused to name their delegates to the National Assembly unless the PCC resolutions were followed. They said that unless the government dropped its move against Kalgan, it would be an indication that the Kuomintang desired a "total national split."

Marshall Threatens to Withdraw

Marshall found both sides very difficult to deal with and began to consider withdrawing from his mission. He informed Chiang that, unless a basis for a cease-fire were arrived at, he would ask the president to relieve him. Chiang said that he understood Marshall's embarrassment, but that it was essential for the government to capture Kalgan.

This was a reversal of Chiang's June position. Chiang, moreover, set conditions for a cease-fire that would permit Kuomintang military operations to proceed for quite some time. Marshall felt that this proposal was of doubtful integrity, and he refused to make the United States a party to it. Marshall then forwarded a message to Washington requesting his recall.

Dr. Stuart advised Chiang of Marshall's cable, whereupon Chiang offered a truce of five days or longer. Marshall replied that a short truce would not allow time for successful negotiations and that a long truce would be too difficult to control. He asked Chiang to accept his proposal of September 27. This specified an immediate cessation of hostilities once certain procedures were agreed to. Chiang counterproposed that Marshall accept his proposal for a five-day truce, whereupon he would then extend the period if it appeared that the Communists were sincere in their negotiations. Marshall then advised Truman of the withdrawal of his request to be relieved of his assignment, since he found this an acceptable basis upon which to proceed.

The Communists Make Trouble

The Communists rejected this proposal. The Communists stated that there should be no time limit to the truce and that discussions in the Committee of Three and the Five-Man Committee should not be limited to the two propositions that the Kuomintang had put forward.

Marshall felt that it was the Communist party that was recalcitrant to a truce at this period. The Communists replied that the government would have to show its sincerity by withdrawing its troops from the Kalgan region. The Communists said they would not bow to the policy of force and hinted that American mediation was not strictly impartial.

Marshall visited Shanghai to talk to Chou. It appeared that there had been a misunderstanding about whether the Communists were to negotiate or carry out the Kuomintang proposals. Chou said the proposal would fix the position of the Communist troops while allowing the Kuomintang troops freedom of movement.

Chou then proposed that all troops resume their positions of January 13, 1946, except in Manchuria, where the positions of June 7, 1946, would be resumed. This would have involved a considerable retreat from the positions the Kuomintang had won since the original cease-fire. After further conferences with Marshall, Chou stated that, if the government would permanently call off its attack upon Kalgan, the Communists would participate in the Committee of Three and the Five-Man Committee.

A group of Third Party forces went to Shanghai to persuade Chou to change his mind. They felt they were having some success in this matter when a number of events occurred. On October 10, 1946, Chiang made a speech accusing the Communists of full responsibility for the truce breakdowns. On the same day, Kuomintang forces captured Kalgan and also made fresh inroads in Jehol and Kiangsu provinces. In addition, the government announced the resumption of nationwide conscription. Sun Fo, president of the Legislative Yuan, felt that Chou had nevertheless been convinced to return. However, the next day, the government announced that the General Assembly, most of whose members had been elected under Kuomintang auspices in 1936, was ordered to convene on November 12, 1946. On this news, Chou announced his refusal to return, and the minority parties strongly criticized the Kuomintang for its "dictatorial action."

Marshall reminded Chiang that the latter had previously stated that a harsh policy would be followed by a generous one and insisted that this was the time for generosity. Marshall submitted a proposal for Chiang's consideration. Chiang made an eight-point counter-proposal. While the Communist reaction to these proposals was unfavorable, Chou nevertheless was persuaded by Third Party forces to return to Nanking. Meanwhile, fighting continued, particularly around points of communication. The Communists also stepped up their propaganda against the United States. Although Marshall and Stuart made strenuous efforts to stop the hostilities and complained to Chou that he was rejecting proposals that he had previously accepted, their efforts were largely unavailing.

Third Party Efforts at Conciliation

The minority parties offered a new three-point proposal, which the Communists proved largely willing to accept. Chiang rejected it, however, and the Kuomintang stepped up its offensive. Finally the Third Party representatives tried to get the two contending parties to agree to informal discussions. Chiang agreed, provided that his eight points governed the agenda. Chou accepted, and a meeting was scheduled for November 4, 1946.

Before the meeting took place, General Marshall had a serious conversation with Chiang in which he urged him to adopt a more conciliatory policy. Marshall pointed out that, although the Kuomintang had been capturing cities, it had not destroyed any Communist armies, that these armies simply refused to give battle and withdrew to the hills. The Generalissimo then agreed that the time had come to halt the fighting. But he stated that he did not want this information to be transmitted to the Third Party forces. However, Marshall informed him that these forces were the only hope in the situation.

Chiang Makes Concessions

On October 30, Chiang informed Dr. Stuart that he would permit a cease-fire order to apply also to Manchuria, and that he would make no additional changes in local administrations along the Changchun Railway, except in localities already occupied by the government.

The Communists were now placing great stress upon the reorganization of the Executive Yuan, while the previous issues of the State Council and local government no longer appeared devoid of solution. The Communists insisted on reorganization of the Executive Yuan before they would name their delegates to the National Assembly, whereas Chiang insisted that delegates to the National Assembly be named first.

The importance of the issue stemmed from the fact that the National Assembly would be controlled by Chiang's delegates, who had been elected in 1936. If the Communists participated in this Assembly, they could be outvoted on any issue that had not previously been settled.

The Communists now placed pressure upon the Third Party forces to stand with them in refusing to name delegates to the National Assembly until the government had been reorganized in accordance with the PCC resolutions. This proved embarrassing to the minority parties, and they urged General Marshall and Dr. Stuart to take the lead in the negotiations. The American negotiators declined because they considered it important for a neutral Chinese group to mediate political matters.

Chiang's Paper-Thin Concessions

Chiang refused to send his delegates to the scheduled conciliation meeting of November 4. He explained that he took this action because he did not believe that the Communists desired American mediation. Marshall regretted this action as he thought it had no bearing on the matter. Chiang thereupon agreed that the time had come for an unconditional cease-fire, and asked the Americans to advise him in this matter. They prepared a draft statement for him. In turn, Chiang submitted to Marshall and Stuart his draft, which, by refusing to consider a reorganization of the Executive Yuan, would, in their opinion, worsen the situation.

Chiang explained that he had to take into account the unanimity of feeling within the Kuomintang that a policy of force should be followed. Since the situation had changed, the PCC resolutions should no longer be given precedence over the 1936 draft constitution. Chiang said that he was alone within the Kuomintang in his belief that matters could be settled peacefully. Marshall prepared a redraft for Chiang, based on Chiang's recommendations, but informed Chiang that the new draft did not have his approval as the representative of the United States government.

Chiang therefore modified the draft when he made his statement of November 8, 1946. But it was inconclusive with regard to governmental reorganization and held the threat of the use of force, although a cease-fire order was issued. Chou reluctantly attended a Committee of Three meeting on November 10, but announced that the convocation of the National Assembly would mean a definite split in China.

Chou did agree, however, to forward the government proposals to Yenan and to work for a cessation of hostilities. The PCC steering committee met and agreed to a reorganization of the Executive Yuan. This reorganization, however, was not to be announced until after the adjournment of the assembly. The National Assembly was postponed for several days while Chiang negotiated with Third Party forces. It was finally convened on November 15. However, the Communists refused to attend, as did the members of the Democratic League, although other Third Party elements did attend. Thus, the Third Party was split and ceased to exist as an effective mediating agent.

Negotiations Break Off

On November 16, Chou asked Marshall to arrange his transportation to Yenan. Marshall asked Chou to take up the subject of his continued mediation with Communist leaders, and stated that he wanted the matter considered as a plain business proposition without questions of "losing face" entering into it.

Both Sides Recalcitrant

Marshall was now doubtful that either side would carry out its agreements. Meanwhile, government military expenditures were consuming 70 percent of the budget, inflation was rife, and half of the government gold reserve had been depleted. Marshall felt that American economic assistance was useless so long as the government was determined to follow a policy of unlimited force. Moreover, there was so much corruption in the government that any aid would be misused.

On December 1, Marshall held a long interview with Chiang. Marshall pointed out that even the most conciliatory government moves had been accompanied by military action that had nullified their effects. He pointed out the danger of economic collapse and the failure of Chiang's predictions concerning his ability to clean the Communists out of certain areas. Marshall concluded that the Communists were too large a force to be ignored, they could not be destroyed through a military campaign, and the only solution was to bring them into the government.

Chiang replied that he was firmly convinced that the Communists never intended to cooperate with the government and that they were acting under Russian influence with the purpose of disrupting the activities of the government. He felt that it was necessary to crush their military forces and predicted that, when this was accomplished, they could be handled politically. Chiang felt that the Communist forces could be defeated in eight to ten months. Marshall disagreed.

Chou forwarded to Marshall the Communist terms for a resumption of negotiations. Those terms called for a dissolution of the National Assembly and the restoration of troop positions as of January 13. They did not include any answer to Marshall's request concerning his mediation activities, thus, in effect, repudiating him. Marshall forwarded their message without comment.

Marshall then refused the advisory position that Chiang offered him, since this would have given him a position with less influence than he had as a mediator and a representative of the United States. Moreover, Marshall felt that the only solution for China was the elimination of corruption and the development of an effective opposition party.

Marshall Encourages Minor Parties

Marshall encouraged the minor party groups to work together and to attempt to develop an effective opposition. He influenced Chiang to stand firm against the reactionary elements in the Kuomintang. In fact, the National Assembly adopted a new constitution that provided for most goals called for by the PCC resolutions. However, Marshall was more concerned by the degree and manner of its enforcement than by its paper provisions. Therefore, he continued his efforts to encourage liberal, minor-party elements in China.

Marshall Mission Ends

The Communists reiterated their opposition to the measures that had been taken. Mediation now seemed hopeless. Therefore, Marshall devoted his final efforts to strengthening democratic elements in China. On January 6, 1947, President Truman announced that he had directed

General Marshall to return to the United States to report in person. Marshall said that the most discouraging factor in the situation was the suspicion both sides had of each other.

United States Policy—December 1946

American policy had been announced in President Truman's statement of December 18, 1946. A united and democratic China was the American aim. Truman announced his willingness to grant constructive aid to China and felt that the plans of January for the political and military reorganization were still sound. The Kuomintang interpreted this as an endorsement of its position while the Communists attacked it as an "apology for U.S. reactionary policy toward China since March. . . ." In January, all American marines, except for a guard contingent at Tsingtao, were withdrawn from China and American personnel were withdrawn from Executive Headquarters. Marshall subsequently was nominated as secretary of state.

Chiang Resumes Negotiations

On January 15, 1947, Chiang informed Dr. Stuart that the Nationalists would like to hold discussions with the Communists at Yenan or Nanking, that both sides should immediately issue a cease-fire, and that agreements should be reached on the reorganization of the army and the political control of disputed areas. Dr. Stuart, acting only as a means of transmission, informed Communist representative Wang Ping-nan of the Nationalist desire to negotiate. But, as requested by Chiang, Stuart said only that the government attached no conditions to the negotiations. Wang replied that the Communists would agree to talk if the constitution were abrogated and the positions of January 13 were restored. He emphasized, however, that these demands were made to clear the ground rather than to break off negotiations. Stuart informed Washington that the Communists were confident and that he believed they meant what they said.

The Communists Reject Chiang's Efforts

The Nationalists now listed their four points publicly. On January 29, the Communists replied that these conditions constituted a fraud. The Nationalists stated that they had no option but to proceed with their plans for democratic political reorganization, and they informed the Communists that their delegation would no longer be welcome at

Nanking. The Communists then accused the Nationalists of selling out to foreign interests and denounced the American government.

On March 10, Molotov proposed that the Council of Foreign Ministers deal with the Chinese problem, but American and Nationalist objections blocked this. The Chinese Foreign Minister informed the United States that the Soviet Union had asked the Chinese to take over the administration of Dairen and Port Arthur and that the railroad from Dairen to Changchun would be jointly operated, but nothing came of the negotiations.

Political Changes in Nationalist China

On March 1, the Legislative and Control Yuans were reorganized. However, there were disagreements between the Kuomintang and the Third Party groupings over distribution of seats within these bodies. Throughout the negotiations, some seats were left open for Communist participation. During this period, Dr. T. V. Soong resigned as Prime Minister. Stuart thought, from the available information, that Soong resigned because Chiang was preparing for all-out war and because Soong saw no way of solving the government's financial problems under these circumstances.

Ineffective Policy of Force

Fighting was picking up that spring, and the Nationalists were losing more men than the Communists. However, despite the Nationalist pledge to Stuart that they would not assault Yenan, the Communist headquarters, the Nationalists made gains there in mid-March, thus making negotiations even more difficult. Despite Nationalist claims of a great victory, Stuart reported that the Nationalists had overextended their lines and the Communists had not suffered manpower losses. The Nationalist victories were deceptive, Stuart reported. However, the Nationalists were now predicting victory in six months, and it was not possible to influence them to a moderate policy.

Student demonstrations were breaking out in Nationalist-controlled areas in this period, and sentiment in liberal Kuomintang circles favored compromise. The government began to suffer reverses in Manchuria and the Northwest. Stuart felt that there was a serious danger of defection from the Nationalist armies. By June, he was warning of potential disaster in Manchuria. Stuart thought that impending catastrophe might aid the liberal elements in the Kuomintang and Chiang might possibly be replaced. Stuart also felt that sectional governments might replace a national government in China.

The Situation Deteriorates

On April 17, the Executive Yuan and the State Council were reorganized. On April 23, the Minister of Information announced that the period of tutelage had ended. Stuart said that it was too early to assess the effect of the changes, and that it must be remembered that many previous reorganizations had been consummated only for their external effects, with little real change in domestic government methods. While Stuart regarded the composition of the State Council favorably, he was concerned by the formation of a political committee—the equivalent of the Politburo in the Soviet Communist Party—headed by Chen Li-fu, leader of a reactionary clique.

During June, Stuart reported, Kuomintang rule had alienated the population in Manchuria. The Kuomintang Central Executive Committee conferred with Stuart and took measures to meet the deteriorating political situation. Stuart regarded these measures as so inadequate that they would have been "farcical had they not been so tragic...."

On July 4, the State Council proclaimed that the Communists were in open rebellion. On July 6, Stuart delivered a message from Secretary of State Marshall in which Marshall informed Chiang that he had predicted the unfavorable consequences of Kuomintang policies. Although the United States sympathized with Chiang's efforts to unify China, the United States could not solve Chinese problems, but it would continue to assist the Nationalists.

Stuart continued to warn of deteriorating conditions in North China and Manchuria. He urged Chiang to undertake radical reforms. Stuart reported to the Department of State that sentiment in the universities was 90–95 percent against both the government and the Communists, but that vigorous reform measures in the government might do something to restore the situation.

The Wedemeyer Mission

The situation in China and Korea had deteriorated to such an extent by July 1947 that President Truman decided to send General Wedemeyer on a fact-finding mission. Right-wing Kuomintang opinion was pleased by his appointment, as it was believed that Wedemeyer's visit was an indication of strong American support. Liberal and opposition groups feared that the American mission would prolong the war. The Communists, of course, denounced it bitterly.

In late August, General Wedemeyer had completed his fact-finding mission. In response to Kuomintang requests for a frank appraisal, in a meeting with top Kuomintang officials, he castigated the incompetence, corruption, and lack of inspiration in the regime. Some in the audience were so furious that they burst into tears. Chiang was fearful that the United States wanted to replace him. The reaction in China became so bitter that Chiang began to issue statements claiming that American and Chinese interests were in opposition and that it might be necessary for the government to work with the Russians.

In his report, General Wedemeyer recommended:

> That China be advised that the United States is favorably disposed to continue aid designed to protect China's territorial integrity and to facilitate her recovery ... with the following stipulations:
>
> That China inform the United Nations promptly of her request to the United States for increased material and advisory assistance.
>
> That China request the United Nations to take immediate action to bring about a cessation of hostilities in Manchuria and request that Manchuria be placed under a Five-Power Guardianship or, failing that, under a Trusteeship in accordance with the United Nations Charter.
>
> That China make effective use of her own resources in a program for economic reconstruction and initiate sound fiscal policies leading to reduction of budgetary deficits.
>
> That China give continuing evidence that the urgently required political and military reforms are being implemented.
>
> That China accept American advisors as responsible representatives of the United States Government in specified military and economic fields to assist China in utilizing United States aid in the manner for which it is intended.

General Wedemeyer warned that a policy of "no assistance" would cut the ground from under the feet of the government and lay open the country to eventual Communist domination. A policy of wait-and-see might force the Generalissimo to carry out "genuine reforms which, in turn, would enable the United States to render *effective aid.*" [Italics supplied] On the other hand, it might lead to such weakness on the part of the government that separatist movements would arise. In this case, a middle group might gain control and establish a modicum of stability with American aid. He warned, however, that such developments were conjectural.

In any case, the necessary political reforms would include the separation of the Kuomintang party from the government, the complete reorganization of the government, reform policies, and the removal of corrupt and undemocratic officials.

Wedemeyer's report warned that a silver loan would be ineffective until the Chinese solved their budgetary problems. Congressional assistance would be helpful if there were an integrated, coordinated program of assistance and if the Chinese took ruthless measures to repair the situation.

General Wedemeyer warned that the Communists had the military initiative in Manchuria and North China. Although it would be quite unwise for Americans to be involved in the fighting, low-echelon and high-echelon advice was necessary. Communist victory was opposed, he said, to American interests. "The only working basis on which national Chinese resistance to Soviet aims can be revitalized is through the presently corrupt, reactionary, and inefficient Chinese National Government." In order to preclude defeat, prompt assistance was necessary. Such aid would lessen the possibility of a Communist-dominated China.

Thus, it was clear that Wedemeyer held out no hopes of Nationalist victory. The most American aid could accomplish was the maintenance of a Nationalist regime in part of China. Moreover, this consequence was dependent upon reforms that the Nationalists had proved stubbornly resistant to in the past and the establishment of a guardianship in Manchuria that would have been dependent on Nationalist, Chinese Communist, and Russian consent. Wedemeyer rejected a guardianship without the Soviet Union, for this would mean war.[15]

Because Wedemeyer thought American military intervention undesirable, he was, therefore, proposing a solution dependent upon agreement with the Soviet Union in a situation in which, according to Wedemeyer's own analysis, Soviet agreement would be contrary to Soviet interests.[16] Moreover, the State Department was so fearful of Nationalist reactions to the trusteeship, or guardianship, proposal that they suppressed the entire report at the time.

Crisis for America

If the State Department accepted Wedemeyer's analysis of the situation, a dilemma was posed for American policy. Unification and coalition were now ruled out. Defeat of the Communists was ruled out as an alternative, unless the United States was willing to rearm and expend its full military might in China, leaving other areas unprotected. The recommended guardianship lacked political feasibility, although under the unlikely circumstances that both the Russian and Chinese Communists accepted it, it might work. If the United States aided Chiang, the aid would be ineffectual unless Chiang instituted reforms he had refused to make in the past. If the United States did nothing, Chiang would fall and the United States would have suffered a disastrous setback in Asia.

The Department of State did little to inform the American public about the policy crisis. Under-secretary Acheson told the House Committee on Foreign Affairs on March 20, 1947, "The Chinese Government is not in a position at the present time that the Greek Government is in. It is not approaching collapse. It is not threatened by defeat by the Communists. The war with the Communists is going on much as it has for the last twenty years."

On the other hand, the United States was in a period of budget balancing and reduction of the national debt. American military and financial resources were quite limited, unless Congress was willing to approve considerably greater expenditures. The Greek and Turkish problems were more limited in scope and the possibility of successful intervention in those areas correspondingly greater than in China.

In addition, Chiang and the Kuomintang regime in China were quite unpopular in the United States. In a speech on the floor of the House on May 7, 1947, influential conservative Republican Congressman George Bender of Ohio stated:

> Ever since President Truman made his fateful speech to the Congress, intense pressure has been placed upon our State Department by Chinese diplomats in this country demanding that the $500,000,000 Export-Import loan be released for use by the present Chinese Government. I charge here on the floor of the House that the Chinese Embassy has had the arrogance to invade our State Department and attempt to tell our State Department that the Truman doctrine has committed our Government to all-out support of the present Fascist Chinese Government.

Mr. Bender's sentiment was not an isolated one.

Apparently American policy had entered an impasse. Unable to aid the Nationalists effectively because of limitations in available American resources and Chinese inability to use aid effectively, it was committed to the continuance of aid that could only be ineffective. In such circumstances, American policy was determined more by the pressures that were placed upon it than by rational orientation to the objectives of global policy.

Reaction and Military Reverses

In China, the reactionary elements were gaining in power within the Kuomintang and anti-Americanism was increasing. Corruption and dictatorial rule were on the increase. Friction among the minor parties resulted in the splitting of the Social Democratic party. On October 28, the Democratic League was outlawed.

During the winter of 1947–1948, rumors of peace negotiations gained some currency. On December 20, Nationalist General Chang informed Stuart that Chiang, although refusing to take any action himself, stated that he had no objection to Chang's attempting to secure Russian mediation. Chiang's secretary confirmed a Russian offer to mediate but said that Chiang would reject it.

By March, Kuomintang forces had almost been eliminated from Manchuria and China north of the Yellow River. Between the Yellow and the Yangtze rivers, there were strong Communist forces. Stuart noted that strong Nationalist leadership was lacking and feared that Chiang was prepared to retreat to Canton. Late in 1947, elections to the National Assembly were held. Almost no minor party candidates had been elected, and the right wing of the Kuomintang was dominant. Chiang withdrew some of his victorious candidates to permit minor party representation.

October 1947—the State Department Reconsiders

By October, the Department of State was prepared to reconsider its China policy. However, it still took the position that the Chinese must be responsible for their own problems. The United States could not assume direct responsibility for the fighting or for the Chinese economy. Although it was not feasible to propose a long-range economic program for China, the administration did propose a program calling for the grant of $570 million in economic aid and assistance. This program was presented to Congress in February 1948. By now, the cold war was on in earnest, and the United States was officially opposed to the entry of Communists into the government of China. Neither President Truman nor Secretary of State Marshall made clear the alternatives, although they did speak of broadening the government by the inclusion of liberal elements.

1948—Politics in China

During March, dissatisfaction with the government reached a high pitch. The Kuomintang Political Committee lost effective control of the Assembly, and Chiang announced that he would not accept the presidency. There was an immediate demand in the Assembly that he revise his position. He thereupon accepted the presidency. Chiang supported Sun Fo for the vice-presidency, but despite Chiang's pressure, Sun lost to General Li Tsung-jen, who rallied liberal support.

Li's victory raised hope of reform, but Li was ignored at the inauguration and thereafter. Dr. Wong Wen-hao, a man of eminent respectability but totally without political following, was named prime minister. Chiang promised Dr. Stuart that he would permit General Ho, the minister of defense, to direct military operations. Chiang immediately broke his promise. According to Stuart, favoritism was continuing to disrupt Nationalist military organization.

Anti-American sentiment had become very great during this period, particularly among the students, who engaged in riots. Economic deterioration was now so bad and inflation so great that the government resorted to drastic measures. However, the Kuomintang government attacked the symptoms by decreeing a price freeze without attempting to reform the currency or budgetary situation. In Shanghai, Chiang's son, Ching-kuo, instituted violent measures to enforce the freeze but was unsuccessful.

August 1948—American Policy

In August 1948, it was considered necessary to reconsider American policy toward China. The Embassy in China advised strongly against a coalition government in the light of what had happened in Europe where coalitions had been tried. Continued or increased support of the Nationalists was recommended, although it was acknowledged that it was probably too late for such measures to succeed.

If the Communists had to be accommodated, it was recommended that this be done within the framework of a loose federation. In the event of a return to regionalism in China, the Embassy recommended aid to non-Communist regional governments. The Department of State agreed that the United States could not support a coalition with the Communists, and it also opposed any further attempts to mediate. But the Department of State also opposed overt participation in the civil war on the ground that this would only give rise to additional anti-

American sentiment. Marshall warned against rigid plans in a situation as fluid as the Chinese situation.

In October, Marshall warned the Embassy that Congressional leaders had stressed that the $125 million in grants Congress had actually voted for China were not to involve the use of American combat troops or American command of military operations. American aid did not constitute a commitment to underwrite the Chinese war effort as this was too vast an undertaking.

Marshall felt that it might still be possible to reduce the Chinese Communists to a negligible factor if the United States took over the Chinese government. But, Marshall said, this would offend all Chinese; it was doubtful if the United States had the personnel to carry it through, and it was impossible to estimate the cost.

Once involved, Marshall continued, the United States would not be able to withdraw, and China would probably become the scene of international conflict. The present Nationalist government, Marshall said, is opposed by 99 percent of the people, according to a high Kuomintang official who supports Chiang. Government troops no longer desire to fight. Many are defecting. In these circumstances, the United States must consider its commitments elsewhere in the world, for they are heavy.

In response to questions from the embassy in China, on October 23 Marshall replied that he would not interfere in internal Chinese politics by recommending Chiang's retirement or a negotiated peace. Marshall did state, however, that the United States would continue to support the Nationalist government so long as it remained an important factor on the Chinese scene. He refused to speculate on the course that would be adopted if it ceased to exist or merged with the Communists.

In November, Dr. Tsiang, head of the Chinese Delegation to the United Nations, inquired about the appointment of American officers to the command of Chinese Army units under the guise of advisers. Marshall sidetracked this request, but assured Tsiang that the delivery of military materiel was being expedited.

Truman communicated to Chiang, in the same period, assurances concerning the delivery of materiel and remarked that the advice of General David Barr, director of the Joint United States Military Advisory Group (JUSMAG) in China, was always available to Chiang. However, JUSMAG informed the American government that no aid short of the employment of American troops could save the situation and that the employment of American troops, under the circumstances, was impossible.

Apparently the United States had given up on China and was attempting to cut its losses.

Communist Victories—Chiang Replaced

By early 1949, the Communists were confident of victory. Chiang had been placed on their list of war criminals, an indication that the Communists had no desire to compromise. Meanwhile, pressure was building up within the Nationalist-held areas for the retirement of Chiang.

Both Chiang and Premier Sun Fo addressed New Year's messages to the people in which they stressed their desire for peace. On January 8, the Chinese Foreign Minister requested the American, British, French, and Soviet governments to act as intermediaries in peace negotiations. The United States replied that, in the light of the results obtained during General Marshall's mission to China, it did not believe that its mediation could serve any useful purpose. On January 21, Chiang retired and General Li became acting president of China.

On January 23, a representative of Li called on Ambassador Stuart and asked American support for a Chinese agreement with Russia that would pledge strict Chinese neutrality in any international conflict, the elimination of American influence in China, and the establishment of real cooperation between China and Russia. The Department of State commented that the request was absurd.

Nationalist China Sues for Peace

In the meantime, the Nationalist government of China sent an unofficial peace delegation to Peiping, although the publicly-announced Communist terms amounted to nothing short of unconditional surrender. However, dissension within the Nationalist regime was gravely impeding both its war and peace efforts. Chiang was interfering in the conduct of the military campaign and also keeping a tight hold on the government's assests. Premier Sun moved the Executive Yuan to Canton against the expressed wishes of President Li.

Rumors were rife that the United States was no longer interested in Chinese resistance. For this reason, the Embassy urged encouragement for potential resistance groups in South China. The State Department, however, refused to make a public statement, although it maintained that continued aid was proof enough of American interest.

Actually, the United States was cutting its losses in China. In a letter to Democratic Senator Tom Connally of Texas, chairman of the Senate Committee on Foreign Relations, on March 15, 1949, Secretary of State Dean Acheson opposed the proposed $1.5 billion in aid for China on the ground that such aid would commit the United States to incalculable future expenditures and prolong the civil war and the suffering of the Chinese people without appreciably changing the final result. Acheson informed Connally of the judgment of General Barr, that the Nationalists had lost no battles because of a shortage of equipment, and stressed the hopelessness of the Nationalist position.

Nationalist China Seeks Aid

During March, Li succeeded in replacing Sun Fo with General Ho as premier. Meanwhile, negotiations continued with the Communists, whose terms amounted to unconditional surrender. The Communists extended their original deadline for acceptance to April 12, but would agree only to minor changes in wording. Li negotiated furiously with the United States embassy, seeking both moral and financial support. He asked whether a spirited defense of the Yangtze that rallied the people to the government would encourage American assistance. Li was told that the government of China had ample reserves. He was advised to get hold of these reserves.[17]

That no American help would be forthcoming was clear. On April 20, the Communist deadline passed, and they attacked along the Yangtze, making, according to the American White Paper, a "ridiculously easy crossing."[18] The government retreated to Canton, but the handwriting was on the wall. The mainland of China would soon be lost to the Nationalists.

The defeat of the Nationalist government was of great consequence for American global policy. The United States today would surely not balk at the $1.5 billion expenditure that in 1949 Acheson thought useless if there were but the most desperate outside chance of holding a portion of the Chinese mainland.

Conclusions

The Yalta agreements on China were dictated by military considerations that seemed urgent at the time. However, when it became evident that Soviet participation in the war against Japan might be undesirable —since Japanese surrender seemed imminent—there was no possible way for the United States to prevent Soviet entry short of the threat of war.

Therefore, the attempts at Yalta to limit Soviet aims in China by making minimal concessions and to secure Soviet cooperation with the Kuomintang regime were strategically sound.

Moreover, the attempt, in addition to being worthwhile in view of the alternatives, did not rest upon a gross misconception of Soviet motivation, despite the efforts of latter-day mythmakers to smell out incompetence or pro-Communist plots. Stalin apparently attempted to carry out his end of the agreement. He did recognize the Nationalist government. According to Titoist sources, Stalin placed great pressure upon the Chinese Communists to cooperate with the Kuomintang.

Stalin may really have believed that the Chinese Communists were radish Communists (red on the outside and white on the inside), just as some Americans may have believed that they were only agrarian reformers.

Regardless of whether or not Stalin really believed what he said, the facts were that the Chinese Communists refused to cooperate with his designs for China, just as the Yugoslav Communists continued their efforts to create a Communist government in Greece—despite Stalin's qualms—until after the Yugoslav split with the Cominform.

The evidence cited to the contrary is inferential rather than direct. The contrary hypothesis rests upon the fact that Soviet troops in Manchuria did not interfere with Chinese Communist attempts to seize arms from Japanese dumps and that Soviet troops occasionally interfered with Nationalist troop movement. These pieces of evidence, however, are susceptible to a different interpretation, which carries greater conviction because it fits in with the remaining evidence.

In the first place, the Communists secured much of their equipment from the Nationalists. It may be that similar methods were used either to turn Russian eyes in other directions or to evade their sentries. But, even assuming Soviet cooperation in the weapons seizure, the evidence need not assume a sinister guise. The Soviet Union had cooperated with Chiang in the past and even had ordered the disarming of Communist forces in 1928. The result was that much of the top leadership of Chinese Communism—the leadership backed by Moscow—was physically destroyed.

If Stalin underestimated the Chinese Communists—and there is strong evidence that he did—who were fewer in numbers and more poorly armed than the Nationalists, he may have permitted them to secure Japanese arms to insure against a repetition of 1928. Stalin never agreed to the liquidation of the Chinese Communists; he agreed only to cooperate with the Nationalists and to recognize the Nationalist government as the government of China.

Soviet interference with Nationalist troop movements may have signified only that the Soviet Union wanted to carry out economic removals without interference and that it intended to secure its "imperialistic" position in Manchuria. In fact, had the Soviet Union counted on Communist victory, it might have regarded the economic removals as ill-advised.

During the civil war, the attitude of the Soviet Union toward the Nationalist government was eminently correct. While Western embassies remained in Communist-occupied Nanking, the Soviet Embassy traveled South with the Nationalists. This was in April 1949. The Truman Doctrine; the Czechoslovak coup; the American intentions of cooperating with the Brussels powers, that is, the intention to form NATO; and the onset of the Berlin blockade had passed or were passing into history.

Soviet behavior had not been notably correct in these matters. It is difficult to believe that the Soviet Union was correct in its behavior toward the Nationalists—ostensibly more correct than the Western powers—if it expected a complete Communist victory in China. There was little point in attempting to conciliate the West. Evidently, Stalin stubbornly refused to recognize that the Chinese Communists had proved him wrong. And evidently, he just as stubbornly intended to deal with the Kuomintang government as the government of China.

Or perhaps Stalin hoped to hold the balance between two Chinas. Perhaps he hoped through organizational methods to influence the Chinese Communists, while influencing the Nationalists because of his ability to moderate Chinese Communist policy. Perhaps he did not want a strong China, or perhaps he did not believe complete victory possible. In any event, there is no ground for the belief that the Yalta accords were responsible for the victory of Communism in China.

The first opportunity for the United States to reconsider its wartime China policy came with the end of war. Six major courses of action were open to consideration: (1) complete inaction; (2) full support of Kuomintang; (3) support of third forces in China; (4) support of a coalition government; (5) support of the Chinese Communists; and, (6) support of the Nationalists only within that part of China controlled by them. The last policy, in effect, would have been based upon the division of China and, therefore, would have represented a break with the traditional American policy of encouraging the formation of a unified national government in China.

Complete inaction was ruled out by past American commitments to China, plans for the United Nations and the postwar world, the presence of Soviet troops in Manchuria, and the necessity of using American marines to assist in handling surrendered Japanese troops in China.

Third forces in China might have been supported within a coalition government. However, third-force elements lacked military capacity, numerical strength, and experience in administration. As the foundation of a government, third forces in China would not have been viable.

American military resources were not available in sufficient quantities to secure complete victory for the Nationalists. Demobilization was in full swing. General MacArthur insisted that he needed more troops for the occupation of Japan than had been assigned to him, and some troops intended for China duty were diverted to his command. Moreover, full support of the Nationalists might have involved a Soviet refusal either to treat with the National government or to withdraw from Manchuria. Even had this alternative been feasible in a military sense, the United States might not have risked these latter consequences. As it was, the fact that military resources for full support were unavailable made it unnecessary even to consider such consequences.

Support of the Nationalists as a regional power in China would have been rejected by the Nationalists. Nor would the Chinese Communists have subscribed to the division of China. Such a division would have been contrary to traditional American foreign policy and—in 1946 at least—support of such a policy would have earned for the United States the enmity of all factions in China.

If the United States had given its support to the Chinese Communists in this period, it would have backed a numerically and militarily inferior regional power against the recognized government of China. Such a policy would have been in gross violation of recognized standards of international law. It would have involved the great danger that all of China could have been moved into the Soviet sphere of influence, the very consequence the Yalta accords on the Far East were designed to avoid.

Nor was there sufficient reason to believe that the Chinese Communists were able to take over all of China against Nationalist resistance. It is true, however, that American career officers were reporting that the Chinese Communists were the most viable political force in China and that Communist victory in a civil war was likely.[19]

The remaining alternative was support for a coalition government. If one were to assume that the Chinese Communists were really agrarian reformers and that the Kuomintang was potentially a trustworthy and democratic organization, support for a coalition government might have had some prospect of success.

However, the belief held by some State Department officers that the Chinese were merely agrarian reformers was incredible. Mao Tse-tung had openly proclaimed both his theoretical and practical adherence to the principles of Marx, Lenin, and Stalin. Mao made no secret of the fact that his agrarian policy was a tactic in the strategic campaign to transform China into a Marxist nation. Did State Department officers think they understood Mao's objectives better than Mao himself? Or were they just naive? Later evidence reveals an amazing ignorance on the part of some officers of the classic works of Communist literature, or, for that matter, an ignorance of Communist organizational methods and practices.

Belief that the Kuomintang was an ordinary Western-style political party also missed the mark by a wide margin. The Kuomintang retained much of the organizational structure that Comintern agent Borodin had created even if it lacked the cohesiveness and efficiency of its Communist counterpart. It was constructed along Leninist lines of democratic centralism. The Kuomintang established a party dictatorship over China. Within the party, the political committee of the party exercised a dictatorship over the party. And, within the political committee, Chiang Kai-shek exercised a dictatorship, even if it was one modified by personal relationships.

Neither the Kuomintang nor the Chinese Communist Party could afford to collaborate with the other. Apart from abundant historical evidence that neither group could be trusted to exercise restraint when it possessed sufficient strength to crush the other, each was well aware of the organizational facts of life.

Coexistence, within the same territory, of two political parties, each organized according to Leninist principles, is a political monstrosity. Such coexistence can persist only until one of the parties can gain sufficient strength to destroy the organization of the other.

It is not possible for governmental machinery to control such parties because the lines of organization, discipline, and loyalty are well-controlled within the party framework. Therefore, a period of coexistence would only provide time for each party to struggle to gain control of the government apparatus and to use the government for its own political ends.

The plan to consolidate Kuomintang and Communist armies ran aground on this issue. Each group would be safe only if it controlled its own armies. In the absence of an overreaching political consensus, military force would decide the fate of China.

Therefore, any agreement reached between the parties was superficial. The Kuomintang wanted consolidation only in order to destroy the Communist armed forces. When this was accomplished, the Communist Party would be destroyed.

In turn, the Communists would not permit consolidation if that would permit the Kuomintang to destroy their independent forces. But the Communists would be willing to consolidate forces in areas where the plans for consolidation permitted the Communists to disrupt the Nationalist military organization.

Therefore, negotiations between the Kuomintang and Communists during the Marshall mission were an elaborate farce. Neither Chinese group can be blamed for the naiveté of American officialdom. Nor can either group be blamed for its role in the breakdown of the truce. It seems clear that each side used the truce to maneuver for advantage and broke the truce when that seemed advantageous.

However, while each group had reason to continue the farce, the facade of negotiations continued. The Kuomintang needed American aid and therefore had to pretend to negotiate. The Communists were able to use American missions as a lever against the Nationalists. Therefore they had a reason to negotiate.

Eventually, the Nationalists found themselves in the most advantageous military position they could expect and therefore risked the cut-off of American aid. And, when it became clear that the Americans were no longer an effective lever against the Nationalists, the Communists no longer had reason to continue negotiations.

American military advice to Chiang, namely, that he was overextending his lines in attempting to displace the Communists, was sound. But American observers failed to reckon with the most important political factor. Chiang's prestige, which was high in this period, stemmed from his role as the unifier of China. If he failed to subdue the Communists, he would be reduced to a regional warlord.

In such a position, Chiang could hardly hope to compete with the Communists, who, from an organizational point of view, had much better leadership, discipline, and morale. The United States failed to recognize that Chiang was engaged in a desperate race against time. Chiang, on his part, must have despaired of the American attitude, for any attempt on his part to explain the facts of Chinese politics immediately would have resulted in the withdrawal of American aid.

There is some evidence that the United States supported a coalition government in order to entrap the Communists. John Carter Vincent, a former State Department official who had served in Communist-controlled territory in China, and who had been "purged" for his policy advice, testified during the hearings on the Institute of Pacific Relations that "the Communists would come into the [Chinese] government on a minority basis and that we could through support of the Chiang Kai-shek government . . . eliminate the Communists. . . . I not only thought that, sir, but General Marshall thought it. It turned out not to have been the case [that the Communists joined the government]."

It is difficult to know how much credence to place in this testimony. But, if true, it casts a peculiar light on the thinking in the Department of State. The Chinese Communists, after all, had gained their political experience in a very rough school, much rougher than that of Washington or corporation politics. If the pundits in the State Department thought themselves capable of outmaneuvering the Chinese Communists in so transparent a manner, they were very wrong indeed. Mao was capable of dealing aces and spades to that crew and trouncing them severely.

In some ways, this explanation would account for subsequent American policy. If Washington believed that it had found a way in which to destroy Communism in China, it must have been extremely disturbed by Chiang's violations of the truce. As American officials did not trust Chiang to keep a secret, they would hardly have informed him of their strategy. Nevertheless, these American officials must have thought that Chiang was destroying the only chance of saving the Nationalist position. Therefore, when the truce broke down, they may have reacted with complete disgust. If it was all Chiang's fault, let Chiang stew in his own juice. The United States washed its hands of the matter.

In any event, of the six "pure" policies that might have been chosen in 1946–1947, none was practicable. The United States was in a box. As a consequence, the only remaining solution was unsatisfactory, but should have been reached by the process of elimination. It was impossible to recognize the ultimate division of China because the Nationalists would have objected and such recognition would have had untoward political consequences. But American policy might have been aimed at giving Chiang sufficient supplies to maintain the Kuomintang within Southern China.

If there is any serious criticism to be leveled at American policy, it lies in the lack of candor of American officials. Congress and the public were informed by Dean Acheson that China was in no danger of collapse. According to the information available to the Department of State, this was outright misrepresentation.

There was a shrewd calculation behind this misrepresentation. If only limited American resources were available, it was important to funnel these resources to Greece and Turkey, where the needs were smaller and there was more chance of effective use. The Wedemeyer report constitutes a sound defense of such an administration policy, although it was not intended as such. Had it been made public, I do not think that the American public would have been willing to pay the costs of effective intervention in China.

Nevertheless, Congress thought it had a right to be informed adequately. Much of what happened in subsequent years can be traced to the refusal of the Department of State to deal with Congress candidly. Even so, the extreme suspiciousness that resulted and the dreadful charges made by some members of Congress were without justification. Nevertheless, Dean Acheson was not without responsibility for the fears and suspicions that eventually made him completely ineffective in the position he held.

Whatever corruption existed within the Nationalist regime, the Li administration in 1949 at last gave evidence of possible reform. The situation was desperate, but the Nationalists were flatly refused support. Whether they could have held at the Yangtze, if support had been promised, is a moot point. But was there anything to lose by promising such aid on the condition of successful defense? Was the administration really concerned about the "suffering of the Chinese people"?

At that time, the United States could have supported a regional government in China with the consent of the Li administration. But it did nothing. Despite a bitter dispute concerning a policy paper on the Formosa issue, it appears clear that the United States was also resigned to the loss of Formosa and prepared to do nothing about it.

If the United States were prepared to accept a Communist China with equanimity, should it not at least have come to terms with the Chinese Communists? Why follow a policy which would result in a Communist victory, while at the same time irritating and incurring the enmity of the Communists?

There is no need to discuss the political uproar that would have resulted from a policy of recognition of and cooperation with the Chinese Communists. Certainly such a policy would have been hazardous politically. But the stakes were exceptionally high. Extremely important strategic interests of the United States were involved. At no time was the issue carried clearly to the American people. Policy was conducted entirely behind a screen of secrecy and under circumstances that aroused suspicion.

Should not, at least, the alternatives have been openly discussed? This may involve the advantage of hindsight, but would the United States today refuse to support a Nationalist government that occupied mainland China below the Yangtze, even if that government were very weak? As late as 1949, the Senate offered to appropriate $1.5 billion, which the administration turned down. Was that so large a sum? Was not China worth that much effort? Had the United States really afforded effective aid to the Nationalists?

Of course, at the time, General Barr, the Direction of JUSMAG,[20] advised the United States government that the Nationalists could not be saved but that they had not lost any battle for lack of munitions. The Department of State was under grave obligation to give serious attention to this field report in determining its policy.

On the other hand, General Barr's statement was more ambiguous than it appears to be, and the United States government was in possession of other field intelligence reports that seemed to conflict with his. Admiral Badger reported, for instance, that the Nationalist defenders of Weihsien were badly outnumbered and that they had an average of six rounds of ammunition per man. Badger, for instance, felt that with considerable American assistance, there was a 50-50 chance, late in 1948, that the armies of General Fu Tso-yi would have been able to hold North China for the Nationalist government. General Barr disputed the accuracy of Admiral Badger's comments with regard to the battle of Weihsien. But both were competent observers, and the historian cannot draw firm conclusions.[21]

There seems little doubt that the Nationalist armies were poorly led, their morale was nonexistent, and Chiang's strategy was disastrous. On the other hand, the State Department overestimated the value of the $2 billion of aid it gave China. Much of this aid was useless from a military standpoint. It was poorly coordinated with military needs. There had been great delays in receipt.[22] The equipment was often defective or vital parts were missing; for instance, Browning automatic rifles often lacked magazines. The supply of rifle ammunition looked large until it was broken down into rounds per man.

Because the Chinese Communists were usually more poorly equipped than the Nationalist troops, it is correct to state that the Nationalists did not lose because of a lack of munitions. However, this does not indicate that some battles would not have gone differently if Nationalist armies had been better equipped. Even General Barr states that General Fu did not have sufficient rifles to equip more than four of his seven armies in the crucial battle of North China.

Whether more massive equipping of the Nationalist troops would have secured victories is difficult to estimate. General Wedemeyer made it clear that the Nationalists lost because of lack of morale and that the main reason for this condition was the corruption and inefficiency of the Nationalist apparatus.[23] Chiang misused the equipment with which the Nationalist government was supplied, distributing it more often on the basis of favoritism than military need. Moreover, much of the Communist equipment was secured from the Nationalists by capture and defection. It is possible that additional aid would only have permitted the Communists to conquer China more quickly.

What appears indisputable is that, by late 1948, the American government had written China off its books. It made no attempt to supply adequate assistance. What it did grant was token aid as a demonstration of American preference for a Nationalist regime in China.

By 1949, American policy was openly based upon Nationalist defeat, and the government of President Li was so informed. The possibility that Li might provide an honest and efficient government that would restore morale and repair the chances of Nationalist survival in the south of China apparently was not considered by the United States. When Li appealed for financial aid, he was told that he should get hold of the government reserves that Chiang had illicitly removed. After the United States informed President Li of this policy, no attempt was made to defend the Yangtze, and the Chinese armies deserted in mass.[24]

It is impossible to estimate the consequences of a policy of aid to Li. By March 1949, the Communists had achieved numerical superiority. There was great dissension among the Nationalists, and Chiang's intrigues were disruptive of effective defense policies. On the other hand, the United States made no effort to support Li in a fashion that might have thwarted Chiang and rallied the Chinese nation for a defense against Communism.

The United States ambassador to China, Dr. Stuart, encouraged a policy of aid. However, Dr. Stuart was instructed by the Department of State that the United States had considered the probable consequences of this policy, its commitments elsewhere in the world, and the resources available to it, and had come to the conclusion that the United States could take no effective action in China.

Although the United States was busily organizing a European alliance against the Russian danger in this period, its Chinese policy was one of retreat and surrender. Although a policy of aid to China might have involved sums of money Congress would have been unwilling to appropriate in 1949, the Department of State made no effort to arouse Congress or the people to the magnitude of the problem and even discouraged the expenditure of monies that the Congress apparently was willing to appropriate. In this sense, the China policy of 1949 may be contrasted to the Korean policy of 1950, although the objectives were of considerably different strategic importance.

Recognition of Communist Crina—1949

There is some evidence, which has not been presented in this chapter, that toward the end of 1949, the State Department was giving serious consideration to the recognition of Communist China. It is likely that British recognition was granted after consultation with the United States.

If this is so, the United States in this period was moving toward a possibly reasonable policy. Whether because of Congressional opposition when rumors of recognition became current or whether the Department never had the intention, no sustained effort was made to explain alternative possible policies to the public. If the intention to recognize the Communist regime existed, it was quickly discarded at the first sign of serious opposition.

As a consequence, until the Korean War, the United States followed a policy that had the advantages of neither recognizing nor sending aid to the Nationalists on Formosa. In fact, one may say that, in this period, the United States did not have a China policy. Instead, it drifted with events and was unable to exploit any opportunities to advantage.

IV

The Rise
of Titoism
(1954)

Yugoslav-American Relations

Relations between the United States and Yugoslavia in the immediate postwar years were more tense than those between the United States
and any other Communist state. A crisis developed during August 1946.
Two American transport planes that deviated from their normal course
and crossed Yugoslavian territory near Bled, the summer residence of
Marshal [Josip Broz] Tito, were shot down.[1] The second plane crashed
on August 19, killing five American soldiers, and the occupants of the first
plane were taken into custody.

Public opinion was volatile and charges were made by both sides.
Secretary of State James Byrnes demanded that the American soldiers be
released and granted safe passage out of the country within forty-eight
hours. He threatened otherwise to take the matter before the Security
Council of the United Nations. Tito complied and also paid indemnities
to the families of the dead men.

The trial of Roman Catholic Archbishop Stepinac during 1946 also
produced friction between Yugoslavia and the United States. The archbishop had cooperated closely with Ante Pavelic,[2] the Axis-supported puppet dictator of Croatia. Public opinion in Yugoslavia demanded reprisals against the archbishop, and this demand accorded with the purposes
of the Communist Party.

A trial was held. According to legal experts, it did not conform to acceptable procedural standards of law. It was quite doubtful that the arch-

bishop had violated existing substantive law. Moreover, the Vatican officially denied the right of the Yugoslav state to try a cleric in a civil court. Nevertheless, Archbishop Stepinac was convicted and sentenced to sixteen years in prison. Americans generally regarded the trial as violating principles of religious freedom.

Socialism, Communist Style

Through the device of the People's Front, the Communist Party of Yugoslavia rapidly imposed a Communist framework on Yugoslavian society. Democratic leaders like Grol and Subasic quickly discovered that they had no place in the new society. Dargoljub Jovanovic, a pro-Soviet agrarian leader, survived a bit longer, even attaining the position of secretary of the Serbian People's Front and a position on the Presidium of the People's Assembly. However, he had criticized the imposition of an economic plan of which Parliament had not been informed, and this led to his arrest in the spring of 1947.

In the autumn of 1946, a cabinet decree divided industrial enterprises into those important to the economy as a whole and those significant to an individual republic. In December, Parliament nationalized all these enterprises. In April 1948, the state nationalized all credit and insurance companies, all ships, fishermen's boats of over fifty tons, transport ships handling more than fifty passengers, all sanitariums, hospitals, spas, printing houses, motion picture theaters, storage houses holding over one hundred tons, and business cellars holding more than three wagon-loads of goods. All immovable property of foreigners was nationalized. The laws were as radical or more so than those of the other Communist-bloc nations.

Agriculture also was handled in a radical manner. In 1945, the laws of Agrarian Reform and Colonization and Agrarian Cooperatives were passed. The land of Germans and Hungarians was confiscated, as were all individual holdings of more than 86.48 acres and land held by corporations or institutions. Individuals who did not cultivate their land were not permitted to retain more than 7.4 to 12.35 acres. The confiscated land was placed in a Land Fund and distributed in diverse ways. In some cases, it was given to individuals formally as private property to a maximum of twelve acres. In other cases, the colonizers settled in a village and formed a *Kolkhoz*, or collective farm, to which the land belonged.

Generally, the land given to individuals would not support them, and they were forced to join one or another version of the cooperatives favored by the state. In the cooperative, the workers in some cases were able to own a small additional parcel of land.

In March 1948, a government decree forbade the transfer of property rights in immovables or the mortgage of immovables without the consent of the state. A decree of 1947 instructed the peasant to sow his land or to face a penalty, possibly confiscation of the land. There were planned quotas and fixed state prices. Only Bulgaria pursued a more radical land policy among the satellites.

In accordance with Communist doctrine, the rulers of Yugoslavia intended to industrialize the country as quickly as possible. The announcement that a planned economy was to be introduced was first made in June 1946. The details were worked out, and in April 1946, the Five-Year Plan was announced. Its professed purpose was to liquidate the economic and technical backwardness of the country, strengthen its economy, and raise the standard of living.

The Yugoslavs aimed to double the 1939 national income by 1951. Heavy industry and transport were featured, although light industry and consumer goods also figured in the plan. The skills of the population were to be improved and increased. Consumers were to live at a considerably higher level by 1951. The problem of obtaining sufficient investment capital to accomplish these ends was not specified.

The plan was administered from a Central Commission of Control, which had the right to direct and to investigate. The newspapers were used to reveal shortcomings. Shock workers, who performed at higher production levels than the normal or who were given special recognition and pay incentives for this, were employed to stimulate enthusiasm. This technique produced much support during the period under discussion; non-Communist students and workers from abroad often participated in some special enterprises or endeavors without pay. The Yugoslavs consistently announced the fulfillment of the planned goals. However, most foreign observers treated the announced percentages with considerable skepticism. The Yugoslav plan was the most advanced of the satellite plans and came closest to approximating the model furnished by the Soviet Union.

Yugoslav Foreign Relations

Yugoslavia's relations with foreign countries continued to deteriorate during 1947. Although Yugoslavia gave up hope of obtaining any modification of its border with Austrian Carinthia, it opened a campaign for Carinthian autonomy. During this period, there were occasional armed clashes on the frontier that disturbed the West. The Yugoslavs were inspiring and aiding the Greek Communists to carry on the civil war in Greece.

Soviet-Yugoslav Relations

Meanwhile, unknown to the outside world, relations between the Yugoslavs and the Russians were deteriorating. The Yugoslavs were the most ideologically-oriented and militant of the Communist parties, and it had been assumed in the West that the ties between Yugoslavia and the Soviet Union were the closest. Apparently causes of friction had existed from the early stages of the war. These causes are attributable to Stalin's attempts to reach agreements with the West, a course viewed by Tito as a deviation from Stalin's duties to support the Yugoslav Communists.

Events continued to deteriorate as the war ended. Rapes committed by soldiers of the Red Army in Yugoslavia caused difficulties. Milovan Djilas had complained to General Korneyev that these incidents were unfortunate, inasmuch as the bourgeoisie were using them to claim that British officers had better morals than those of the Red Army. Korneyev protested and carried the protest to Moscow, which took his side. This affair seemed to blow over when Stalin accepted Djilas' explanation in April 1945.

During the autumn of 1945, Colonel Stepanov, a member of the Soviet military mission to Yugoslavia, persisted in efforts to recruit agents for Soviet intelligence from among the Yugoslav partisans. One of those he approached quoted him to Yugoslav authorities as saying, "There was *at present* [italics added] nothing to suspect comrade Tito of, that he was working as he should for the time being, but . . . this was not the case with others."

During May 1945, in a speech at Ljublijana, Tito said: "It is said that this war is a just war, and we have considered it as such. However, we seek also a just end; we do not want to pay for others; we do not want to be used as a bribe in international bargaining; we do not want to get involved in any policy of spheres of influence." Tito was referring to what he regarded as the Soviet Union's appeasement of the Western powers in the case of Trieste, and his speech was recognized as such by the Soviet Union.[3] In the exchange of letters preceding the break, Stalin and Molotov stated:

> As is well known, after a series of territorial concessions for the benefit of Yugoslavia which the Soviet Union extracted from the Anglo-Americans,

the latter, together with the French, rejected the Soviet proposal to hand Trieste over to Yugoslavia and occupied Trieste with their own forces, which were then in Italy. Since all other means were exhausted, the Soviet Union had only one other method left for gaining Trieste for Yugoslavia—to start war with the Anglo-Americans over Trieste and take it by force. The Yugoslav comrades could not fail to realize that after such a hard war the USSR could not enter another.

The Soviet Union was grossly offended by Tito's earlier speech and by what it regarded as the inadequacy of Yugoslavia's explanations. Under instructions from Moscow, the Soviet Ambassador, Sadchikov, informed Edward Kardelj on June 5:

> We regard Comrade Tito's speech as an unfriendly attack on the Soviet Union, and the explanation by Comrade Kardelj as unsatisfactory. Our readers understood Comrade Tito's speech in this way, and it cannot be understood in any other. Tell Comrade Tito that if he should once again permit such an attack on the Soviet Union we shall be forced to reply with open criticism in the press and disavow him.

Kardelj, according to Sadchikov, said, "Tito had done great work in liquidating fractionalism in the CPY and in organizing the people's liberation struggle, but he was inclined to regard Yugoslavia as a self-sufficient unit outside the general development of the proletarian revolution and socialism." Whether Kardelj actually criticized Tito in this fashion is not known, but the whole situation was something less than comradely.

During May 1946, Tito and other Yugoslav delegates went to the Soviet Union for conferences with Stalin at which he showed great deference to the Yugoslavs, entrusting them with Albanian party relations, despite the hostility between the two parties, thus apparently offering to place Albania in a Yugoslav sphere of influence. Stalin said that the question of joint-stock companies could be decided as the Yugoslavs desired, that the Poles did not want them either, and that this was all right with the Soviet Union. However, when negotiations were under way in Belgrade the Soviet representative, Yatrov, revealed that he had orders to form companies that would have given the Soviet Union monopolies in whole branches of industries. It also seemed to the Yugoslavs that the Russians were not interested in the development of Yugoslav industry, but desired to use Yugoslavia as a base for raw materials.

The Soviet representative wanted a joint-stock company with a monopoly in oil exploitation. Moreover, he insisted that the resources themselves were not to constitute any part of Yugoslavia's capital contribution. He asked exemption from taxes of various kinds, the normal rate of social security payments, the obligations arising under Yugoslav law, and coordination with the Yugoslav economic plans. Yatrov also insisted that the companies would have to operate on a paying basis, that sales to Yugoslavia should cover all costs, while sales to the Soviet Union should occur at the most favorable world-price levels, thus implying that Yugoslavia would have to make good any losses occurring in this fashion. Negotiations dragged on into 1947, and finally agreements were signed for air transport and river shipping. Yugoslavia rejected Soviet demands in the fields of oil, lead, iron, and many others.

The Soviet representative also suggested the formation of a Soviet-Yugoslav bank that would have been a Soviet creature rather than a joint enterprise. Its proposed activities were to have so wide a scope that the Yugoslavs feared they would result in control of the entire Yugoslav economy by the Soviet Union.

Kardelj went to Moscow for a meeting with Stalin in March 1947 after the two joint-stock companies had already begun to injure the Yugoslav economy. Stalin professed that things would be done as the Yugoslavs desired and agreed to advance Yugoslavia credits of $135 million which Yugoslavia was to use to purchase heavy industrial equipment from the Soviet Union. Actually, the Soviet Union had only shipped industrial equipment with a value of $800,000 before the agreement was revoked in 1949.

The next serious development in the cleavage between Yugoslavia and the Soviet Union is related to the formation of the Communist Information Bureau: Cominform or Informburo. The creation of the Cominform had been foreshadowed in early June 1946 when Stalin had informed Tito that the revival of the Third International in any form was out of the question, although it would be desirable to organize an information organ that would meet from time to time, exchange experiences, and make decisions without binding any party that did not agree.

The Cominform was called into being and met for the first time at Sklyarska Poremba, Poland, at the end of September 1947. The Yugoslavs now believe that the object of the body was to bind them so closely to the organization that they would be unable to follow an independent path. Although there is no evidence that they believed this at the time—and unlike the Pole, Gomulka, they did not oppose the formation of the body—it is quite likely that the object was to do precisely that. The Russians probably desired to give an air of internationalism to their dictation. In fact, the whole problem of satellite nationalism was probably bothering them. Both Bulgaria and Yugoslavia had enacted state secret laws that differentiated sharply between state and party and were used to cut off the respective Russian ambassadors from access to requested information.

If the Soviet purpose was that suspected by the Yugoslavs, its procedure was shrewd. When the Italian, French, and Polish parties were subjected to criticism, Andrei Zhdanov, who led the Soviet delegation and who was Stalin's second-in-command in the Soviet Secretariat, turned the criticism over to the Yugoslav comrades who proceeded to denounce and instruct the other parties, thus depriving themselves of possible future support[4] and establishing the validity of this kind of interparty criticism and discipline.

Difficulties in Soviet-Yugoslav relations were evident at this first gathering of the Cominform, for Yugoslav delegates ostentatiously forgot to thank the Soviet Union for the liberating influence of the Red Army. The delegates of the other East European countries were more ceremonious. The Yugoslavs also used this forum to assert that their resistance activities against the Germans had commenced prior to the German attack on the Soviet Union. Their poor manners were quite evident.

Meanwhile, from June onward, the Yugoslavs had been negotiating with Georgi Dimitrov and his fellow Bulgarian Communist Party leaders the formation of a Balkan federation that was to include all the East European "popular democracies" and Greece, once it had become a "popular democracy." According to the agreement reached at Bled in August 1947, a preliminary step would be taken when Bulgarian Macedonia was joined to Yugoslavian Macedonia as one of the federal republics of Yugoslavia.

Early in January, Anatoli Lavrentiev, the Soviet ambassador, presented a telegram from Stalin requesting that someone from the Yugoslav politburo, if possible Djilas, leave for Moscow to discuss various issues, particularly in connection with Albania. Djilas left with Svetozar Vukemanovic and Vladimir Popovic, stopping first in Bucharest, and then proceeding to Moscow. Events dragged on in Moscow with little result. Toward the end of the month, Georgi Dimitrov was in Rumania and, at a press conference, he spoke of the Balkan Federation or Confederation, calling it premature but desirable. On January 29, *Pravda* attacked Dimitrov's statement. Telegrams were sent to Belgrade and Sofia demanding top-level delegations for important discussions.

Dimitrov, Traicho Kostov, and Vassil Kolarov constituted the Bul-

garian delegation. Kardelj and Vladimir Bakaric were assigned by Yugoslavia to negotiate along with Djilas. Meanwhile Albania requested that
two Yugoslav divisions be sent to southern Albania in addition to the air
force regiment already stationed in Albania. Although Stalin had informed
Djilas in January that Yugoslavia "is free to swallow Albania any time
she wishes to do so," Vyacheslav Molotov now sent a sharp cable to the
Albanian and Yugoslav parties disapproving of the arrangements already
made and threatening publicly to announce Moscow's disagreement unless the military arrangements were cancelled.

On February 10, the conference of the Soviet Union, Bulgaria, and
Yugoslavia got under way, after a prior indirect allusion to Tito's absence. Molotov called the relations between Yugoslavia and Bulgaria,
on the one hand, and the Soviet Union, on the other hand, inadmissible
both from the party and the state point of view. Stalin attacked both
the Bulgarian-Yugoslav Alliance and the proposed federation. Stalin, however, did ask that three federations be formed immediately. They would
consist of Poland and Czechoslovakia, Rumania and Hungary, and Bulgaria and Yugoslavia. Evidently the policy was divide and rule.

Stalin denounced the Yugoslavs and Bulgarians for not keeping him
informed of their activities. He called their alliance "Comsomolist...
preventive war" in policy. Moreover, he quarreled with their policy of
supporting the Greek Communists. Although he admitted that he had
given poor advice to the Chinese Communists and that it was a good
thing they had not followed it, he insisted that his policy was correct in
Greece. The next day Molotov bluntly ordered the Yugoslavs to sign an
agreement providing for mutual consultation on matters of foreign
policy.

The Rupture

On February 12, the Paris *Figaro* printed a report from Bucharest
to the effect that Tito was in disfavor among the Soviet bloc and that
the Communist Party of Rumania had ordered the removal of his pictures from all windows in which they appeared alongside the portraits
of Stalin, Dimitrov, and Petru Groza, the Prime Minister of Rumania.
At a reception in Tirane, Gagarinov, the Soviet *chargé,* replied to a toast
offered to Stalin and Tito by Josip Djerdja, the Yugoslav envoy, "I drink
to Tito provided Tito is for unity in the democratic bloc." Towards the
end of February, Krutikov, the Soviet assistant minister of foreign trade,
informed Bogdan Crnobrnja, the head of the Yugoslav trade delegation,

that it was not necessary to send another trade delegation to Moscow. The trade talks had been stalled for two months anyway.

The top group of Yugoslav leaders must have known that a break of serious proportions between Yugoslavia and the Soviet Union was possible at least since early January. They claim to have discovered from undisclosed sources that Moscow had proof from seized Gestapo records that Andrija Hebrang, the secretary of the Croatian Communist Party and chairman of the State Planning Commission, had betrayed the party as the result of torture.

Since Moscow had not disclosed this information to Belgrade, it could have meant only one thing to the Yugoslavs, namely that Hebrang was being blackmailed by the MVD, the Soviet security agency, to act as Moscow's agent within the Yugoslav party. In January, Hebrang was transferred from the chairmanship of the State Planning Commission to the Ministry of Light Industry, a demotion which, in the various Communist parties, usually precedes a purge.

On March 1, a meeting of the Central Committee of the Yugoslav Communist Party was called. Although Yugoslav accounts of the meeting did not explicitly state so, it was clear from the revealed proceedings that the top leadership had carefully stage-managed the meeting in order to prepare the Central Committee for the events that were to follow in the next few months.

Tito opened the meeting by stating that relations with the Soviet Union had reached an impasse. Economic relations, he said, were unequal, and the Russians did not desire to help Yugoslavia to build a strong army. Tito said that the delay in the conclusion of the trade negotiations was a form of economic pressure to which the Yugoslavs must stand up. Kardelj described Stalin's attitude toward the Yugoslav delegation to Moscow as insulting.

Djilas and Svetozar Vukmanovic announced that the Soviet Union was trying to make Yugoslavia dependent upon it and that Moscow had opposed party organizations within the army.[5] Kardelj pointed out that there were differences between Moscow and Belgrade as to whether socialism should develop through the equal progress of nations working toward that goal or through the enlargement of the Soviet Union. He stated that it had been improper for the Soviet Union to recruit Yugoslav citizens for its secret police.

Boris Kidric, a member of the Yugoslav Central Committee, said that the Soviet Union was doing grave economic damage to Yugoslavia because of its failure to reach a trade agreement and that strict economy would be necessary to overcome these difficulties. Tito said that independence was more important than economic benefit. He added that he still favored federation with Bulgaria but that the time was not ripe. There were ideological differences with the Bulgarian party. If the two parties were combined, the Bulgarian would constitute a Trojan horse within the Yugoslav party.

Moreover, Bulgaria would be an economic drag upon Yugoslavia. Tito complained that the Soviet Union was attempting to use Yugoslavia like a pawn on the chess board. Djilas said that the Soviet Union would not stop with economic pressure. Aleksandur Rankovic, the Yugoslav Minister of Interior, said that the men in the Bulgarian party who had been trained in Bulgaria rather than in the Soviet Union were falling into disfavor. The meeting decided to reject all Soviet demands and to keep the proceedings of the meeting secret.[6]

On March 18, Soviet General Barskov announced to the Yugoslavs that, on orders from Marshal Nikolai Bulganin, all Soviet military advisers and instructors were being withdrawn because they were "surrounded by unfriendliness, and treated with hostility in Yugoslavia." The next day, Armyaninov, the Soviet *chargé*, announced that all Soviet civilian specialists were ordered to leave Yugoslavia.

On March 20, Marshal Tito wrote a letter on behalf of the Yugoslav party to V. Molotov, as representative of the Communist Party of the Soviet Union (CPSU).[7] Tito referred to the events of March 18 and 19 and to the attempts of the Soviet commercial *attaché*, Lebedev, to obtain information from the government bureaus. With respect to the latter, Tito wrote that a government decree forbade bureau employes to grant this information, but that it could have been obtained, as Lebedev had been informed, by application to the Central Committee of the party.[8] Tito rejected the Soviet claims of unfriendliness and hostility and asked that the Soviet Union inform him what the trouble was. He cautioned the Soviet Union that it was receiving information from unreliable sources.

While Tito waited anxiously for the Soviet reply, international pressure on Yugoslavia accumulated. Italian sources accused Yugoslavia of mobilizing on the Trieste border. In an attempt to influence the Italian elections, scheduled for April, the United States announced that it would attempt to carry through revisions in the Italian peace treaty. Foreign Minister Georges Bidault of France announced that the United States,

France, and Great Britain would support the return of the Trieste territory to Italy.

The Soviet answer, dated March 27, was written by Stalin and Molotov[9] and delivered to Tito by Anatoli Lavrentiev, the Soviet Ambassador, who was accompanied by Armyaninov. Before Tito had finished reading the letter, Lavrentiev asked when an answer would be delivered. Tito said the letter would be considered, and he then dismissed Lavrentiev.

The Soviet reply brought up all the old grievances and rejected Yugoslavia's explanations. Moreover, it claimed that Soviet representatives and Pavel Yudin, the Soviet Cominform representative, had been spied upon by the Yugoslav secret police.[10] It charged that rumors circulating among the leading comrades in Yugoslavia stated that "the CPSU is degenerate," that "great power chauvinism is rampant in the USSR," that "the USSR is trying to dominate Yugoslavia economically," that "the Cominform is a means of controlling other parties by the CPSU," that "socialism in the Soviet Union has ceased to be revolutionary," and that "Yugoslavia alone is the exponent of 'revolutionary socialism.' "[11] Djilas, Vukmanovic, Kidric, and Rankovic were referred to as "questionable Marxists." The Soviet letter threatened, "We think the political career of Trotsky is quite instructive."

The Soviet indictment continued, stating that the Communist Party of Yugoslavia (CPY) had only a semi-legal status, decisions of the party organs were never published in the press, there was no democracy within the party, and that the secretary of the party was also Minister of State Security.[12] It charged that the state controlled the party rather than the other way around, that the People's Front rather than the party was the leading force in the country, and that the class struggle was not being carried on.[13] Tito was particularly charged with these failures. The Soviet letter charged that Vladimir Velebit of the Yugoslav Foreign Office was a British spy and criticized the Yugoslavs for keeping him on duty when informed of this by the Soviet Union.

When Tito had read the letter thoroughly, he phoned Kardelj, Rankovic, Djilas, and Kidric. While they were coming, he drafted a reply. The episode approaches the comic for three of these four individuals certainly were slated for a purge if the Russian demands were met, and the position of the fourth was precarious for the Russian note had also referred to "others" as "questionable Marxists." They naturally supported Tito in his defiance of the Soviet Union. They rejected his suggestion that he resign. Then, they made a nominal offer to resign. Tito rejected this offer, stating it would "wreck our Central Committee."

Up to this point, the exchange of letters had been kept secret from the Central Committee of the CPY. It was decided to hold a plenum of the CC on April 12, 1948. The Yugoslavs did not explain the delay, but the obvious inference is that time was given to Rankovic and the secret police to make sure that nothing would go wrong. On April 11, Tito and Stalin exchanged cold telegrams of greeting on the third anniversary of the signing of the treaty of friendship and mutual assistance linking the Soviet Union and Yugoslavia.

The meeting of the Central Committee CPY was carefully staged. Tito opened the meeting by informing the members of the CC of the conflict and its history. Then he read the text of the proposed Yugoslav reply (dated April 13, 1948, in the final version). Although the letter attempts to answer the Soviet criticisms of Yugoslavia, to assert the faithfulness of Yugoslavia to the cause of the Soviet Union, and to restate the transgressions of the Soviet Union, the statement of doctrinal purity is qualified by a doctrine of state sovereignty that flies in the face of Russian primacy. "No matter," it says, "how much each of us loves the land of Socialism, the USSR, he can, in no case, love his country less, which also is developing Socialism—in this case the FPRY (Federal People's Republic of Yugoslavia), for which so many thousands of its most progressive people fell. We know very well that this is also similarly understood in the Soviet Union."

Tito emphasized the question of sovereignty in his final remarks to the Central Committee: "Comrades, remember that it is not a matter here of any theoretical discussions, it is not a question of errors committed by the Communist Party of Yugoslavia, of ideological deviation on our part. . . . Comrades, the issue here, first and foremost, is the relationship between one state and another."

Other members of the Central Committee stood up and repeated in general the statements that had been made by Tito. The last man to speak was Sreten Zhujovic. In apparent naiveté, he said: "Comrades, I appeal to your revolutionary conscience. I am against sending such a letter to the Soviet Party. Do not forget that tremendous matters are involved."

As he continued to speak, Tito rose and paced, muttering, "This is treason to the people, the State, and the Party." Although Tito kept repeating this phrase, Zhujovic, who either did not hear him or was incapable of understanding the situation, kept on speaking. Finally, Tito asked him whether he thought Tito was a Trotskyite. Zhujovic replied, "No, but ... ," and the other members of the Central Committee took Tito's cue and placed Zhujovic on the defensive. Zhujovic was finally accused of reporting to the Soviet ambassador. Finally, it was agreed to send the letter prepared by Tito and to set up a committee to decide the cases of Hebrang and Zhujovic.

The letter was personally delivered to Molotov by the Yugoslav ambassador, who spent forty-five minutes explaining it. When he ended, he asked Molotov whether there were any questions. Molotov had none, but expressed his surprise that the ambassador shared the viewpoint of the others in Belgrade. But then Molotov, in all probability, had previously received a full report from Lavrentiev, who had had another conference with Zhujovic.

Moscow, at this point, began circulating the correspondence to the other Cominform members. On April 16, Yudin delivered a letter from Zhdanov, with additional comments by Bela Rakosi.[14] The Yugoslavs denounced the release of the letters by the CC of CPSU without the approval of the CC of the CPY, or without waiting for the reply of the Yugoslavs to the letter of March 27. Meanwhile, additional criticisms were received from the Czechoslovakian and Rumanian parties. On April 19, a Bulgarian delegation, including Dimitrov, passed through Belgrade on its way to Prague. According to the Yugoslavs, Dimitrov told Djilas to "be firm," although his tone "altered visibly" as Vlko Chervenkov, a leading Bulgarian Communist, and some others entered the coach. Shortly thereafter, a letter arrived from Chervenkov denouncing the Yugoslavs.

On May 4, a new letter arrived from the Soviet party. Apart from the usual boring and repetitious charges, it denied that the Yugoslavs had contributed to their own independence; this honor was now assigned to the Red Army. The Yugoslavs were warned, "In his time Trotsky also rendered revolutionary services, but this does not mean that the CPSU could close its eyes to his crude opportunist mistakes which followed later, making him an enemy of the Soviet Union." The letter finally proposed that the matter be discussed at the next meeting of the Cominform.

The plenum of the CC, CPY, met on May 9 to discuss the latest Soviet letter. It agreed to a brief reply (dated May 17) rejecting the Soviet demand that the matter be discussed at the Cominform meeting. It professed continued loyalty to the Soviet Union, however.[15] The plenum also agreed to expel Hebrang and Zhujovic and to institute charges of treason against them.

On May 19, a letter arrived from Mikhail Suslov, secretary of the CC, CPSU, asking the Yugoslavs to be sure to attend the Cominform meeting. On May 20, the CC, CPY, decided unanimously not to attend. On May 22, the Soviet Union accused the Yugoslav party, in particular Tito and Kardelj, of deviation and of tacitly admitting their guilt by refusing to appear before the Cominform. Stalin informed the Yugoslavs that the matter would be discussed at the Cominform whether they attended or not.

Shortly thereafter, Wladyslav Gomulka, of the Polish party, suggested that he and Jakob Berman come to Belgrade to discuss the question with the Yugoslav comrades.[16] Tito replied that the Poles were free to come, but that the Yugoslav decision had been taken with full thought. On May 25, Tito's birthday, Dimitrov was the only Communist leader outside Yugoslavia to wire congratulations. That day, *Borba*, the Yugoslav party newspaper, published the decision of the Yugoslavs to convene a party congress at which all party matters—including the impending break with the Soviet Union—would be discussed. The Congress was to be held beginning July 21, 1948.

An offical invitation to attend the Cominform meeting, scheduled for Bucharest, arrived. On June 20, the Politburo and CC, CPY, sent a letter to the Conference of the Information Bureau declining the invitation to attend. On June 28, the Resolution of the Information Bureau concerning the situation of the Communist Party of Yugoslavia was released. The long, tiring charges were repeated.

The arrests of Hebrang and Zhujovic were called "disgraceful." The CPY was described as "sectarian-bureaucratic," as following the "military methods . . . of Trotsky," of imposing a "Turkish, terrorist regime." "The Information Bureau considers that, in view of all this, the Central Committee of the Communist Party of Yugoslavia has placed itself and the Yugoslav Party outside the family of the fraternal Communist Parties, outside the Communist front and consequently outside the ranks of the Information Bureau."

The resolution then accused the CPY of believing that it could curry favor with the imperialist powers to maintain its independence. But, said the Informburo, its independence could only be lost in this fashion, and Yugoslavia would degenerate into an ordinary nationalist bourgeois state. In effect, appealing to loyal Moscovites to stage a revolution inside Yugoslavia, the Cominform did not "doubt that inside Yugoslavia there are sufficient healthy elements, loyal to Marxism–Leninism . . . Their task is to compel their present leaders to recognize their mistakes . . . and to rectify them. . . . Should the present leaders of the Yugoslav Communist Party prove incapable of doing this, their job is to replace them. . . ." It is interesting that the Yugoslavs did not find it necessary to purge a single figure of national party rank after the arrests of Hebrang and Zhujovic.[17]

On June 29, the plenum of the CC, CPY, published its reply, along with the Cominform charges, in *Borba*. On July 5, the Congress of the CYP unanimously supported the position taken by its Central Committee. Rankovic had done his job well. In August, the Soviet Embassy instructed its agents in the Yugoslav government and party to flee the country. On August 12, Arso Jovanovic, the chief of staff, was shot while trying to cross the border to Rumania. Major General Branko Petrichevich and Colonel Vladimir Dapchevich were soon apprehended. Major General Pero Popivoda escaped from Yugoslavia.

Aftermath

Yugoslavia's defection was a severe blow to the Kremlin and probably persuaded the Russians to tighten their hold in other satellites. The loss of Yugoslavia greatly eased Soviet pressure on Italy and eliminated the Soviet foothold on the Adriatic. However, for a period to come, Yugoslavia was to play a lonely role as an independent Communist state, removed from the shelter of the Soviet sphere but supremely resistant to capitalist and bourgeois lures.

By August, reports from Belgrade stated that Yugoslavia's treaties with the satellites were considered scraps of paper. Yugoslavia delivered notes of protest to Rumania and Hungary, alleging efforts to incite civil war in Yugoslavia. Although Yugoslavia and the Soviet Union signed a new trade accord in December, it reduced trade between the two countries to an eighth of its previous level. Tito and Kardelj stated to the National Assembly that conditions between Yugoslavia and the Soviet bloc could hardly be worse. Yugoslavia's five-year plan was suffering greatly as a result. Kardelj made the interesting statement that conditions were now ripe for improving relations with Italy.

In January, the Soviet Union created the Council for Mutual Economic Aid (Comecon), the Soviet answer to the Marshall Plan. Shortly after the formation of Comecon, a virtual boycott was established on trade with Yugoslavia. This boycott reached full force in May when Hungary refused to forward trade between Czechoslovakia and Yugoslavia. Yugoslav protests concerning its exclusion from Comecon were ignored.

Early in 1949, Yugoslavia accused its Cominform neighbors of provoking border incidents. These disturbances grew increasingly more serious throughout 1949. During the summer, the Yugoslavs denounced the Russians for refusing to support their claim to Austrian Carinthia. In July and August, the Yugoslavs claimed they broke up a Soviet spy ring involving white Russian emigrés and the secretary of the Soviet Embassy.

During January, rumors spread that General Markos Vafiades, the first leader of the Greek revolt, had been removed for Titoism. During June, Yugoslavia, according to reports from Denmark, had given definite assurances to the United States and Great Britain that it had ceased all military assistance to the Greek rebels. Since the Yugoslavs had been a major instigator and supplier of the Greek revolt, this boded ill for the rebels.

The Yugoslavs finally closed the border between the two countries in June. In July, Foreign Minister Kardelj stated that the Cominform was responsible for Yugoslavia's decision. Zachariades, the new leader of the Greek Communists, had issued a call for an independent Macedonia, presumably at the Kremlin's instigation. This move, apparently designed to embarrass the Yugoslavs, had cost the Greek rebels much of their support within Greece and had alienated the Yugoslavs. Kardelj stated bitterly that the Greek revolution had been sacrificed to the Cominform campaign against Yugoslavia. Tito, however, also called upon Great Britain and America to take seriously Yugoslav demands to the United Nations to restrain the Greek "monarcho-Fascists" from provoking border clashes.

During August and September of 1949, there were reported satellite troop movements near the Yugoslav border. Rumors of a secret Cominform meeting also spread. On September 24, Laszlo Rajk, the Hungarian Foreign Minister, was condemned to death for his role in the "Titoist plot." On September 28, the Soviet Union denounced its alliance with Yugoslavia on the basis of the evidence produced at the Rajk trial. Yugoslavia responded by accusing the Soviet Union of inciting rebellion in Yugoslavia. The Soviet Union then accused the Yugoslav diplomatic representatives in the Soviet Union of being spies.

The other Cominform members also denounced their treaties with Yugoslavia. Yugoslavia took the lead in denouncing its treaty with Albania. On September 26, ten members of the Yugoslav legation in Budapest had been ordered out of Hungary by the Hungarian government. Yugoslavia complained to the Soviet Union, Great Britain, and the United States, of Hungarian violations of the peace treaty and failure to pay reparations to Yugoslavia. Charges and countercharges filled the air without surcease.

Conclusions

American relations with Yugoslavia had been worse than with any other Communist country. The United States viewed Yugoslavia as the most Communist and the most hopeless of the nations of the Communist bloc and was consequently greatly surprised by the break.[18] The rupture between Yugoslavia and the Cominform was greeted hopefully by the West, but there was some doubt about the stability of the Yugoslav regime. No initiative was taken at the time to support the regime.[19] Apparently only the monolithic unity of the CPY permitted it to survive. Many commentators are surprised that the Russians did not permit the satellite armies to invade Yugoslavia. It is doubtful that the West would have blocked the move. Nevertheless, the Yugoslav regime continued to maintain itself. As its ideological trappings were accommodated to the advantages of aid from the West, the strongest army in Western Europe came to protect its Italian and Greek borders.

A major diplomatic and strategic victory accrued to the West without its efforts and even in spite of them. The moves of the West against Yugoslavia, particularly with respect to Trieste, and the violations of Yugoslav air space must have made the rupture quite difficult and could well have split the regime, thus producing a Russian rather than a Western victory.

V

The
Communist Coup
in Czechoslovakia
(1954)

In a previous publication, I advanced the thesis that any analysis of the foreign policy of a state is at best only one of a number of available hypotheses.[1] It was stated that a hypothesis had to account for the available evidence in the simplest fashion possible. The present paper is a case study designed to explore the limits within which the available material on the Czechoslovak coup restricts the range of probable hypotheses and, if possible, to assess one of these hypotheses as the most probable.

The Communist coup in Czechoslovakia is often called the consequence of Communist ideology. It is asserted that the Communists had the intention all the time or that it was just a matter of "timing a stroke which completes Russian designs already laid during the negotiations in Moscow and Kosice in 1945 or even before the visit of President Benes to Moscow in 1943."[2] Or, it is said that the Communists "had only gained what they had had already."[3]

These explanations are not very helpful. It is true that the Communist Party did not support Czech democracy because of principle. But, if it only took what it had, why shock world sensibilities by so overt a coup? And, if the coup had been planned as early as 1945, why wait until 1948? Would it not have been simpler and less risky to install a Communist regime with the advance of the Red Army? The Lublin Committee, an ostensibly multiparty group that was established on Soviet territory during the war, was transformed into the Polish government in that fashion. Is it not more likely that the Communist Party of the Soviet Union was prepared to tolerate Czech democracy under some conditions and that its capacity for tolerance was exhausted when these conditions no longer existed?

If so, the problem is to determine the condition or congeries of conditions that triggered the decision to subvert the democratic government. In short, what are the restraints that inhibit Soviet absorption of weak neighbors? If no restraints existed, the triggering of the coup would have occurred much earlier.

If one examines the genesis of Soviet policy toward Czechoslovakia during World War II, it appears that the Soviet Union was never willing to place trust entirely in the laissez-faire of politics in Czechoslovakia. Czechoslovakia was an important military *glacis*. It was only 400 kilometers from France, and it flanked Bavaria. The uranium deposits near Jachymov assumed a new importance by 1945.[4] Before the war, Czechoslovakia had been the sixth industrial nation in Europe. Despite the postwar disorganization, Czechoslovakia could be expected to improve its position, since the Nazis, during the protectorate, had fostered the growth of capital industry in order to support their war efforts.

However, Czechoslovakia had followed a consistent policy of friendship with the Soviet Union. Its foreign policy was dependably anti-German. The expulsion of collaborationist Germans—a goal of all Czech parties—would force the Czechs to depend upon the Soviet Union for protection.[5]

The Soviet Union has rarely relied upon goodwill alone for its protection. On December 12, 1943, the Soviet Union negotiated an alliance with Czechoslovakia that was directed against Germany and her associates despite a Soviet agreement with Great Britain not to conclude an agreement with any of the small powers concerning frontiers or other postwar matters until the cessation of hostilities.[6] At the same time, a form of pressure was maintained on the London government-in-exile by the refusal of the Communists in Moscow to participate in the London cabinet. They maintained that a new government would have to be formed when Czechoslovakia was liberated.

The question of the future status of Subcarpathian Ruthenia had been left open in the 1943 discussions between President Eduard Benes and Marshal Stalin, although it was apparent that Benes was prepared to cede Subcarpathian Ruthenia to the Soviet Union if that country insisted. Therefore, it was particularly shocking to the government in London when the Red Army fostered a Ruthenian National Committee pledged to union with Russia.[7] Although the Soviet Union claimed it could not suppress a spontaneous nationalist movement, the ruse fooled no one. The unsuccessful attempt of the Soviet Union to negotiate a separatist agreement with the collaborationist Slovak regime was also disappointing to the London government.

During 1945, it was agreed that the Czech government go first to Moscow and then return to Czechoslovakia in the wake of the Red Army. A new government, including Communists, would be formed in Moscow. In the meantime, Zdenek Fierlinger, the Social Democratic Ambassador of the Czech government to Moscow, had been playing the Communist game rather than representing his government. It had become clear from his behavior that considerable pressure was to be exercised by the Soviet Union.

In Moscow, it was agreed that the six parties having allied approval and a few nonparty technicians would organize a National Front government. Four of the parties were Czech: the Communists, Social Democrats, National Socialists, and People's. Two were Slovak: the Communists and Democrats. The Premier was to be Fierlinger, the fellow-traveling Social Democrat, although he had held no position of consequence in the party prior to the war. The Communist, Vaclav Nosek, was named Minister of the Interior and was in charge of the police. Klement Gottwald, a leading Communist, received one of the vice-premierships and several other important ministries. Thus, Communists and fellow travelers had many of the key positions in the cabinet.[8] Slovakia received virtual autonomy as a result of Communist insistence. Since the collaborationist People's Party, the popular party in Slovakia, had been outlawed, the Communists hoped, by posing as the champions of Slovak independence and by artificially restricting the parties in that nation, to be able to take over politically.

The agreement formally reached in Kosice, which formed the basis for the coalition government, differed little from a mimeographed text prepared by Gottwald in Moscow and presented to the various parties in March in that city.[9] The Kosice program provided for the "democratization" of the army and cooperation with officers of the Red Army. Partisan units, often of Communist persuasion, were incorporated into the army. The bulk of the postwar army had been organized in Soviet territory, and many of its officers were Communist or pro-Communist.

A Provisional National Assembly was to be elected by "national committees" rather than by the population as a whole. This body was to prepare for the election of a Constituent National Assembly that was to draft a constitution for the country. As the composition of the Provisional Assembly had been decided upon in advance by the parties and as firm party discipline existed, the peculiar form of election for the Assembly was not of major significance.

However, the extensive powers of the self-appointed and often Communist-dominated national committees were used in the meantime to distribute land under the seizure program, thus placing many in the debt of the Communist Party. These committees often arrested and tried collaborationists. It has been claimed that they often acted against those whose only crime was anti-Communism while exculpating genuine collaborationists who joined the Communist Party.[10]

The Kosice program called for land and labor reform. It extended to the fields of culture and education. German and Hungarian influences were to be minimized. Slavonic influence was to predominate, and the Slavonic Institute was to be reestablished. All anti-Bolshevik remarks were to be removed from textbooks—raising an interesting question with respect to academic freedom; however, American occupation policy in defeated countries suffered from a similar ambivalence—and the study of Russian was to be encouraged.

After liberation, the Central Council of Trades Unions (URO and ROH), which developed as part of the resistance movement during the war, proclaimed itself the only trade union organization in the Czech lands and adhered to the Kosice Program. It was the governing body of the Revolutionary Trades Unions Movement; a similar movement developed in Slovakia, and the two movements united in mid-1946. The unions in this body were organized vertically and by 1946 included 2,100,000 workers of whom 86 percent were Czech. It was the largest organization in the nation.

The ROH had the right under law to represent all workers, to regulate its own organization, to create or dissolve any individual branches, to see that workers performed their functions as citizens, to see that the worker's right to work was protected and that he was employed to the best of his capacity. The ROH was given the right to participate in and make suggestions to all legislative and executive groups considering legislation or decrees affecting workers. It had a right to representation on all public bodies not popularly elected and the right to expect support from all public and private bodies in carrying out its objectives. The revolutionary guards of the labor organizations were later used as factory police.

The president of the ROH was a Communist, the secretary-general a Social Democrat, and the editor of its newspaper a National Socialist. Communists were reputed to dominate the Central Council,[11] although elections at the Workers' Council level in 1946 seemed to indicate a waning of Communist strength. The picture that emerges, however, is that of a labor organization with the power of livelihood over the individual worker, with the right to interfere in the exercise of his citizenship prerogatives, with the ability to paralyze the economy, and with an armed force upon which it could call.

Because the economic programs of the government were national objectives endorsed by all the parties, the ROH refused to use the strike to increase wages, although it also refused to give up the right to strike. However, as the president of the Central Council declared in September 1946, "But we would not hesitate to use this weapon [the strike] if anyone would try to revive the conditions of the First Republic after the working people have brought about order in production and economy."[12] The labor unions were one of the weapons used by the Communists in carrying out the coup of February 1948.[13]

Thus, the Communist Party secured control of many areas of physical power in the state and was likely to be the most powerful political force. If the Soviet Union, thus, made concessions to democratic procedures, and if the Czechoslovak Communist Party was forced to compromise certain issues, Czechoslovakia was not free to govern without the Communists or to conduct a foreign policy opposed to that of the Soviet Union.

Nevertheless, the Communists had made concessions they could have avoided had they reduced the rules of the game to physical force. Despite the sympathy of the Western allies for Czechoslovakia, they gave no indication that they would intervene on her behalf any more effectively than they had done for Poland. Had Czechoslovakia been converted into a people's democracy in 1945, it would have been just one more country in the lists of those communized by force in the immediate postwar year.

The hypothesis I am advancing is that the Soviet Union did not communize for ideological reasons alone, that questions of military security and of political reliability were weighed in the balance. If the governments seemed reliable, if the position of the Communist Party was firm enough, and if the security interests of the Soviet Union were served, it might not choose to exert the energy involved in a coup, particularly if this would involve international political difficulties.

In the following pages, the events from the restoration of the republic to the coup will be described without fitting them into the hypothesis. They will then be analyzed to see whether they fit within the range that has just been stated.

Party and Nationality Problems

Although the Kosice Program had been agreed to by all parties, it soon became evident that the Marxist parties, i.e., the two Communist parties and the Social Democrats, split with the other parties on economic matters, while the other five parties split with the Slovak Democrats on the nationality issue.[14] Moreover, as 1946 wore on, the right wing of the Social Democratic Party gained in strength, thus weakening the Communist-Social Democratic bloc.

During 1946, two issues came to a head. One was settled by the organization of a Slovak Labor Party[15] and a Slovak Freedom (Catholic) Party, both of which adhered to the Kosice Program. The other issue centered on voting procedures. Voting in Czechoslovakia was compulsory. However, the right-wing parties had been outlawed on the ground that they had collaborated with the enemy. Therefore, the individuals who supported these parties would have had no option other than voting for one of the left-leaning but non-Marxist parties.

The Communists proposed that the option of casting a blank ballot be provided so that dissatisfaction with the governing parties could be manifested. The non-Marxist parties thought that this maneuver would deprive them of many votes that would otherwise be cast for them. Consequently, they opposed this. The issue was finally cast into the Provisional Assembly where no agreement proved possible, and, on a straight party vote, the Marxist parties barely carried their position.[16]

In the elections of May 1946, the Communists polled 38 percent of all valid votes and the Social Democratic Party 12.33 percent, indicating that, as in some other European countries, the Social Democratic Party was caught in a vise as a result of its cooperation with the Communist Party. Those who approved of its policies often preferred to vote Communist, and those who disapproved of its compromises with the Communists often seceded to one of the non-Marxist parties. Thus, the Social Democrats had suffered a considerable decline from their postwar strength.

The National Socialist Party received 18.33 percent; the People's Party, 15.34 percent; the Democratic Party, 14.33 percent; and the Freedom Party, 1 percent. The Slovak Labor Party received 0.67 percent. The Marxist parties had a total of 51 percent. The Communist Party emerged as the strongest party, more than twice as strong as its nearest competitor.

Moreover, the right-wing vote did not have to look for any place to go; there were only a few non-Marxist alternatives.

However, one element in the situation disturbed the Communists greatly. In Slovakia alone, they polled only 30.37 percent of the vote, while the Democratic Party received 62 percent. It had been agreed that the cabinet and other governing bodies would be divided according to the proportion of the vote rather than equally, as before the election, so the Democratic Party would dominate the Slovak National Council.

Although the Communist, Klement Gottwald, became premier of Czechoslovakia, the most powerful post in the state, the Communists started to cast baleful glances at the situation in Slovakia. Moreover, as the Marxist parties had only a bare majority of the vote, they could not in combination carry a constitutional provision in the Constituent National Assembly that, according to the 1920 Constitutional Charter, required a vote of 60 percent of all the deputies.

Less than a week after the elections, a Czech football team defeated a Slovak team in Bratislava. A riot followed the game, and accusations and counteraccusations were made. The Socialists stated that the riots indicated the growth of anti-Czech separatism in Slovakia, while the Communists alleged Catholic intimidation in the elections[17] and proof of an underground separatist plot.

A commission dispatched by the Communist Minister of the Interior to investigate the matter claimed to find documentary evidence of the plot, whereupon the Communists demanded the invalidation of the elections to the national committees and the subordination of the Slovak National Council to the central government.[18] The Slovak leaders denied the charges, but a new agreement subjecting the existing powers of the Slovak National Council to more effective control by the central government was negotiated. It was agreed that the Council could legislate only on matters not affecting the whole of the republic; whether or not a matter affected the whole of the republic was to be decided by the central government. Moreover, the executive powers of the Slovak Board of Commissioners, appointed by the National Council with the consent of the central government, were limited to decrees promulgated by the National Council. In all other matters, the executive power in Slovakia was to rest with the central government, particularly with respect to the economic integration of the country.

The changes were not a victory for the Communists; the other Czech parties had always been opposed to Slovak autonomy and had agreed to the previous state of affairs only under strong Communist pressure. President Benes himself warned the Slovaks in February 1947 that there must be a definitive solution of their status within the state, that the state could not survive another crisis on the issue, that the Slovaks could not remain independent if they separated, for the Soviet Union would absorb them. The Czechs, according to Benes, could not permit separation for, faced by 65 million Germans, they required a common frontier with the Soviet Union in self-defense.

There were increasing indications toward the end of 1946 that strength within the Marxist bloc was flowing back from the Communists to the Social Democrats.[19] It is possible that this change in attitudes stemmed partly from the more independent position being taken by members of the Social Democratic Party as its middle and right wing gained at the expense of the left. It also may have been related to that fact that many Czechs had joined the Communist Party to save themselves from the depredations of the Red Army. By Soviet and American agreement, occupation forces had been withdrawn during November 1945.

Although it has been claimed that the Czech Communists attempted to exploit this element of fear,[20] its strength was beginning to decline. Evidence of this could be found in the press. Although no organization opposed to the principles of the National Front government was permitted to exist and, therefore, to publish a newspaper, the Soviet protests against alleged anti-Soviet remarks in the official press of the People's Party were successfully brushed aside.

The Economic Situation

Moreover, confidence was increasing as the economic situation improved despite its poor condition at the end of the war. Shortly after the war, $240 million of UNRRA (United Nations Relief and Rehabilitation Administration) aid was required to prevent severe hardship. In addition to the food shortage, German economic measures in Bohemia and Moravia had changed the pattern of production and made the economy dependent upon raw materials that were lacking at the end of the war. German financial policy was responsible for a postwar inflation that pushed the prices of the goods beyond competitive world levels.

In 1945, Czech trade was only 3.9 percent of 1937 exports and 5.5 percent of 1937 imports in value (volume was much smaller in proportion). By the end of 1946, however, production had risen to 80 percent of the 1937 level.[21] Because of the inflation elsewhere in the world, Czechoslovak products became competitive. By the end of 1946, the value of Czechoslovak exports slightly exceeded the 1937 total, although imports fell just a bit short of the 1937 figure. The 1946 harvest was not far short of prewar standards, and the livestock population rose rapidly.

If the Communists were losing strength politically, this loss of strength was reflected in the Czechoslovak economic program. The nationalizations carried out in 1945 had represented a compromise. Sixty percent of Czechoslovak industry had been nationalized. Although this large program went further than the non-Marxist parties had desired, the Communists were also dissatisfied. The Two-Year Plan, which went into effect on January 1, 1947, specified that no further nationalizations were to take place while the plan was in progress; this was a victory for the non-Marxists.

The plan was prepared in the General Secretariat of the Economic Council in which all National Front Parties, as well as nonparty technicians, were represented. It was adopted by the National Assembly virtually without change. The plan had among its goals the surpassing of the 1937 level of industrial production by 10 percent; raising agricultural production to prewar levels; increasing the number of residential, industrial, and administrative buildings; improving water and sanitary facilities; reaching the 1937 level in transportation; raising the economic level of Slovakia to that of the Czech lands and raising the level of backward places in the Czech lands; and, after these tasks were completed, increasing the production of consumer goods.

The Czechoslovak plan increased productive capacity rather than the standard of living; in this respect, it was more similar to Soviet planning than to that of the British Socialists, for instance. Although there is no evidence of great political opposition, as long as the standard of living compared with the prewar standard, there was a certain amount of consumer resistance to the lack of variety and quality imposed by the plan. Moreover, the fact that a considerable proportion of industry remained outside the plan and that the economy was dependent to a great extent upon foreign trade that, in the case of the capitalist countries at least, could not be well integrated with the plan caused some difficulties.

Foreign Policy Considerations

Although, in the political and economic sense, Communist influence was waning in Czechoslovakia, the psychological pressure of the neighboring Soviet Union, the fear of Germany, and the large size of the Communist Party and its control of effective points of physical power made it impossible to govern without the Communists. The arguments for a pro-Soviet orientation in Czechoslovak foreign policy were reinforced by American and British support for the Hungarian position at the Paris Peace Conference of 1946. More damaging to those favoring a bridge to the West was the early demobilization of the American army and the failure of the United States effectively to counterbalance Soviet influence in Eastern Europe.

The Czechoslovaks were, if anything, even more anti-German than were the Russians. The speech of Secretary of State James Byrnes at Stuttgart in September 1946, therefore, produced a profound shock in Czechoslovakia. If Russian efforts to woo the Germans were later to deflate the Soviet stock, the Stuttgart speech weakened the faith of the Czechoslovaks in the foreign policy of the Western powers.[22]

Winston Churchill's proposals in 1946 for a United Europe also caused dismay in Czechoslovakia. The Czechoslovaks desired a policy that ringed Germany with states obligated to unite in defense against possible German expansionism. A proposal calling for a European partnership including the Germans—with Germany perhaps as a major partner —and cooperation between the Germans and French caused the Czechs to fear their eventual isolation.

Economy, Foreign Policy, and the Marshall Plan

Superficially, Czechoslovakia had returned to a state of prosperity by early 1947. However, careful scrutiny of the trade ledgers revealed dangerous weak spots. Although Czechoslovakia ran large trade surplusses with the Soviet Union and Switzerland, its balances with the United States and Great Britain were negative.[23]

The growing lack of convertibility of national curriencies made it difficult to balance the surplusses against the deficits, particularly when dollars were needed. However, imports from the United States and Great Britain had to be maintained at a high level if the goals of the two-year economic plan were to be met. Credits or loans were needed; imports from dollar areas and exports to nondollar areas would have to be cut if the internal targets were to be met. Although no specific areas were mentioned, it was clear that some of the cuts in exports would have to be made from the shipments to the Soviet Union, thus embarrassing the economy of that country.

The announcement of the Marshall Plan Conference in Paris appeared to most Czechoslovaks as a last-minute lifesaver. A Polish delegation, including Hilary Minc, the Minister for Industry and Trade, was in Prague at the time, and this Communist delegation was even more enthusiastic than the Czechoslovak officials.

The announcement that Soviet Foreign Minister Molotov had quit the Paris Conference shattered the euphoria of the Polish–Czechoslovak talks. Minc said that Molotov must have had excellent reasons for his stand and that the Soviet Union had taken the proper course. However, he pointed out, the Soviet Union was a great country while Poland and Czechoslovakia were small countries with all the problems of small countries. They needed the credits that the Marshall Plan offered. Minc said he was certain that the Soviet Union would not object if they went ahead and made arrangements to adhere to the Marshall Plan.[24]

The Poles proposed that the two countries send missions, headed by officers of cabinet rank, to the Paris discussions. Czechoslovak Foreign Minister Jan Masaryk urged greater caution and suggested that the ambassadors to France of the two countries be utilized. Masaryk further suggested that the ambassadors maintain a reserved attitude until they could understand the aim behind the Marshall Plan and the conditions attached to it.

The procedure suggested by Masaryk was discussed at a meeting of the Czech cabinet in July and adopted unanimously after the Communists[25] had been told by Masaryk that Bodrev, the Soviet *chargé,* had been informed of the pending decision and had raised no objections.

Meanwhile, the Czechoslovak cabinet was debating the proposed Franco-Czechoslovak treaty. The Communists protested against the clause in the projected treaty that would make the alliance applicable only against Germany; they demanded that the treaty also apply against states associated with Germany. Although the democratic parties admitted the weakness of the treaty in this respect, they declared, nevertheless, that it was desirable even without such a provision. The cabinet was unable to come to an agreement, and, at the suggestion of Hubert Ripka, a National Socialist, it was decided to send a delegation to Moscow to discuss the treaty and general economic matters. Shortly thereafter, Moscow requested an immediate conference. Since Ripka was ill, Masaryk, Gottwald, and Prokop Drtina, the National Social Minister of Justice, were sent.

The delegation left for Moscow on July 8, the same day the Poles announced that they would not participate in the Marshall Plan.[26] After the delegation arrived, Gottwald had a preliminary conference with Stalin without the knowledge of the other members of the delegation.

Apparently all the important decisions were made at this preliminary conference. Gottwald informed the other members of the delegation, before the main conference, that Stalin was furious and demanded Czechoslovak withdrawal from the Marshall Plan.

At the conference, Stalin declared that the aim of the Marshall Plan was to isolate the Soviet Union and that it held no immediate economic advantages for Czechoslovakia. Stalin rejected Masaryk's request that Czechoslovakia participate in the Marshall Plan discussions and withdraw gracefully later. Stalin said that Sweden and Switzerland were hesitating and that such a move would influence their decision unfavorably. "In the Soviet Government no one doubts the friendship of Czechoslovakia for the Soviet Union. If you take part in the Conference you will prove by that act that you allow yourselves to be used as a tool against the Soviet Union. Neither the people nor the Government of the Soviet Union would tolerate that."

When Stalin was informed by Masaryk and Drtina that Czechoslovakia depended on the Western countries for 60 to 80 percent of its raw materials, Stalin offered to purchase pipelines, electric motors, and other products that Czechoslovakia normally sold to the West, while providing wheat in return. Although Czechoslovakia needed the wheat badly, the other elements of the plan involved an additional imbalance in trade with the West and a subsequent reduction in the Czech standard of living. Masaryk privately drew the conclusion that the Soviets did not desire, and even feared, the recovery of Western Europe. Masaryk thought that Stalin expected war and was basing his strategy upon that expectation.[27]

The Czechoslovak delegation also consulted Stalin about the projected treaty with France. All the Czechoslovak parties would have preferred a more inclusive treaty: the democratic parties because they wanted the treaty to apply in case of trouble with Hungary and the Communist Party probably because it was thinking of the United States as a possible ally of the Germans.

However, the primary object of the democratic parties was to create a contractual bridge with a Western power.[28] Therefore, they desired the treaty badly, even if it applied only against Germany. The Communists apparently feared just this contingency. Stalin denied that he opposed the treaty, but declared that he wanted a really good treaty for Czechoslovakia, one that gave a guarantee of immediate aid in case of attack and that applied to allies or satellites of Germany.[29]

Stalin pointed out that France had deserted Czechoslovakia at

Munich and that it was necessary to have a strong treaty, that Czechoslovakia was not a country with great land space and would need aid fast. He mentioned that Great Britain, although offering to extend her alliance with the Soviet Union to fifty years, was also attempting to weaken it by eliminating the clause on immediate aid and the clause applying the treaty against the associates of Germany.

Apparently Stalin's moderation disturbed Gottwald, who feared that the other delegates might draw the conclusion that Stalin did not forbid its completion. Gottwald then asked Stalin whether signing of the treaty might not have an adverse effect upon the Anglo-Soviet negotiations.[30] Stalin affirmed this objection and that sealed the fate of the treaty. Although France later offered to modify the treaty to apply it to states that joined Germany in acts of aggression, the Czechoslovak Communists continued to find objections to the treaty, and negotiations for it were never completed.

Onset of the Coup

All the signs pointed to an approaching crisis. During the spring, the Communist leaders, Gottwald and Rudolf Slansky, secretary general of the party, had expressed the need for the Communist Party to secure a majority of the votes in the coming elections in order to end the policy of compromise with the other parties.[31] The Communists evidently believed that it had become necessary for them to gain firm control of the policies of the Czechoslovak nation. The democratic parties, although disposed to orient Czechoslovak foreign policy primarily toward the Soviet Union, desired to maintain a bridge to the West. Moreover, the economic needs of Czechoslovakia entailed relations with the West. After the Marshall Plan episode, Masaryk still expressed a hope of obtaining Western aid, at least in the form of "normal commercial loans for specific purposes."[32]

As the needs of the Czechs for foreign aid increased and as the negotiations with the Russians for a foreign trade pact were bogging down, the Communists began to make desperate efforts to consolidate their domestic political position. On September 5, 1947, bombs were sent through the mails to the offices of Zenkl, Drtina, and Masaryk. Although it was later proved, despite interference from the Communist-controlled Ministry of the Interior, that the plot had originated within a local unit of the Communist Party, Slansky accused the National Socialist Party of staging this attempted assassination.[33]

On September 11, 1947, the Communist Party reached an agreement with Social Democrats Fierlinger and Josef Vilim, secretary general of the Social Democrat Party, that the Communist and Social Democratic parties were to follow a common line. The National Socialist Party later rejected an invitation to join this united socialist front. Many Social Democrats were affronted by this agreement. Vaclav Majer, the Social Democratic Minister of Food, handed in his resignation, although President Benes refused to accept it.

In late September, the Cominform was established. In its announcement, the Cominform vigorously attacked the socialist parties and accused them of betraying the cause of the working class. This charge increased the resentment within the Social Democratic Party of the pact with the Communist Party. During November, complicated maneuvering by Vilim led to a Social Democratic Party Congress in which Fierlinger[34] was replaced as party president by Bohumil Lausman, an opportunist who had been won temporarily to an anti-Communist position.[35]

In October, the Communist Party engaged in new efforts to reshape the Slovak Board of Commissioners more to Communist liking. The Communists accused the Democratic Party of conspiring with the outlawed Slovak People's Party and with maintaining relations with Ferdinand Durcansky, an *emigré* Axis collaborator, to plot against the republic. These changes were not entirely without foundation, and there were indications of linkages between some Democratic Party deputies and Karol Sidor and Durcansky.[36] However, leaders of the National Socialist Party thought that the charges went far beyond the available evidence and that they were spread in this form by the Communists in order to destroy the Democratic Party and to take over Slovakia. There was evidence that the Communist-controlled police had inspired denunciations of Slovak Democrats by *agents provocateurs*.

By November, the Communists demanded the right to include representatives of the ROH within the Slovak Board of Commissioners, in effect, to "pack" it. They also demanded the right to include representatives of the ROH and other "nonpolitical" groups in the Czechoslovak National Front. They were effectively resisted by the other parties. The Slovak National Council, however, was reorganized, and the Democratic Party lost three seats. One of these went to the Freedom Party, another to the Labor (Social Democratic) Party, and the third to a pro-Communist nonparty technician.

During November, President Benes informed Valerian Zorin, the retiring Soviet ambassador to Prague, that the Communist Party would lose the forthcoming elections. He reported the impression that Zorin also expected this result.[37] In Moscow, in this period, suspicions were expressed concerning Czech foreign policy. M. Lebediev accused the Czechs of desiring to throw the Communists out of the cabinet as the French had done. Anastas Mikoyan ominously informed Czech representatives, "Your disagreements and your internal struggles are your own business; what interests us is your relations with the U.S.S.R.; we will trust you if you remain our allies."

During the autumn, a series of purges was initiated in the Soviet satellites. Especially disquieting was the fact that Nikolai Petkov, the second postwar premier of Bulgaria—who had fallen into disfavor with Russia despite the fact that he was widely considered a crypto-Communist—was tried and executed even in the face of American protests. Moreover, the alarming information spread that, at a meeting of the executive committee of the Communist Party, Gottwald warned of a reactionary coup against the government and announced that the Communist Party might be forced to take drastic measures to protect its position.

During November, shortly after the execution of Petkov in Bulgaria, Petr Zenkl and some others called on American Ambassador Lawrence Steinhardt to discuss the Czechoslovak situation with him. Zenkl expressed fear that the Communists were preparing to destroy the democratic system and doubted that a fair election could be held while the Communists controlled the police. Steinhardt replied that he knew Stalin and was sure that Stalin wanted to maintain Czechoslovakia as a display of cooperation between East and West.

Zenkl referred to the execution of Petkov and the ineffective American protests. Steinhardt replied that Bulgaria had been a defeated enemy country. The situation in Czechoslovakia was quite different, he said. Czechoslovakia was an ally for whom the United States had great regard. Moreover, American troops were in Bavaria on the Czechoslovak border.[38] The United States, he said, would take an active interest in anything that happened in Czechoslovakia. Steinhardt said that he would also be there to represent the United States if anything were attempted. Zenkl said that he did not doubt the friendship of the United States or of Steinhardt for Czechoslovakia.[39]

During November and December, Nosek, the Communist Minister of the Interior, began a purge inside the intelligence service and the S.N.B., the mobile security police. Although he was forced to dismiss the Communist, Captain Porkony, as head of Intelligence, because he falsified evidence in the bombing plot, he was able to retain Porkony within the service and to intensify the replacement of non-Communist technicians by Communists. Weapons, including submachine guns, were discovered in the home of a Communist deputy. The Communists were forced to disavow the deputy, and they were clearly embarrassed by the disclosure.

During December 1947, the Czechoslovak–Bulgarian treaty negotiations bogged down because of cabinet disagreements. The Bulgars wanted the treaty to apply to any aggressor, not just to Germany and its associates. The Bulgars were evidently concerned with their neighbors, Greece and Turkey. Although Gottwald stated that such a wording of the treaty had the approval of Stalin, President Benes personally opposed such terms. Jan Masaryk wrote to Moscow that Czechoslovakia would sign such a treaty if the Soviet Union would be a party to it, whereupon Moscow replied that the terms of the treaty concerned only Czechoslovakia and Bulgaria.[40]

Meanwhile the economic crisis continued. During November 1947, it was reported that Czechoslovakia was in dire need of American loans or credits because of Soviet demands that practically exhausted Czechoslovak export capacities in heavy goods. These were the products, moreover, that Czechoslovakia traditionally traded to the West. Instead of decreasing, the Russian demands were increasing.[41]

By the middle of November, the terms of a five-year trade pact between the Soviet Union and Czechoslovakia were being completed in the Moscow negotiations. At the same time, the United States was growing more doubtful about advancing credits to Czechoslovakia.[42] Although Ambassador Steinhardt intervened energetically to secure credits for Czechoslovakia,[43] some American officials thought that American credits would serve only to advance the integration of the Czechoslovak economy with that of the Soviet Union. On the other hand, the failure of the United States to act reduced the alternatives available to the democratic parties and strengthened the arguments of the Communists.

Toward the end of November, reports circulated that the trade negotiations were lagging. It was noted that the failure of the Soviet Union to deliver promised grain had resulted in a serious shortage as a result of the great drought in Czechoslovakia, and that the Czechs were unsuccessfully attempting to get grain elsewhere.[44] In an effort to secure goodwill for the Communist Party, Premier Gottwald, without the knowledge of the cabinet,[45] appealed to Stalin to increase scheduled grain deliveries by 150,000 tons. Stalin responded by promising 200,000 additional tons of grain, and also promised to grant credits to Czechoslovakia.[46] Although many observers doubted that the transportation system between the Soviet Union and Czechoslovakia would permit the fulfillment of Stalin's promise, early deliveries were made with great publicity. Gottwald also delivered a personal attack on Majer, the anti-Communist Minister of Food, accusing him of failure to solve the food situation.

By the middle of December, the negotiations for a five-year trade pact were concluded successfully. The agreement provided for the exchange of $500 million in goods. The Czechs were to get food, fodder, cotton, fertilizer, oil products, ore, and other materials. The Russians were to get oil piping, rails, machinery for generating power, general industrial machinery, sugar, textiles, and chemicals, among other products.[47] The pact accounted for 16 percent of the Czech foreign trade, 40 percent of her grain requirements, and 25 percent of her cotton requirements.[48]

Hubert Ripka, the Czech trade negotiator, states that the pact was, on the whole, advantageous for Czechoslovakia. The Soviet Union cut back its demands for industrial products and increased its delivery schedule for food products. However, to pay for the increased grain, Czechoslovakia had to step up its deliveries of consumer goods products to the Soviet Union. This would require the Czech worker to tighten his belt over the next several years.[49]

Later in December, Premier Klement Gottwald urged a new five-year plan designed to increase Czechoslovak heavy industry by 80 percent. To carry out this program, 30 percent of current production would have to be diverted to the production of capital goods.[50] Taken in conjunction with the trade pact, the plan required a considerable reduction in the Czech standard of living. Although the effects of the plan would not be felt quickly enough to influence the forthcoming elections, the long-term effect would probably be disastrous politically for the parties that proposed it. Even so, the Social Democratic Party was disposed to support the Communist Party on these economic objectives.[51] As a result, many right-wing Social Democrats left the party, thus decreasing the influence and resistance of the anti-Communist wing of that party.

The Coup Is Organized

During January 1948, the situation built up to a climax. Early in January, the case of the bomb plot was brought into Parliament when Drtina demanded the dismissal of the police who destroyed the evidence of Communist complicity. The Communists responded with threats and accused the National Socialists of intending to stage a "Reichstag fire trial."

Toward the end of the month, Hubert Ripka was visited by an unnamed Communist deputy, who informed him that he feared the worst unless thoughtful persons on both sides could agree on a compromise. This deputy then suggested a confidential meeting between Gottwald and Slansky on one side and Ripka and Zenkl on the other. As Ripka viewed the suggestion as an effort to intimidate the National Socialists into accepting the Communist reorganization of the Ministry of the Interior, he refused to accept.[52]

When Ripka met Gottwald on ministerial business, Gottwald accused the National Socialists of attempting to make a van der Lubbe[53] of him. He accused the National Socialists of fostering reaction and raising the trouble about the police only so they could claim the elections were rigged after they lost. Ripka retorted that he was aware of the survey of public opinion carried out by Communist Minister of Information Vaclar Kopecky, according to which the Communists would lose 8 to 10 percent of their vote.[54]

This was ominous, as the Communists had no intention of permitting such a reduction of their power in the state. Moreover, before the interview was broken off, Gottwald asserted strongly that the Communists would never give way on the issue of the security police. Since, as later events confirmed, they could not count on the support of the Social Democratic Party on this issue, this could only mean that they were prepared, or wished others to believe them prepared, to resort to force to maintain their control of the police.

By February, it was evident that the drama was coming to a close. Word came back to Czechoslovakia that Hungarian Communists were predicting the emergence of the Communists as the masters of Czechoslovakia by the end of the month.[55]

The next issue that arose was a minor one from a superficial standpoint. It concerned a proposed 25 percent pay increase for civil servants. The URO and the Communist Party opposed the increase on the ground that it would lead to inflation. They warned that they would have to resort to strikes to secure increases for all other workers if the increase for civil servants went through. As the civil servants were underpaid, the specific Communist objections were not especially relevant. However, if they intended to depress living standards generally as a consequence of the projected five-year plan, this was hardly the time to increase wages.

Even more important was the possibility that the Communists could split the Social Democratic Party from the other democratic parties on this issue. Thus, if they could bring matters to a head on the economic issue rather than on the police issue, they had a good chance of carrying a majority with them.

The democratic leaders understood this as well as the Communists. Therefore, the anti-Communist Social Democrat Majer introduced a compromise before the cabinet that was much closer to the Communist than to the National Socialist position. The National Socialists, however, accepted this compromise as soon as their proposal was beaten. The wavering Social Democrats were kept in line despite the threats of Antonin Zapotocky, president of the URO and his delegation. Majer's resolution was then passed over the Communist opposition. Zapotocky said the URO would not accept the decision and that the unions would answer the government through the congress of unit committees.[56] Gottwald shouted, "You will pay us back for that!"[57] The vehemence of the Communists was indicative of the pressure[58] under which they were acting and of the seriousness of the situation. Time was very short indeed.

Before the meeting of the Czechoslovak cabinet on February 13, 1948, it was learned that Minister of the Interior Nosek had dismissed eight non-Communist police commissioners in Prague and had ordered their replacement by Communists.[59] Because the police commissioners had control of the arms used by the police, this seemed to be an obvious preparation for a coup. The matter was introduced at the cabinet meeting and the representatives of all parties except the Communist Party voted for a resolution ordering Nosek to reinstate the dismissed police commissioners.

The unity of the non-Communist parties interfered with the plans of the Communists, and they sought to provide another issue on which to force a cabinet split. According to reports circulating on February 16, the secretariat of the Communist Party had worked out a plan of radical socialism that the National Socialists and the bourgeois parties would be forced to oppose and that the Social Democrats would support.

According to these reports, the Communists hoped that rejection of this proposal by the bourgeois parties would precipitate a cabinet crisis, permitting Gottwald to form a new cabinet from Communist, Social Democratic, and URO elements. This cabinet would stage an election in which it would win more than 50 percent of the votes. According to the informant, Slansky assured the secretariat of the party that everything had been cleared with the Cominform and Zhdanov.[60]

Ripka, Zenkl, and other leaders of the National Socialist Party thought it dangerous to permit the Communists to choose the issue on which the break was to come. Because Nosek had not carried out the resolution of the cabinet with respect to his dismissals of the Prague police commissioners, they saw an opportunity to parry the Communist gambit by handing in their resignations on this issue if Nosek continued to disregard the cabinet decision. The democratic leaders hoped in this fashion to demonstrate to the public that the regime was in danger. Then, if a cabinet crisis was provoked, they hoped to be able to advance the elections to an earlier date, before the police had a chance to rig them.

Gottwald abruptly adjourned a cabinet meeting when the other parties refused to discuss any other issue, unless he would force Nosek to comply with the cabinet resolution. The People's and Slovak Democratic parties agreed to act in unison with the National Socialist plan to cause a cabinet crisis over this issue if Nosek did not comply. Majer, the Social Democrat, promised to go along with the anti-Communist grouping. Representatives of the democratic parties then proceeded to inform President Benes of their plans. He advised them to hold firm to the course they had chosen and agreed that it was necessary to insist upon the cabinet resolution regarding the police.

Benes also told them that Premier Gottwald had conferred with him and had accused the National Socialists of plotting to install a cabinet of technicians, thus eliminating Communist participation in the cabinet. Benes said he had replied that he would never accept a cabinet that did not include representatives of all the parties or that did include representatives of other groups.[61] In effect, he was warning Gottwald that he would not approve a cabinet including URO elements or excluding the democratic parties at the same time that he was assuring him of continued Communist participation in the cabinet.

The Coup

Soviet troop movements were reported on the Czech periphery in mid-February 1948. On February 19, Valerian Zorin, the Soviet Deputy Minister of Foreign Affairs and ex-ambassador to Czechoslovakia, arrived in Prague ostensibly to check on the deliveries of Russian wheat and to participate in a scheduled celebration of Soviet–Czechoslovak friendship. The mission was a relatively minor one for so important an official.[62]

Ambassador Steinhardt arrived in Prague on February 19 from the United States.[63] Shortly after his arrival, the ambassador received a visit from Zenkl. The ambassador informed Zenkl that the United States was in no position to help or aid the Czechoslovak democrats, except by expressions of sympathy or moral support. Ambassador Steinhardt asked whether the democratic parties would take any steps to prevent a coup. Zenkl noted the difficulties of the situation. The democratic parties had no arms with which to defend themselves, while the Communists had caches of arms and the control of the police. He was not sanguine about the situation.[64]

In the meantime, the Social Democratic ministers attempted to persuade the Communists to give way on the police issue. Gottwald shouted at them, "If you do not march with us, you will be liquidated like the others."[65] The National Socialists, Democrats, and People's Party agreed not to participate in the cabinet meeting of February 20 unless first informed about whether or not the cabinet decision of February 13 had been executed. The Social Democrats also agreed to abstain from cabinet meetings until that issue had been settled satisfactorily. When the Communist reply was unsatisfactory, the three parties decided that their ministers would hand in their resignations that afternoon. The Social Democratic Party promised to call a meeting of its executive committee to determine its position.

At four P.M., the twelve ministers belonging to the three parties handed their resignations to Benes. Benes congratulated them on the course they had chosen and promised not to accept the resignations. He said that he would not compromise on the issue and that the important thing was to hurry the elections. The Communist losses would exceed all their forecasts.[66]

That same day, the state radio service, which was under the control of the Communists, attacked the twelve "reactionary" ministers. The radio urged all workers to meet in the Old City Square Saturday morning, February 21. Communist squads took physical reprisals against those workers who refused to participate in the rally. Gottwald spoke at the rally, and accused his opponents of being agents of foreign reaction. Committees of Action were urged by the premier.

According to plan, Committees of Action, supposedly representing the people, but actually set up through Communist channels, came into action throughout the country. Later that day, Gottwald called on the president and demanded that he accept the resignations of the ministers. Benes refused. Later, factory committee representatives called on Benes and repeated the demand. He again refused and had his position printed in the newspapers.[67] Benes declared that he would not accept a cabinet of technicians, a cabinet that excluded the Communists, or one that excluded any other party.

The democratic parties would have preferred that Benes insist upon the resignation of the entire cabinet. They were disturbed by the fact that their requests to see the president on February 21 had been refused although he had received several Communist delegations. Meanwhile, Benes was deluged by a flood of Communist-inspired telegrams and messages. Also, the police were required to take oaths to support the government of Klement Gottwald and to take orders from Minister of the Interior Nosek.

On Sunday, February 22, the Communists staged a packed congress of union unit committees. The democratic parties staged counterdemonstrations throughout the state against a background of increasing Communist violence and intimidation. That day the Communists began to arrest some of those who took part in the demonstrations.

Later that day word arrived from Jina, Chief of the Political Division in the Office of the President, that President Benes was depressed by the brutal methods of the Communists. He requested the democratic parties' agreement to his appeasing the Communists. Benes wanted to accept the resignations of the democratic ministers and then to persuade the Communists to accept a cabinet of all the parties.[68] Although the parties could not prevent the president from accepting the resignations of their ministers, they refused to approve such actions.

Later that night, Communist-controlled S.N.B. (Corps of the Security Police) mobile police units occupied Prague, and several secretaries of the National Socialist Party were arrested. Gendarmes with submachine guns were stationed at the homes of leading members of the democratic parties.

During the afternoon of February 23, President Benes, who had received Gottwald and Nosek that morning, conferred with the leaders of the National Socialist Party. He said he had informed Gottwald that he would not permit him to make a *putsch.* Then he called Gottwald's demands the equivalent of Munich and said, "... I will act no differently from what I did then. I want to have no part in this second Munich you are preparing."[69] This was ominous inasmuch as Benes had acceded to the Nazi demands at Munich without accepting responsibility for them. In effect, Benes was stating that he would not participate in the Communist plans, nor would he oppose them.

Nevertheless, Benes informed Gottwald that he would not accept a cabinet list obtained by intimidation or by the artificial splitting of parties.

But he qualified this posture of opposition: "If the Communists persist in their threatening attitude, and if they insist that I bow to their demands, I shall refuse, and I shall resign myself rather than comply."[70] Benes was very worried about the massing of the Red Army. "I think as you [Ripka] do that Moscow will not run the risks which an armed intervention would involve. However, I cannot rule out the possibility of seeing their troops cross our frontiers. In that case what could we do?" Benes ruled out Ripka's demand that they fight, even if it meant defeat. "No one will help us. Moscow knows that. . . . They take themselves for realists; at bottom they are only fanatics. Their whole policy is a provocation to war."

On February 21, one of the leaders of the Slovak Democratic Party had been arrested, while Communist printers refused to print its newspaper. On February 23, the secretariats of the three anti-Communist parties were raided and their files seized. That day, the Minister of the Interior announced discovery of a plot against the republic. Unofficial Communist charges were circulated that the American embassy was involved in the plot. Newsprint deliveries to the papers of the democratic parties ceased. General Bohumil Bocek, Chief of Staff of the army, announced his resolution to oppose "all tendencies which hide a desire to provoke a reactionary reversal of our foreign policy."[71] Thus, Bocek blossomed forth as a collaborator of the Communists.

Meanwhile, the Social Democrats had been following a hesitant policy. On February 20, Lausman had promised not to participate in a government from which the other parties were excluded. He claimed to have refused all Communist offers. However, Lausman refused to accede to the request of his party comrade, Majer, that the Social Democratic ministers resign immediately.

A meeting of the central executive committee of the Social Democratic Party was scheduled for Monday, February 23. During the crisis, the Social Democratic paper, *Pravo Lidu*, followed an unhesitating anti-Communist line. As late as the night of February 22, Lausman had promised not to participate in a cabinet that did not include the other parties.

On February 23, when the Communists were already resorting to direct action, the central executive committee of the Social Democratic Party met. The Fierlinger wing of the party, with the help of Lausman, defeated a motion by Majer calling for the resignation of the Social Democratic ministers. It then passed a resolution calling for talks with the Communists and participation with the URO in a conference designed to create a Central Committee of Action to set up a new National Front. That evening, Lausman and Vilim were received by Benes. On February 24, Fierlinger's men, aided by a Communist mob and the police, occupied the editorial offices of *Pravo Lidu*, against the resistance of Majer.[72] The secretariat of the party was also seized by force.

On February 23, Minister of National Defense Ludvig Svoboda made a speech pledging fidelity to the revolutionary cause. Although Majer was still an accredited minister in the cabinet, a Communist mob forcibly ejected him from his governmental office, despite appeals for aid to the Minister of the Interior. The renegade Catholic People's Party deputies, led by two men named Petr and Plojhar, took over the offices of *Lidova Democracie*, the People's Party newspaper, by force. The independent liberal daily, *Svobodne Noviny*, was seized by force, as was Melantrich, the publishing house of the National Socialist Party, and its paper, *Svobodne Slovo*.[73] Several editors were arrested, and the general manager was prevented from occupying the premises. *Mlade Fronta*, the Young Communist publication, "hail[ed] with joy these measures which, at last, have freed our press from traitors to the nation."

On February 23, the Communists created the new National Front, consisting of Communists, Social Democrats, URO elements, and some renegades from the other parties. On February 24, Alois Neumann and Emanuel Slechta, two National Socialists, agreed to participate in a Gottwald cabinet without the knowledge or approval of their party. Benes was informed by the party, when it learned of this, that the action of the two National Socialist deputies was unauthorized. On the same day, Benes appealed by letter to Gottwald again to "discuss the matter of a new and lasting cooperation . . . reasonable agreement is possible because it is absolutely necessary."

The Communists replied that they refused to cooperate with the three parties.[74] *Rude Pravo* threatened a general strike unless Gottwald's demands were satisfied. At noon on February 25, the radio announced that Benes had accepted the resignations of the twelve ministers. The chancellory responded, however, to a telephone inquiry that no decision had yet been reached. By four P.M., Benes had approved the new ministerial list submitted by Gottwald.[75] The Communist coup had been carried out successfully.

Factors Precipitating the Coup

It seems that one factor alone would have been sufficient to necessitate the coup. That was the five-year plan advocated by Klement Gottwald in December 1947, a plan calling for an 80 percent increase in heavy industrial capacity. To accomplish that objective, 30 percent of the productive facilities for consumption would be diverted. This would have been so unpopular that it could be carried out only under a dictatorial regime. No free people will tighten its belt to that extent unless there is a clear and present danger.[76]

Although the Czechoslovaks desired to cooperate with the Soviet Union, their image of the West differed greatly from that broadcast by the Kremlin. Therefore, that particular clear and present danger did not exist for the Czechs. Moreover, the National Socialist, People's, and Democratic parties were sure to exploit the issue of increasing heavy industry. Because of the agreement of 1946 that cabinet posts were to be distributed according to strength in Parliament, over a period of years the Communist Party would lose its key positions in the government and, thus, its ability to veto policies to which it objected.

Although the Communist Party was making propagandistic use of the five-year trade agreement with the Soviet Union, and although the economic terms of that agreement were not completely unfavorable to Czechoslovakia, the agreement would produce a further decline in the level of consumption, thus driving an additional nail into the coffin of the Communist Party.

In addition, the failure of Czechoslovakia to join the Marshall Plan was unpopular because that plan held the promise of mitigating Czechoslovakia's economic problems. Yet this may have been the very reason why the Czechs, as well as the Poles and the Rumanians, were not permitted to join. Had they joined, their trade and production schedules would have been tied to Western credits and Western needs rather than to Soviet needs.[77] As a member of the Marshall Plan Council, Czechoslovakia automatically would have negotiated with the West; the very bridge the Russians desired to deny them would have been created in an aggravated form. The iron curtain would have been pierced. As the organization of the West increased, disorganization would have appeared in the Soviet bloc. The stability and viability of the Soviet bloc were in question, and that involved the vital security interests of the Soviet Union.

The monolithic unity of the Soviet sphere has been asserted so frequently that the cracks in that monolithic structure are often overlooked. However, it is just those cracks, those symptoms of impending disorganization, that the Soviet Union desired to repair.

The series of purges in the satellites, beginning in 1947, constitute evidence of a "nationalist" opposition to Moscow policy. The Balkan federation proposed by Dimitrov infuriated Stalin because it appeared to envisage a bloc of Communist states combining to act as a counterweight against the Soviet Union.

It is significant that Stalin demanded on February 10, 1948, that three federations be formed immediately, and that his suggested federations would group those states between whom the greatest national friction existed. The federations he proposed included Yugoslavia and Bulgaria, in dispute over Macedonia; Hungary and Rumania, in dispute over Transylvania; and Czechoslovakia and Poland, in dispute over the Teschen region.[78] Federations of this character would have weakened the Communist parties in the satellites by permitting Stalin to play off the parties within each federation and to play off one federation against the others. Stalin's plan would have hardened the organizations along the most divisive lines.

Stalin had definite problems of leadership. Gomulka opposed the formation of the Cominform, and he also opposed Zhdanov's policy of collectivization and forced industrialization.[79] However, it is apparent from Rumanian and Czech responses to the Marshall Plan that others were in opposition, even if their positions were not as overt as those of Gomulka. Kostov argued economic policy with Stalin during the February 1948 meetings in Moscow and had to be shouted down. At the Cominform meeting, Slansky supported Gomulka on the partisan issue against Zhdanov.[80]

As late as April 1949, Czechoslovakia maintained its trade pattern with Yugoslavia despite the Cominform boycott. It was only after Hungary refused to transship[81] and after Mikoyan made a trip to Prague that Czechoslovakia broke off her trade relations with Yugoslavia.

Was the Cominform itself an attempt to get the various Communist parties into face-to-face relations with the Moscow bosses and to play the party organizations against each other in order to assure Moscow's leadership? Even if this were not so, the problems of maintaining unity in program and action apparently were becoming formidable.

Why could not Moscow have played down the industrialization program, thus reducing the friction resulting from the economic problems of Czechoslovakia and the satellites?[82] No categorical answer can be given to this question. The sharp dispute with respect to this issue between Zhdanov and Gomulka at the sessions establishing the Cominform would indicate that the imposition of forced industrialization within the satellite bloc was an important reason for establishing the Cominform.

Gottwald advocated the five-year plan shortly after the Cominform meeting. According to reports a twelve-year plan for Poland and a five-year plan for Czechoslovakia were formulated at the Cominform meeting. These plans called for an abnormally high level of investment, which required forced savings and which was to be accomplished by reducing consumption, by the direction of labor to specified jobs, and by other harsh measures.[83]

According to an escaped Czech civil servant, the Communists were using Czechoslovakia as a source for economic reconstruction of the Soviet Union and as a source of military supplies. He reported that the Communists were attempting to build an Eastern Ruhr in Czechoslovakia and Poland and that they were attempting to integrate the economies of Eastern Europe and East Germany.[84]

It is necessary now to turn back to the German problem. The plans for Anglo-American bizonal fusion in Germany had been viewed gravely by the Soviet Union. Increases in the level of permitted production in the Western zones were matched by planned increases of two to three hundred percent in the Soviet zone. The failure of the Moscow meeting of Foreign Ministers in March-April 1947, the Truman Doctrine, the Brussels Pact, French adherence to the Anglo-American program with respect to Germany, and the veto of the Soviet proposal for four-power control of the Ruhr must have confronted the masterminds of the Kremlin with a nightmare,[85] especially when during the summer, JCS 1067, providing for the dismantlement of German heavy industry, was formally revoked. Moscow envisaged the enlistment of the Ruhr productive capacity in the service of the Western powers. The Soviet leaders had no hope of matching this productive capacity, but they may well have believed that draconic measures were necessary in order to achieve a situation approaching parity.

Rejection of the Marshall Plan and insistence upon forced industrialization produced convulsions in the Soviet sphere of Europe. The difficulties it caused within the various Communist parties and the harsh measures required to keep the various populations in check involved great material costs—if not moral costs—for the Kremlin. Moreover, this crisis occurred at a time when unrest was evidently so great within the Soviet Union that increases in the standard of living had to be promised the Russian people. It is doubtful that these steps were taken for purely ideological reasons. Stalin generally was able to subordinate ideology to considerations of the consolidation and maintenance of Soviet power.

Russia feared war, and, as in 1937,[86] it was stepping up the rate of industrialization to meet that danger. After the defeat of the Chinese

Communists in 1926–27, the rupture of the Soviet-Kuomintang entente, and the international isolation of the Soviet Union,[87] the first five-year plan and farm collectivization were ordered.

If the reasons stated above have validity, the Soviet leaders thought it necessary to impose the five-year plan on Czechoslovakia because of its great industrial capacity. From that standpoint, Czechoslovakia was the key European satellite. Therefore, the coup clearly had to be imposed at approximately the time the five-year plan was carried through. However, to say that this consideration would have been sufficient to produce the result is not equivalent to stating that it did produce the result.

A hypothesis must account for all the evidence, and some pieces of evidence produced in the body of the paper have not been accounted for. Gottwald and Slansky were speaking of the necessity of winning a majority in the election during the spring, roughly half a year before the Cominform meeting and the order to force through the five-year industrialization program.

No totally convincing answer can be offered if that fact is offered as an objection to the hypothesis because sufficient information is not available. However, there is evidence that many programs planned by the Soviet Union are in the consideration and planning stages for months before the orders for their execution are issued. The developing cold war would undoubtedly have given rise to talk in top Communist circles of certain strategic needs, including firm control of such strategic areas as Czechoslovakia. Moreover, the resolution to win a majority in the elections in order to have that type of firm control does not of itself implicate the intention of dispensing with parliamentary devices or of resorting to force.

It must also be remembered that the statements by Gottwald and Slansky occurred just after announcement of the Truman Doctrine, in which the American president supported aid to Greece and Turkey with a general declaration of American resistance to aggression. Although the efforts of the democratic parties to build a bridge to the West were both justified and sensible from the standpoint of Czechoslovakia, there is no gainsaying the fact that the democratic parties' purpose in building a bridge to the West was to weaken the dependence of Czechoslovakia upon the Soviet Union. However, this is just what the Soviet Union could not afford, for it required to organize Czechoslovakia in its bloc of nations.

While the Soviet Union had secured relatively easy victories on the

Marshall Plan and French alliance issues, the remarks made by Mikoyan and Lebediev reveal growing suspicion of the motivation of the democratic parties. Although the democratic parties had every reason to resent the brutal methods of the Soviet Union and the Czech Communist Party, it is undeniable that the rift between the parties was widening as conditions returned to normal within the country. The position of the Communist Party was correspondingly weakened.

If the democratic parties had no intention of forcing the Communist Party out of the cabinet, one wonders whether they might not have discovered such an intention had their position become sufficiently strong at the elections. Certainly the Communists feared this, and they were probably correct in fearing it; in any case, the mobilization of the Czech economy in the service of Soviet objectives could not have been achieved had the democratic parties held power.

There is no evidence that the coup had been planned as early as the spring. But there is reason to believe that the Communists were cognizant of the importance of controlling the government and that they, therefore, were beginning to consider the possibility of a coup. The Czech Communists were probably under pressure from Moscow, and certainly were under pressure from Belgrade, where the Tito forces disliked the moderate methods of the Czech Communists. It is even possible that the Czech Communists made efforts to avoid this eventuality and that their requests to confer with the democratic parties were not merely attempts to intimidate them. I express no firm conviction on this point.

The point to be emphasized is that the coup was not a mere exercise of the power of the Communist Party. That power could have been exercised with greater ease and less risk in 1945 or 1946. It represented a decision based on Soviet estimates of the international situation and of its security requirements in that situation. It also reflected the suspiciousness with which the Soviet Union viewed the external world and the relatively high priority given to security considerations when the international situation worsens.

There is a Soviet syndrome: danger→industrialization program→ rigid political controls and purges.[88] The syndrome continues to operate until external factors change or internal correctives come into force.

The point I should like to maintain is that Soviet policy was responding to American policy just as American policy had responded to Soviet policy. If the Soviet Union, given the estimates of its security requirements and of the political reliability of non-Communist Poles or

Bulgarians, saw fit to destroy democracy in those areas, it did not imply a decision to destroy it everywhere the Red Army went regardless of security and reliability.

If, on the other hand, the Americans were shocked by the brutality of the action and feared that it portended other action requiring defensive measures, it did not imply a decision to attack the Soviet Union. But the very fact that the United States took these measures, and the fact that the Soviet Union had suspicions, led to changes in the calculus of security and reliability invoked by the Soviet Union.

In other words, suspicion and force kept feeding themselves particularly given the low tolerance of the Soviet Union for restraint where the opposition is very weak. It is unlikely that there was a master plan to take over Czechoslovakia from the very beginning.

On the other hand, evidence strongly indicates that the Soviet Union had no intrinsic regard for democratic government. If Stalin permitted Czechoslovak democracy to survive in the period between 1945 and 1948, that indicated only that he was not prepared to risk the displeasure of the West or to increase the risk of war under the international conditions then existing. There may also have been a desire to secure the cooperation of non-Communists in the economic reconstruction of Czechoslovakia.

If the Communists resorted to force in 1948, it would seem to indicate only that they considered cooperation with the West less likely than in 1945, that their need for heavy industry had increased since 1945, or that they considered war a present danger.

In all likelihood, the Soviet Union viewed the Truman Doctrine and changes in Allied German policy as indications of belligerent motivation. This interpretation, as all Westerners know, had no foundation in fact. However, the American fears that the Czechoslovak coup indicated a Soviet intention of waging major war may have been lacking in foundation also. Nevertheless, those fears *did exist,* as the war scare of March 1948 demonstrates.[89]

VI

The Korean War
(1955)

The division of Korea at the 38th parallel between the United States and the Soviet Union, which had no significance except to assign areas of responsibility to the occupying American and Soviet forces for purposes of military government, has made it difficult ever since to treat Korea as a single entity. Diplomacy failed to bridge the differences in objectives between American and Soviet Russian foreign policies with respect to Korea. At the 1945 meeting in Moscow of the foreign ministers, Secretary of State James Byrnes proposed the establishment of a joint Soviet-American Commission to unify policies on currency, trade and transportation, telecommunications, electric power distribution, coastal shipping, and other important matters. He also proposed a Four-Power trusteeship to "endure for no longer period than necessary to allow the Koreans to form an independent, representative and effective government."

The Soviet Union submitted a counterproposal for a joint commission to coordinate economic matters, and to set up a provisional government. Molotov also proposed a Four-Power trusteeship to last five years. Although most Koreans opposed a trusteeship, the United States accepted the Soviet plan after making a few technical amendments.

American-Soviet Differences

The Soviet-American Commission met for the first time in January 1946, but immediately disagreed over the interpretation of the terms of its commission. Byrnes stated that the United States' representatives wanted to treat Korea as a whole and that the Soviet representative was simply interested in coordinating the activities of the two sections of Korea. From this time forward, different concepts underlying the administration of the two zones made the application of uniform policies even more difficult.

Another source of difficulty for the United States was precipitated partly by the character of the American occupation. When Lieutenant General John R. Hodge began his duties, he viewed the population as potentially hostile and doubted the ability of any Korean grouping to represent the country. As a consequence, he dispersed the existing provisional Korean government under Lyuh Woon Hyung, which had been set up prior to the landing of the American forces. General Hodge used the Japanese police force to maintain order among the Korean population. There were a number of incidents as a result of this decision. Moreover, the decision to set up a trusteeship was very unpopular. Virtually every Korean grouping except the Communist Party opposed it. The Korean parties claimed that they were a liberated rather than an occupied country, and, from the standpoint of United Nations declarations, their case was a good one. The decision that the United States and the Soviet Union would accept the surrender of the Japanese reflected, however, the essentially military character of decisions in this period.

The Soviet representative on the Commission insisted that only those parties cooperating with the occupying authorities and accepting the trusteeship proposal should be consulted on the formation of a Korean government. The Russian position was not without logic, but it was clear that, in this case, such a decision would turn Korea over to Communism, fail to represent the will of the Korean people, and be tantamount to treating Korea as a defeated country.

At the same time, a policy debate was going on in high military circles concerning the strategic importance of Korea. Some military figures held that Korea was of great importance because of its geographic relation to Japan. Others felt that Korea had little or no strategic value. Although it is not certain that a definitive decision concerning the strategic importance of Korea had been reached in this period, an interim decision was made to reject the Soviet contention that only groups accepting the plan for trusteeship be consulted by the Commission. The differences in policies and objectives between the United States and the Soviet Union had become so pronounced by this time that further discussions seemed useless. As a consequence, the Joint Commission adjourned *sine die* in May 1946.

The United States, during this period, followed a policy of cooperating more closely with the non-Communist Korean groupings in its zone of occupation. Koreans replaced the Japanese police and, after the adjournment of the Joint Commission, Koreans were assigned to many government positions. This policy increased the cooperation between Koreans and Americans, although a few of the better organized Korean groups—particularly the one headed by Syngman Rhee—were permitted by these measures to multiply their advantage over more loosely organized or less favored groups in South Korea.

The impasse between the United States and the Soviet Union impeded all efforts to unite the country. Diplomatic negotiations, conducted through private channels, renewed the hope that a compromise might be reached. A year later, in May 1947, the Joint Commission was reconvened. An agreement was reached to consult all Korean democratic parties and social organizations. All interested groups were invited to submit applications to the Joint Commission so that their participation could be considered. Thirty-eight applications were received from North Korea, all representing groups participating in the Democratic People's Front. Four hundred twenty-two petitions were received from South Korea representing many different shades of political opinion including the Democratic People's Front.

But the Soviet Union and the United States again disagreed over the criteria for participation. To surmount the impasse, the United States proposed a meeting of the Four Powers in September 1947, with the object of establishing a provisional Korean government. Although Great Britain and China agreed to the American proposal, the Soviet Union rejected it. By May 1947, however, the American policy of encouraging the formation of self-governmental activities in South Korea had already culminated in the formation of an interim government.

The Wedemeyer Mission

During the summer of 1947, General Wedemeyer visited South Korea, following his mission to China. He reported to the State Department on the efficiency and skill of the North Korean Army and war industry. He warned that American withdrawal from Korea would probably constitute a signal for unification of the country under Communist auspices. Therefore, he recommended a trusteeship for Korea, with both the United States and the Soviet Union serving as trustees.

The State Department objected to the Soviet Union as a trustee, although General Wedemeyer pointed out that its participation in a trusteeship could not be avoided short of war, which he did not advocate, and that it would be better to have the Soviet Union as a member of a commission governing all of Korea than to allow the Soviet Union to govern the northern section single-handedly. His proposals were rejected by the Department of State, and, for reasons that are not entirely clear, the report was not made public.[1]

The United Nations and Korea

By September 1947, the United States informed the Soviet Union of its intention to carry the Korean question to the United Nations. Secretary of State George C. Marshall told the General Assembly of the United Nations that Korea remained divided at the 38th parallel with no solution in sight. The Korean economy, he said, had been crippled by the artificial division between the two zones. The Assembly, by a large majority, voted to include the problems of Korean independence on its agenda, despite a Soviet counterproposal that Soviet and American troops simultaneously be withdrawn from Korea.

The Soviet proposals were rejected. On November 14, the Assembly adopted a resolution by a vote of 43 to 0, with 6 abstentions, recommending that the occupying powers hold elections in their respective zones not later than March 31, 1948. (The resolution had initially been proposed by the United States.) The Assembly recommended that, after this first step, a Korean national assembly and a national government, with its own security forces, be established. This national government, according to the resolution, would then arrange for the withdrawal of occupation troops.

The Assembly created a United Nations Temporary Commission and recommended that it be present in Korea during the period of elections and that it be granted the privilege of free travel and observation, that it be available for consultation on the other political measures leading to the establishment of a Korean national government and the withdrawal of occupation forces. The Temporary Commission was to report to the General Assembly and to make further recommendations to the General Assembly concerning measures likely to maintain the independence of Korea.

The Temporary Commission

Nine nations, including Australia, Canada, China, El Salvador, France, India, the Philippines, Syria, and the Ukrainian Soviet Socialist Republic, were named to the Temporary Commission. The Ukraine, however, declined to serve. The members of the Commission arrived in Korea in January. The Soviet Union refused the Commission permission to enter the Soviet zone.

The Temporary Commission sent the General Assembly a report stating that the people of Korea desired self-government and were fit to govern themselves, and that they relied upon the United Nations. It was not certain, the Commission reported, whether the people favored a separate government for South Korea, as advocated by Syngman Rhee, or desired to wait until unified elections could be held. The Commission observed that it would recommend elections either designed to establish a government of South Korea only or designed to select representatives of the South Korean people who could then consult with the Commission, or it could explore or note other possibilities for establishing the national independence of Korea, or it could express its inability to carry on its mission under the prevailing circumstances and return its mandate to the General Assembly.

Despite Canadian and Australian doubts concerning the wisdom and legality of the procedure, the Interim Committee of the United Nations ordered the Commission to implement the resolution in those areas of Korea accessible to it, namely, in South Korea. After expressing concern over the role the Korean police and rightist youth organizations might play in an election, the Commission decided in April 1948 that free elections could be held. With the cooperation of the zonal authorities, elections were held on May 10. About 80 percent of the eligible voters registered and, despite a leftist boycott, an estimated 92.5 percent of these used their franchise and brought to power Syngman Rhee and his party. The Commission reported that, so far as its observations could determine, a free election had been held, "bearing in mind the traditional and historical background of the people of Korea."

EVENTS IN NORTH KOREA

During this period, the North Korean People's Committee, or provisional government, under Kim Il Sung[2] invited all South Korean political parties and organizations to attend a joint meeting. The invitation was accepted by some rightists and liberals, including Kim Koo and Kim Kiusic, as well as by Communists. North Korea gained some support for its position from liberals. On May 7, the Soviet Commander, General Korotkov, notified the head of the Communist Party in North Korea of arrangements to withdraw Soviet forces, evidently with the hope that American forces would also be withdrawn. Although American military authorities in Korea did not give credence to the announcement, the Soviet forces were reduced severely in the following period.*

ROK—Government of South Korea

On the last day of May, the elected Assemblymen of South Korea—representing approximately two-thirds of the population of Korea—convened and chose Syngman Rhee as temporary chairman. He took the position that the Assembly represented all of Korea, adding that seats were being reserved for North Korean representatives and that he would open negotiations with the Soviet Union for a solution of the Korean problem. Rhee expressed the hope that American troops would remain in Korea for security reasons until Korea had been unified. The Assembly proceeded to adopt a constitution and to elect Rhee as president.

During August, the United States granted partial recognition to the Rhee government as the government of all Korea (Republic of Korea or ROK). On August 15, the United States Military Government was terminated. These steps were taken despite the fact that the Temporary Commission had refused to recognize the Rhee regime as the government of Korea. The Rhee regime, for this reason, refused to consult with the Temporary Commission, although required to do so by the resolution of the General Assembly.

Government of North Korea

In the meantime, the Korean Democratic People's Republic had been established in the Soviet zone. General elections, which were not supervised by the Temporary Commission, were held in August. The North Korean government also professed to represent the whole of Korea and stated that candidates for its parliament from the south had been elected in an "underground" fashion. The Korean Democratic People's government regarded the Rhee government as illegitimate and pledged itself to remove that government. Its attitude was reciprocated by that of the South Korean government.

On September 18, the Soviet government informed the American Em-

---

*We now know from *Khrushchev Remembers* (Strube Talbott, editor, Little Brown, 1970, pp. 367-73), that Stalin withdrew the remaining Russian forces in 1950 when he learned that Kim Il Sung intended to attack in the near future so as not to risk involvement. Perhaps he reduced Russian forces in 1948 to encourage American withdrawal to avoid the danger of great power involvement if war occurred [M. A. K. 1975].

bassy in Moscow that all Soviet military forces would be withdrawn from Korea by the end of December at the request of the Supreme National Assembly of North Korea. Two days later, the American Department of State announced that it agreed, in principle, to the withdrawal of occupying forces at the earliest practicable date, but that the question must be considered within the larger problem of the unification and independence of Korea. The American government announced that the question was under consideration at the General Assembly of the United Nations. Behind the announcement was the belief of the American government that the South Korean government would not prove viable—given the superior armed forces of the North—should the American forces be withdrawn completely. As we see, this reluctance to withdraw was soon overcome for strategic reasons.

South Korean Elections Approved

The General Assembly met in Paris in December 1948. Requests for participation in the debate were received from both governments in Korea. The South Korean request was granted, and the North Korean rejected. By a large majority, the Assembly declared that the Rhee regime was "a lawful government" with "effective control over . . . part of Korea . . . " and that "it is the only such government in Korea." The General Assembly did not, in this act, recognize the ROK government as *the* government of Korea, although the United States took the resolution as an excuse for granting full recognition in January. The General Assembly resolution recommended the withdrawal of all occupation forces from Korea at the earliest practicable time.

The resolution also recommended that a new seven-nation commission proceed to Korea to lend its good offices in negotiating unification, the integration of security forces, and the removal of economic barriers, as well as to supervise the withdrawal of occupation forces.

American Decision to Withdraw

Actually, the decision to withdraw the American forces in Korea had been reached by the United States as a result of a high-level military study carried out some time in 1948. The decision was made primarily on economic grounds and because the United States Army had a complement of only 630,000 men. The United States had four under-strength divisions in Japan, slightly more than one division in Europe, and five understrength divisions in the United States.[3] Under these circumstances, it could not afford its military commitments in Korea. Only after this study had been made was the United States willing to facilitate the passage of the United Nations recommendation for the withdrawal of the occupation forces from Korea.

Lines Are Drawn

When the United Nations Commission reached Korea, it was informed by Rhee that the ROK government was the government of all Korea and that the Commission had the function only of vindicating its claim and not of negotiating with the government of North Korea, thus preventing the Commission from carrying out its mission. Although the Commission was unable to establish contact with North Korea, it did note that there was a good deal of military "posturing" on both sides of the 38th parallel. In fact, both sides were threatening to use military force to invade the other, and frequent border clashes were taking place.

In May 1949, the United States agreed to the establishment of a Korean Military Advisory Group to replace the Provisional Military Advisory Group, with the purpose of assisting the development of Korean security forces. The United States transferred military equipment and supplies to the ROK forces. However, it provided only light arms, very few aircraft, some light artillery and some light tanks. According to General Roberts, head of the Military Advisory Group, "The South Koreans were not adequately armed because the United States feared they would attack the North Koreans.[4] The United States also had granted large amounts of economic aid.[5]

By 1949, the United States apparently had come to the conclusion that Korea was not a sufficiently important strategic asset to warrant the commitment of scarce American manpower and military supplies. Although the United States was not indifferent to the fate of the government of the Republic of Korea and attempted to bolster its international prestige, its economic viability and its ability to defend itself were distinctly subsidiary objectives of American foreign policy.

Moreover, the United States was apparently disturbed by the hostile treatment accorded the United Nations Commission by the Rhee government and fearful that it might engage in a military campaign against the North that would either lead to its collapse or possible American involvement. By August, the Department of State and the Joint Chiefs had agreed that American defense in the Pacific was to be centered on Japan, the Ryukyus, and the Philippines.[6]

The United Nations Commission reported to the General Assembly in September that, according to reports, the Soviet Union had completed the withdrawal of its forces from Korea, but that it had not been able to verify these reports. It stated that, by June 29, all American forces, with the exception of the Military Advisory Group, had been withdrawn. Progress toward unification, it said, was blocked by bitterness. The General Assembly continued the mandate of the Commission and strengthened its mediatory powers.

Events Preceding Hostilities

During the fall of 1949, official spokesmen for the governments of North and South Korea were threatening to engage in military efforts against each other. Both sides were precipitating border incidents. By September 1949, the situation was becoming quite serious. The elections in North Korea were postponed, and South Korean police forces were alerted to the possibility of surprise attack.

On September 8, an UNCOK (the United Nations Commission in Korea) report laid the blame for the division of Korea upon the Soviet-sponsored North Korean regime. It specifically noted: "There is much ... posturing on both sides of the parallel ... [that] holds serious danger of provoking open military conflict. . . ." Shortly thereafter, the South Koreans appealed to the United States for additional military aid.

In October, the Senate passed an administration bill for $150 million in military aid to the Republic of Korea. That same month, the General Assembly of the United Nations voted to extend the life of UNCOK. Toward the end of the year, local elections were held in North Korea. According to figures released by the North Korean government, 99.99 percent of the eligible (3.8 million registered) voters exercised their franchise and cast 89.9 percent of the vote for the United Democratic Front, an apparent coalition of left-wing parties, as in the People's Republics of Eastern Europe, that was, in fact, controlled by the Communist Party.

Early in January 1950, ROK authorities complained to UNCOK that North Korean plans for armed attack were maturing. The next month, ROK officials informed UNCOK that North Korea had a definite superiority in armed strength. On January 12, Secretary of State Dean Acheson made a speech to the National Press Club stating that the defense perimeter of the United States did not include Korea or Formosa. He also stated that the United Nations could be relied upon if Korea were attacked. He also favored the continuance of aid to Korea.

The next day, at a closed session of the Senate Committee on Foreign Relations, Acheson was reported to have stated that South Korea was capable of repelling an invasion from the North, "unless other influence were brought to bear." On January 19, by a vote of 193–191, the House of Representatives defeated the Korean aid measure. Two days later, President Truman requested that the House reverse its vote "in order that important foreign policy interests of this country may be properly safeguarded." A letter written by Dean Acheson was released in which he expressed his concern over the effects of the House vote in Korea and other areas where "our encouragement is a major element in the struggle for freedom." He called the vote "disastrous for the foreign policy of the United States. . . ."

On the last day of the month, the House Committee on Foreign Affairs approved a new bill extending aid both to the Chinese National- ists on Formosa and the ROK government. The administration was re- ported to have accepted the aid to China provisions reluctantly in order to secure approval of aid to Korea. The bills were passed and became law early in February 1950.[7]

On February 13, UNCOK established two committees. The first was to observe "developments which might lead to military conflict" and the other was to observe "developments which will assist in bringing about unification." On March 3, Economic Cooperation Administration head Paul Hoffman told the Senate Committee on Foreign Relations that the Truman administration would ask $100 million in aid for Korea for the fiscal year beginning July 1, to cover the second year of a proposed three- year program of aid. On March 7, Dean Acheson testified that the object of the proposed aid was to strengthen the ROK regime so it could with- stand the threat of the expanding Communist influence of the North Korean regime and to serve to create the foundation for the peaceful unification of Korea. The aid bill became law late in May.

Meanwhile, intelligence cables from CINCFE (Commander-in-Chief Far East) regularly carried reports of a scheduled invasion of South Ko- rea. The weekly intelligence cable of March 10 carried a report that the People's Army would invade South Korea in June, but a comment ap- pended to the report devalued it. According to the comment, the People's Army would be prepared to invade by June, but the preparation would not necessarily precipitate civil war. The intentions of the Communists in Korea, it said, were related to their program in Southeast Asia. It was likely that military moves would be held in abeyance until the Soviets were able to observe the effects of their activities in such places as Indo- china, Burma, and Thailand. If the Soviet Union were satisfied with progress in those areas, the Soviet Union would be willing to allow South

Korea to ripen for future harvest. However, if checked elsewhere, the Soviet Union might divert its efforts to South Korea.

On March 25, 1950, the FEC (Far East Command) intelligence report commented that, according to its evaluation, there would be no civil war in Korea that spring or summer. It was believed that the Communists would emphasize political moves, guerrilla activity, and psychological activity in order to cause the ROK government to collapse.

During April, events seemed to confirm CINCFE's intelligence predictions and to indicate that conditions were so bad within the South Korean government that its collapse could be expected. On April 1, ROK army authorities announced that 700 guerrillas had crossed the border from the North. Later that month, the army announced that it had destroyed all but 150 of the 700 fighters.

On April 3, American authorities expressed grave concern over the mounting inflation in Korea, while President Rhee contended that the economic threat was that of deflation. The United States also expressed concern over Rhee's proposed postponement of the scheduled general elections from May to November. Rhee was informed that American aid was predicated upon the existence and growth of democratic institutions with free popular elections, in accordance with the Korean constitution, as the foundation of those democratic institutions.

On April 3, Premier Lee Bum Suk announced his plans to retire. The Korean National Assembly, by a vote of 88–2, disapproved Rhee's proposed appointment of Defense Minister Sing Sung Mo as temporary premier. The appointment was termed unconstitutional. The Assembly demanded a permanent appointment and indicated its desire that the premier be responsible to it rather than to the president. Nevertheless, on April 22, the retiring premier handed the seal of office to Sing Sung Mo.

On May 10, the ROK defense minister told a press conference that "North Korean troops [are] moving in force toward the 38th parallel and . . . there was imminent danger of invasion from the North." On May 12, UNCOK sought information from two officers on the staff of General William L. Roberts, chief of the United States Military Advisory Group in Korea (USMAG or MAG). They confirmed the evidence of the North Korean build-up, but denied that danger was imminent and also declared that the ROK forces were capable of repelling any attack from the North.

ROK general elections were held on May 30. About 90 percent of the eligible voters exercised their franchise. The opposition candidates led by the Democratic Nationalists had demanded that some presidential powers be transferred to the premier and that the premier be made responsible to the Assembly (a demand that had previously been narrowly defeated in the Assembly). On June 1, with only one district unreported, it was announced that independent candidates had won 128 seats. The Democratic Nationalists had won only 22 (fewer than in the previous assembly); the Korean Nationalists, the National Society, and the Korean Youth Corps—all supporting President Rhee—had won only 45 seats, a loss of 28 from their previous total. Many of those who ran as independents, however, were expected to support President Rhee.

John Foster Dulles, special adviser to the Secretary of State, arrived in Korea from Japan on June 17. He inspected conditions along the barricades at the 38th parallel. On June 19, he addressed the National Assembly and pledged to continue American aid and support to South Korea.[8]

Hostilities Begin

Early in the morning of June 25, 1950, Far Eastern time, hostilities began in the vicinity of the 38th parallel. The areas of attack were the Ongjin peninsula, the Kaesong area, and Chunchon. North Korean landings were made from the sea. Kaesong quickly fell. An ROK cabinet resolution of the twenty-fifth stated that ROK forces were opposing vigorously the "lawless act of aggression." The North Koreans, on the other hand, accused the South Koreans of beginning the attack and claimed that their forces were pursuing the aggressors.

President Truman was in Missouri late on the night of June 24 when word first arrived of the commencement of hostilities. Although State Department officials began to work immediately on the matter, Truman was not recalled to Washington until Sunday. On June 25, a cable from Ambassador John Muccio in Seoul reported, "According to Korean army reports which are partly confirmed by Korean Military Group field advisers reports, North Korean forces invaded Republic of Korea territory at several points this morning. . . . It would appear from the nature of the attack and the manner in which it was launched that it constitutes an all-out offensive against the Republic of Korea."

At American initiative, an emergency session of the United Nations Security Council was called on June 25. Ernest Gross, the American representative on the Security Council, informed the Secretary-General, in requesting the session, "The American Ambassador to the Republic of Korea has informed the Department of State that North Korean forces invaded the territory of the Republic of Korea at several points in the early morning hours of June 25.[9] An attack of the forces of the North Korean regime under the circumstances referred to above constitutes a breach of the peace and an act of aggression."

On the same day, UNCOK reported to the Secretary-General, "Government of Republic of Korea states that about 04:00 hours 25 June attacks were launched in strength by North Korean forces all along the 38th parallel. Commission wishes to draw attention of Secretary-General to serious situation developing which is assuming character of full-scale war and may endanger the maintenance of international peace and security. It suggests that he consider possibility of bringing matter to notice of Security Council."

At the meeting of the Security Council that day, Ernest Gross informed the Council that the report of UNCOK to the Secretary-General had confirmed "this wholly illegal and unprovoked attack by North Korean forces. . . ." That same day, the Council adopted a United States-sponsored resolution[10] that noted "with grave concern the armed attack upon the Republic of Korea by forces from North Korea," determined "that this action constitutes a breach of the peace," and called "for the cessation of hostilities"[11] and called "upon the authorities of North Korean forces to cease hostilities forthwith and to withdraw their armed forces to the thirty-eighth parallel. . . ."

The resolution was adopted 9–0. The Soviet Union was boycotting Council meetings on the ground that—until a representative of the People's Republic of China replaced the Nationalist delegate—all meetings were illegal. Yugoslavia abstained on the ground that sufficient information had not yet been received to convict the North Koreans of aggression.[12] The Yugoslav delegate offered a resolution that would have invited the North Korean government to state its case before the Security Council. This resolution was defeated 6–1 with 2 abstentions.

On Sunday, in the Blair House Conference, the president, the secretaries of state and defense, and the joint chiefs agreed on the advisability of evacuating American nationals from Korea. The navy was to be used for that purpose. There was some discussion of the possibility of Russian or Chinese intervention in the matter; Russian entry was viewed as the more likely possibility.

On June 26, UNCOK reported to the Secretary-General its conviction that North Korea would not accede to the resolution or accept the good offices of UNCOK. It pointed out that the critical operation might terminate within the next few days and the cease-fire resolution become academic. It suggested that the Security Council might consider inviting both parties to agree to a neutral mediator or request member governments to undertake immediate mediation.

In another cable that day, UNCOK reported that, on the basis of observer reports ending forty-eight hours before the beginning of hostilities and "judging from actual progress of operations, Northern regime is carrying out well-planned, concerted, and full-scale invasion of South Korea; second, that South Korean forces were deployed on wholly defensive basis in all sectors of the parallel, and, third, that they were taken completely by surprise as they had no reason to believe from intelligence sources that invasion was imminent."[13]

On June 26, President Truman issued a statement in which he stated his gratification with the action of the Security Council. The South Korean Ambassador delivered an appeal for aid, reminding the United States that, although military aid had been authorized by Congress, none had been delivered as yet. At a high-level Blair House conference that evening, it was decided to extend air and sea support to ROK forces south of the 38th parallel. Since Communist assault would prejudice American security interests in the Pacific and interfere with American actions in Korea, the Seventh Fleet was ordered to prevent any attack on Formosa. As a corollary, the president called upon the Nationalists on Formosa to cease all air and sea operations against the mainland of China. It was also decided to step up aid to the French forces in Indochina. President Truman made a public statement the next day releasing this information.

On June 26, General MacArthur was instructed to furnish the ROK government with military supplies from the American stores in Japan. Officials of the ECA said that aid to the ROK government was being placed upon an emergency basis.

On June 27, under strong American urging, the Security Council passed a resolution recommending "that the Members of the United Nations furnish such assistance to the Republic of Korea as may be necessary to repel the armed attack and to restore international peace and security in the area."[14] The same day, Truman authorized MacArthur to conduct air missions south of the 38th parallel. A naval blockade of the Korean coast south of the 38th parallel was authorized. The American objective at this time was to hold a beachhead in Korea and to use that beachhead to evacuate American nationals.

The same day, the American ambassador to the Soviet Union, A. Kirk, delivered an *aide-memoire* to Andrei Gromyko accusing the Soviet government of violating its obligations as a member of the Security Council and stating: "In view of the universally known fact of the close relations between the Union of Soviet Socialist Republics and the North Korean regime, the United States Government asks an assurance that the Union of Soviet Socialist Republics disavows responsibility for this unprovoked and unwarranted attack, and that it will use its influence with the North Korean authorities to withdraw their invading forces immediately."

By June 28, decisions in Washington were being influenced considerably by the information feedback from CINCFE. Also, General MacArthur was already implementing the directives issued to him by the JCS. The American Far East Air Force and naval elements of FEC were conducting combat operations south of the 38th parallel in support of the ROK. Ammunition and other supplies were being delivered to ROK forces by air lift and by sea; moreover, a small advance echelon of GHQFEC had been established in Korea.

On June 28, Great Britain offered military assistance to the ROK. In the House of Commons, Prime Minister Clement Attlee announced that British naval forces in Japanese waters had been placed at American disposal on behalf of United Nations efforts in Korea. Canada announced that it was considering what action it might appropriately take. The Council of the Organization of American States, which then characteristically supported American policy, issued a resolution giving its "firmest support" to the United Nations decision on Korea. A French Foreign Office spokesman welcomed the United Nations vote, but cautioned that French commitments in Indochina would limit the assistance it could extend to Korea.

At his press conference that day, Secretary of State Acheson expressed gratitude for the "almost unanimous world reaction. . . . In all parts of the world where free opinion exists there has been an immediate response—a response to the realization that this was, if ever there was in the world, a test of whether the United Nations is going to survive." Acheson expressed the view that it was of great importance that all action since June 25 had been "under the aegis of the United Nations."

President Truman told the American Newspaper Guild: "The recent unprovoked invasion of the Republic of Korea by Communist armies is an example of the danger to which undeveloped areas particularly are exposed. It is essential that we do everything we can to prevent such aggression and to enforce the principles of the United Nations Charter."

According to *Pravda*, on the other hand: "The events in Korea . . . reveal with all clarity that the imperialist warmongers will not stop half way in pursuit of their objects. As is known, on June 25, the provocative actions of troops of the puppet Government of South Korea, directed against the Korean People's Democratic Republic, unleashed military operations on the territory of Korea. In reply to this, security detachments of troops of the People's Democratic Republic undertook active measures and, carrying out their Government's orders, went over to the counter-offensive. . . .

"As is clear from . . . [President Truman's statement], he has instructed the air and naval forces of the United States to give armed assistance to the Korean people [and] at the same time . . . has instructed the American Seventh Fleet to 'prevent attack on Formosa,' which is an order for the actual occupation by American armed forces of part of the territory of China. This order signifies that the Government of the United States . . . has undertaken a direct act of aggression against the Korean People's Democratic Republic and against the People's Republic of China.'"

Ohio Republican Senator Robert Taft charged that the "bungling and inconsistent foreign policy" of the administration was responsible for the war in Korea. Senator Taft felt that the sending of troops to Korea reflected a wise decision, but he declared that it represented a reversal of Acheson's policies. Consequently, Senator Taft demanded that the Secretary of State resign. He also qualified his approval of the troop decision by reminding the president of Congressional sharing of responsibility in war situations and suggested that senate approval be sought.

On June 29, 1950, President Truman denied that Secretary Acheson had been reversed or that his actions in Korea required Congressional approval. On the same day, Dean Acheson, in an address before the American Newspaper Guild, appeared to limit American objectives to Korea. He informed his audience: "This action pursuant to the Security Council Resolutions is solely for the purpose of restoring the Republic of Korea to its status prior to the invasion from the north and of re-establishing the peace broken by that aggression."

On June 29, Prime Minister Jawaharlal Nehru of India gave public support to the Security Council actions with respect to Korea. Thirty-three of fifty-nine member states notified the Security Council of their attitudes toward its resolutions. Twenty-eight offered support while five including the Soviet bloc and Yugoslavia, opposed the resolutions. The Soviet Union termed the resolution of June 27 "illegal" because neither it nor representatives of (The People's Republic of) China were present at the voting. That same day, the Soviet Union officially rejected the American *aide-memoire*. It declared that the American request would result in an act of "interference . . . in the internal affairs of Korea" and protested that such action would be "inadmissible."

That same day, General MacArthur visited the front lines in Korea. Military events were taking a bad turn for the South Korean forces as North Korean units were penetrating deeply into the countryside. As a result of his observations at the front and policy recommendations to JCS on the basis of these observations, an important decision was made in Blair House on June 30. General MacArthur had reported that a beachhead in Korea could not be held by South Korean troops, even though they were supported by the American air force and navy.[15]

The decision made by Truman, the secretaries of state and defense, and the Joint Chiefs on June 30 was to permit the bombing of specific military targets in North Korea, to use the navy to blockade the entire coast, and to employ American ground forces to hold the Pusan area. The latter was a serious decision, for the only ground forces available were in the skeletal Eighth Army. Units of the First Marine Division were not available for combat until August. Practically no other forces were available throughout the Pacific area. MacArthur was named Supreme Commander of American forces in Korea at this meeting.

Shortly thereafter, the Chinese Nationalists offered to send 33,000 Nationalist soldiers to participate in the defense of the ROK. On July 1, Secretary of State Dean Acheson expressed his appreciation for the offer, but felt that in view of the threat that Formosa might be invaded, the representatives of General MacArthur should hold discussions with the Taiwan authorities before any final decision was made. Acheson stated clearly that his expression of opinion represented the opinion only of the American government and not that of the United Nations.

On July 4, the United States officially informed the Soviet Union of the blockade it had established off the coastal areas of Korea. The Soviet Union replied that the blockade was illegal and stated that it would hold the United States accountable for any incidents.

The United Nations Security Council held its fourth meeting on the Korean question on July 7. It was reported to the Council that forty-four of fifty-nine members of the United Nations had expressed official approval of United Nations action by that date, and that five member nations were already participating in military action.

At its meeting that day, the Security Council recommended that all member nations providing military force and other assistance make them available to a unified command under the United States. The United States was requested to designate a commander of these unified forces, and the use of a United Nations flag was authorized. The United States was requested to furnish the Security Council "with reports *as appropriate* [italics added] on the course of action taken under the unified command." Senator Warren Austin accepted for the United States the responsibilities imposed by the resolution. President Truman designated General MacArthur as Supreme Commander United Nations Command (SCUNC) on July 10, 1950.

Prime Minister Nehru of India expressed the opinion on July 7 that the return of the Soviet Union to the Security Council and the admission of China to the United Nations were necessary conditions to "bring the Korean conflict to a prompt and peaceful conclusion."

On July 14 a spokesman for the Department of State emphasized that the United Nations was the proper forum for settling the Korean conflict. He insisted that the United States did not contemplate bilateral negotiations with the Soviet Union, and that the "minimum and irreducible" conditions for a solution were a "cease-fire and a return to the thirty-eighth parallel."

On July 15, Stalin replied to Nehru's suggestion by stating his desire for a solution to the Korean problem. Stalin felt that a solution would have to be found by the five great powers and that it would be "expedient" to hear "representatives of the Korean people" by which he presumably meant representatives of North Korea. Dean Acheson rejected Nehru's proposed solution for the Korean problem. Meanwhile North Korean officials announced plans to hold elections on July 25 for provincial, district, and village councils in "liberated areas."

On July 10, Trygve Lie circulated requests for aid to fifty-two member states of the United Nations. He did not send requests to members of the Soviet bloc, to Yugoslavia, which had expressed disapproval of the United Nations action, or to the United States, as it was already contributing heavily to the military efforts of the United Nations Command.

By July 18, a spokesman of the State Department was able to announce that fifteen to twenty nations were holding bilateral talks in Washington with representatives of the Korean Unified Command with respect to the aid they could furnish in support of the United Nations action in Korea.

Three days later, United Nations Secretary-General Trygve Lie announced that eleven nations had pledged aid of various kinds. Only Bolivia had pledged ground troops, however, and that was in the form of thirty commissioned officers. On July 23, Thailand agreed to supply a contingent of 4,000 men. Two days later, Turkey pledged 4,500 troops. On July 26, Australia, New Zealand, and Great Britain promised to supply ground forces. Meanwhile, fifteen other states pledged aid of various kinds. On July 29, India offered to send a field ambulance and surgical team, while Mexico offered to extend its military cooperation to the United Nations Command.

Military events in Korea, however, were not transpiring favorably. On July 26, the first report of the Supreme Commander was presented to the United Nations Security Council. MacArthur reported great difficulties in building United Nations forces up to the point at which they could match the North Koreans, who, he said, still had military superiority. MacArthur significantly complained that the North Koreans were equipped in excess of their internal capacities. This was the first indication of the later charge that the Soviet Union or China had equipped or was equipping the North Koreans.

On the last day of July, the U.S. delegate to the United Nations, Warren Austin, introduced a resolution in the Security Council condemning North Korea for "continued defiance of the United Nations." The resolution called upon all states to use their influence with North Korea to prevail upon that government to cease its defiance, and it also called upon members of the United Nations to refrain from assisting or encouraging North Korea. On July 29, General MacArthur flew to Formosa and pledged further American aid to Chiang.

In August, according to the principle of rotation in effect, the representative of the Soviet Union was due to assume the presidency of the Security Council. The Soviet Union ended its boycott of Council activities and, on August 1, 1950, Jacob Malik assumed the presidency of the Council. The agenda proposed by Council President Malik consisted of two items: the recognition of a representative of the People's Republic of China as the representative of China on the Security Council and the peaceful settlement of the Korean question.

Warren Austin protested that the resolution he had introduced on July 31 should take priority. He denied that the question of Chinese representation and that of the Korean question were linked, and he assailed the item calling for the "peaceful settlement of the Korean question" as a Soviet "propaganda title."

Malik maintained that President Truman had been the first to link the Chinese and Korean issues when he interposed the Seventh Fleet in the straits of Formosa. Representative Gladwyn Jebb of Great Britain also denied that the two items were linked. Moreover, he maintained that the more important item, Korea, should be considered first.

On August 3, 1950, Malik contended that the Korean matter was a civil war, essentially national in scope, and therefore, not subject to United Nations intervention. Although American representatives had implicitly described the Korean hostilities as a civil war, Malik's arguments did not prove persuasive to most Council members. Malik was overruled by the Council on the order of the items and then on the individual items. Finally, the American resolution was given priority by an 8–1 vote with 2 abstentions.

Not a man easily to be beaten, Malik introduced a new resolution on August 4. This resolution would have invited representatives of the People's Republic of China and of the Korean people (evidently meaning the people of North Korea) to present their case before the Security Council; it would have called for a halt to hostilities and simultaneously for the withdrawal of foreign troops.

On August 8, Malik introduced a resolution endorsing the appeal of the North Korean government for an "end to the savage bombing by the American air force."

In the meantime, the Council was unable to take action that the United States desired. Austin accused Malik of misusing his position as president of the Council to prevent a peaceful solution in Korea. The United States then introduced a resolution to adjourn Council meetings until August 10 to enable Malik to communicate with his government so that he could obtain permission to cease obstructing Council action. This resolution was adopted 9–1, with 1 abstention. Particularly irking to the Council was Malik's refusal to continue the Council's invitation to a representative of the Republic of Korea or to hand down a ruling refusing to invite the ROK representative. The Council could not overrule the president unless he made a ruling.

Meanwhile, events were going poorly in Korea, and United Nations forces were compressed in a pocket around the port of Pusan. On August 14, Yugoslav delegate Ales Bebler told the Council that "a bold departure from the vicious circle in which we seem to be moving" was necessary. However on August 22, Austin continued the barrage of charges and countercharges. He accused the Soviet Union of selling equipment to North Korean forces even after withdrawal of the Soviet army of occupation from North Korea.

On August 26, MacArthur's speech, prepared for delivery to the Veterans of Foreign Wars, was published despite a presidential directive that it be withdrawn.[16] In the speech, MacArthur said:

> As a result of its geographic location and base potential, utilization of Formosa by a military power hostile to the United States may either counter-balance or overshadow the strategic importance of the central and southern flank of the United States front line position.
> Formosa in the hands of such a hostile power could be compared to an unsinkable aircraft carrier and submarine tender ideally located to accomplish offensive strategy and at the same time checkmate defensive or counter-offensive operations by friendly forces based on Okinawa and the Philippines.

The statement by MacArthur caused consternation in official quarters because it cast doubt upon the officially stated American position that the Seventh Fleet was operating in the Formosa Straits only to protect the United Nations forces in Korea.

On August 25, Secretary of the Navy Francis P. Matthews urged preventive war against the Communist powers. The next day, G. N. Craig, national commander of the American Legion, said that any new Russian move would mean war. Hanson Baldwin stated in the *New York Times* that Matthews' speech was a trial balloon launched by Secretary of Defense Louis Johnson. The White House disavowed the Matthews speech. On September 1, Major General Orvil A. Anderson was suspended as commandant of the Air War College for urging preventive war. A campaign was clearly under way to persuade the American government to compete more forcefully with the Communist powers.

Late in August, Congress appropriated an additional $90 million in economic aid for the Republic of Korea. On September 1, Sir Gladwyn Jebb, of the United Kingdom, assumed the presidency of the Security Council. One of his first acts was to invite a representative of the Republic of Korea to attend the session of the Council. His ruling was upheld by a vote of 9–1, with 1 abstention.

A Soviet proposal to invite a representative of North Korea was defeated 8–2, with 1 abstention. Representative Austin returned to the fray with the charge that heavy rail activity had been noted in areas of Norh Korea adjacent to China. He also charged that American fighter planes had shot down an unescorted Soviet bomber off the west coast of Korea after the Soviet plane had opened fire.[17]

On September 6, the Security Council voted for the American resolution originally proposed on July 31 by 9–1 with 1 abstention. Because the negative vote was cast by the Soviet Union, the resolution was vetoed. The Soviet counterproposal for the cessation of hostilities and the withdrawal of foreign troops was defeated by the Council.

At that session of the Council, Malik contended that the downed bomber had been on a training flight, and that it had not been equipped for combat. He stated that it had been just off the Soviet-controlled island of Kwang-Tao when attacked by eleven American fighter planes, that it had been eighty-seven miles off the west coast of Korea, and that it had been preparing to enter the Soviet base of Port Arthur. According to Malik, two Soviet planes had seen the action at a distance. The Soviet protest was rejected by Ambassador Kirk in Moscow on grounds that the action was a United Nations matter; the State Department also refused to receive a protest on the same grounds.

A Soviet resolution forbidding United Nations forces to bomb in North Korea was beaten by 9–1, with 1 abstention. General MacArthur's fourth report to the Security Council claimed that much Soviet equipment of 1949–50 vintage was being used by North Korean forces. He also claimed that North Korean veterans of the China campaigns had been released to North Korea in the period preceding the hostilities.[18]

In late August 1950, the front was relatively stable. On September 1, the North Korean offensive began. By September 14, the United Nations forces had been strengthened sufficiently to begin a counteroffensive. On September 16, the Inchon landing took place, and United Nations forces opened operations along the Naktong River; they advanced to the suburbs of Seoul the next day.

By September 22, Supreme Commander MacArthur was proclaiming that the North Korean forces were sustaining record losses. United Nations forces burst through the Pusan perimeter. On September 28, General Walter Walker announced that North Korean forces were in rout and that they no longer existed as an organized body. He stated that United Nations forces were in close pursuit and would annihilate them before they reached the 38th parallel. On September 30, General Mac-Arthur broadcast an unconditional surrender demand to the North Korean forces.

Thirty-Eighth-Parallel Decision

The problem of what should be done when the 38th parallel was reached came to the fore. A JCS communication to CINCFE on September 15 informed MacArthur that the following conclusions had been approved by the president concerning the United States course of action with respect to Korea:

(a) Final decisions cannot be made at this time inasmuch as the course of action best advancing United States national interest must be determined in the light of—

(1) Action by the Soviet Union and the Chinese Communists;

(2) In consultation with friendly members of the United Nations; and

(3) An appraisal of the risk of general war;

(b) The United Nations forces have a legal basis for conducting operations north of the thirty-eighth parallel to compel withdrawal of the North Korean forces behind the line or to defend against these forces.

(c) The joint chiefs of staff were authorized to direct General MacArthur to plan for the possible occupation of North Korea but to execute such plans only with the approval of the president.

(d) General MacArthur should undertake no ground operations north of the thirty-eighth parallel in event of occupation of North Korea by Soviet or Chinese Communist forces. In this event, air and naval operations north of the parallel should not be discontinued; and

(e) In the event of employment of major Chinese Communist units south of the thirty-eighth parallel, the United States would (1) not permit itself to become engaged in a general war with Communist China; (2) authorize General MacArthur to continue military action as long as it offered a reasonable chance of successful resistance [deleted].*

General MacArthur informed the Joint Chiefs that he could protect his forces only by occupying North Korea. He submitted a plan of operations calling for "an attack north along the western coastal corridor by the Eighth United States Army and an amphibious landing by the United States Tenth Corps at Wonsan on the east coast of North Korea." This plan received the approval of the Joint Chiefs of Staff on September 29, 1950. Thus, the decision to cross the parallel was taken before the General Assembly was given an opportunity to consider the matter.

On the day that the Joint Chiefs gave MacArthur permission to cross the parallel, Australia, Brazil, Great Britain, the Netherlands, Norway, Pakistan, and the Philippines submitted a resolution to the General As-

---

*I have some reason to believe that the deleted material called for continued air and naval action against Communist China, designed to force her to withdraw from South Korea, in the event that American group forces were forced to evacuate.

sembly of the United Nations recommending: (1) that all appropriate steps be taken to insure conditions of stability throughout Korea; (2) that all constituent measures be taken, including the holding of elections under the auspices of the United Nations, for the establishment of a unified, independent, and democratic government in the sovereign state of Korea; (3) that United Nations forces should not remain in Korea any longer than necessary to achieve the first two objectives; and (4) that all necessary measures be taken to accomplish the economic rehabilitation of Korea.

Although the resolution did not specifically authorize the crossing of the 38th parallel by the United Nations forces, its recommendations implied consent to the forcible reunification of Korea. Evidently, the nations of the Soviet bloc accepted this interpretation of the proposed resolution for they attempted diversionary measures in the Political and Security Committee of the General Assembly.

U.S. Representative Austin supported the proposed resolution. He said: "Faithful adherence to the United Nations objectives of restoring international peace and security in the area counsels the taking of appropriate steps to eliminate the power and ability of the North Korean aggressor to launch future attacks. The aggressor's forces should not be permitted to have refuge behind an imaginary line.... The question of whether this artificial barrier, the 38th parallel, shall remain, and whether the country shall be unified now must be determined by the United Nations.... The artificial barrier ... has no basis for existence either in law or reason."

On October 2, Andrei Vyshinsky introduced a counterproposal jointly sponsored by the Soviet Union, the Ukraine, Byelorussia, Poland, and Czechoslovakia. The resolution sponsored by the Communist powers recommended: (1) that the belligerents in Korea immediately cease hostilities; (2) that the United States and other foreign states having troops in Korea withdraw those troops; (3) that, after the withdrawal of foreign troops, all-Korean elections to a National Assembly be held as soon as possible for the purpose of establishing a government of a unified and independent Korean state; (4) that a joint commission composed of the representatives of North and South Korea be elected at a joint assembly of the deputies of the Assembly of the People's Democratic Republic of North Korea and of the National Assembly of South Korea to organize and conduct the all-Korean elections, and that the joint assembly also elect an interim committee to carry out the functions of governing the country and to operate pending the elections and the establishment of a Korean government; (5) that a United Nations committee "with the indispensable participation in it of the states bordering on Korea" be established to observe the holding of elections; (6) that to rehabilitate Korea, ECOSOC (the Economic and Social Council of the UN) should draw up plans immediately to provide the necessary technical and economic aid; and (7) that after the establishment of the all-Korean government the Security Council should consider admitting Korea to United Nations membership. Vyshinsky also introduced two companion resolutions calling for the dissolution of UNCOK on the ground that it had been established illegally. He called on the United States to cease its "inhuman and barbarous" bombings in Korea.

Although Australian delegate Percy Spender rejected any possibility of returning to the situation that existed before the outbreak of hostilities, Sir Benegal Rau of India professed to see some good in both the United States and Soviet resolutions. He announced that India would abstain on both resolutions and that a compromise should be drafted.

On October 3, 1950, the substance of an interview between Chinese Premier Chou En-lai and Indian Ambassador Kavalam M. Panikkar became known. Chou had informed Panikkar that China would be compelled to intervene in the Korean war if American forces crossed the 38th parallel; on the other hand, Chinese forces would not intervene if only South Korean forces crossed the parallel.[19] This information caused a wave of apprehension throughout the General Assembly. The consequences threatened to be serious for the United States.

General MacArthur already had been authorized to cross the parallel by the American Joint Chiefs of Staff; but as he was technically the United Nations Supreme Commander, lack of support from the United Nations for the crossing would have proved embarrassing. The United States Mission to the United Nations countered the information coming from India by revealing privately to other delegations that American intelligence information proved beyond a doubt that China would not intervene in the Korean hostilities under any circumstances.[20]

The American arguments must have proved convincing to the majority of the delegations, for on October 4, the Political Committee rejected the Indian proposal to establish a committee to consider compromise proposals by a vote of 24–32, with 3 abstentions. The Political Committee then reported favorably on the eight-power resolution and rejected the Soviet resolutions.

On October 7, the General Assembly approved the eight-power resolution by 47–5, with 8 abstentions. The resolution also established a commission consisting of representatives of Australia, Chile, the Netherlands, Pakistan, the Philippines, Turkey, and a seventh member to be specified by a plenary session of the General Assembly, to be known as the United Nations Commission for the Unification and Rehabilitation of Korea (UNCURK). After the vote, the United States delegate, Warren Austin, overcome by emotion, with tears in his eyes, thanked God for the decision that had been taken.

On October 8, Eighth Army intelligence reported the entry of Chinese soldiers into Korea, athough, as yet, there were no indications that the build-up was as big as it later turned out to be.

On October 15, 1950, President Truman and General MacArthur met on Wake Island to discuss policy matters. Apparently little of real importance was discussed while the two met with Truman's top level advisers. However, Truman and MacArthur met privately for forty minutes before this, during which time areas of disagreement may have been discussed. A few days later, Truman denied that he and the general still differed on the matter of Formosa.

Meanwhile, the governments represented by the United Nations Commission on the Unification and Rehabilitation of Korea (UNCURK) established an interim committee to consider the problems involved in the unification and rehabilitation of Korea. On October 12, this interim committee advised the United Nations Command to assume governmental and civil administration of those parts of Korea not recognized by the United Nations as being under the jurisdiction of the Republic of Korea. The interim committee also established a schedule of stages for the administration of North Korea from the stage of pacification to that of the withdrawal of non-Korean United Nations forces.

The plan to have the United Nations Command assume governmental and civil administration in North Korea was received with dismay by the Syngman Rhee government of South Korea. On October 15, President Rhee sent messages to United Nations member states protesting that the plan was wrong in principle and in practice, and that it disregarded the sovereign rights of the Republic of Korea. On October 17, Rhee announced that he was sending civil administrators into the North as a temporary measure and that a bloc of 100 seats had been set aside in the ROK National Assembly for delegates to be elected in the North. At the same time, South Korean Foreign Minister Ben Limb criticized proposals emanating from United Nations sources that elections be held in all of Korea.

On October 30, it was reported that MacArthur would not allow the five ROK-appointed governors to assume their posts. The issue, however, involved little more than prestige, for MacArthur was virtually forced to appoint South Koreans recommended by and responsive to the wishes of the ROK government. Moreover, it was soon to become academic, for Chinese volunteer forces reconquered North Korea. ECOSOC and ECA plans for the rehabilitation of Korea were progressing during this period.

On October 8, United States Air Force planes strafed an airfield sixty miles north of the Korean border in Siberia. On October 10, the United States Embassy in Moscow refused to accept a note of protest from the Soviet Foreign Office. One week later, Representative Austin informed United Nations Secretary-General Lie that the attack had occurred, but that it had been inadvertent. On October 19, United Nations forces entered the North Korean capital of Pyongyang. By the end of the month, United Nations forces were approaching the Yalu river border between Korea and Manchuria. During this period, North Korean resistance noticeably stiffened, and counterattacks occurred.

In November 1950, domestic opposition to the Rhee government increased, and many United Nations members began to speculate that the Communists would win free elections. On November 3, the National Assembly refused to confirm Rhee's appointment of Paik Nak Choon as premier by a vote of 100–21, with 2 abstentions. On November 13, because of growing concern with police brutalities and the use of the police as a political instrument by the Rhee forces, the National Assembly of South Korea overrode two presidential vetoes to pass bills limiting police powers in the punishment of Communist collaborators and increasing the power of the National Assembly in subsequent investigations of the abuse of the police power. As the result of a compromise, John Chang, Korean Ambassador to the United States, was approved as premier on November 23 by the Assembly by a vote of 148–6.

Meanwhile, concern with the United Nations machinery for combating aggression was coming to a head. Dissatisfaction with United Nations machinery had been expressed by the Senate Committee on Foreign Relations in formal hearings in 1949 and 1950. On September 20, 1950, Secretary of State Acheson addressed the General Assembly of the United Nations and said that it "can and should organize itself to discharge its responsibility promptly and decisively if the Security Council is prevented from acting." He offered four proposals designed to strengthen the collective security system. These proposals corresponded to a draft jointly submitted several days later by Great Britain, France, the United States, Canada, the Philippines, Turkey, and Uruguay.

The seven-power resolution was finally adopted on November 3 by a vote of 52–5, with 2 abstentions. Known as the Uniting for Peace resolution, it specified:

(1) "that if the Security Council, because of lack of the permanent members, fails to exercise its primary responsibility for the maintenance of international peace and security in any case where there appears to be a threat to the peace, breach of the peace, or act of aggression, the General Assembly shall consider the matter immediately with a view to making appropriate recommendations to Members for collective measures, including in the case of a breach of the peace or act of aggression the use of armed force when necessary, to maintain or restore international peace and security;"

(2) that "if not in session at the time, the General Assembly may meet in emergency special session within twenty-four hours of the request; therefore, such emergency special session shall be called if requested by the Security Council on the vote of any seven members, or by a majority of the Members of the United Nations;"

(3) that there be established "a Peace Observation Commission . . . which could observe and report on the situation in any area where there exists international tension the continuance of which is likely to endanger the maintenance of international peace and security. Upon the invitation or with the consent of the state into whose territory the Commission would go, the General Assembly or the Interim Committee when the Assembly is not in session, may utilize the Commission if the Security Council is not exercising the functions assigned to it by the Charter with respect to the matter in question . . ."

(4) that "each member of the United Nations . . . survey its resources in order to determine the nature and scope of the assistance it may be in a position to render in support of any recommendations of the Security Council or of the General Assembly for the restoration of international peace and security;"

(5) that "each member [state of the United Nations] maintain within its national armed forces element so trained, organized and equipped that they could promptly be made available, in accordance with its constitutional processes, for service as a United Nations unit or units . . ."

(6) that "the Secretary-General . . . appoint, . . . a panel of military experts who could be made available, on request, to member states wishing to obtain technical advice regarding the organization, training, and equipment for prompt service as United Nations units . . ."

(7)   that there be established "a Collective Measures Committee . . . and [that] . . . the Committee . . . study and make a report to the Security Council and the General Assembly . . . on methods, including 'making available armed forces,' which might be used to maintain and strengthen international peace and security in accordance with the Purposes and Principles of the Charter, taking account of collective self-defense and regional arrangements. . . ."

Chinese Intervention

Strengthening the machinery of the United Nations may have occurred none too soon from the standpoint of the United Nations Command in Korea. On November 1, enemy jet aircraft were encountered for the first time in Korea. Enemy ground resistance began to stiffen. Nevertheless, a spearhead of the twenty-fourth Division drove to within fourteen miles of the Korean-Manchurian border. On November 3, a tactical retreat was ordered on the right flank of the United Nations lines. Two days later, MacArthur ominously announced that "elements of alien Communist forces" had moved into Korea from across the Yalu River. United Nations air forces bombed the crossing points, being careful not to bomb Manchurian territory; but enemy reinforcements continued to pour across from China. On November 14, the United States Defense Department estimated the Chinese Communist forces in Manchuria at 60,000 to 70,000 men.

The seriousness of the situation was not apparent to the general public. On November 24, General MacArthur announced a "general assault" by United Nations forces. "If successful," he said, "this should for all practical purposes end the war, restore the peace and unity in Korea, enable the prompt withdrawal of United Nations military forces, and permit the complete assumption by the Korean people and the nation of full sovereignty and international equality." He told reporters that the "boys would be home by Christmas."

The same day, the Joint Chiefs suggested to MacArthur that United Nations forces, except for the South Koreans, should not hold the terrain dominating the approaches to the valley of the Yalu, and that the hydroelectric works on the Yalu should be spared. This, the Joint Chiefs felt, would permit the unification of Korea, while lessening the chances of Chinese involvement. They expressed the concern that America's allies in the United Nations command felt. The next day, MacArthur rejected the suggestion. He said that neither Russia nor China considered the hydroelectric works a major factor. He felt that stopping the attack on them would provoke China, and he advocated sending American troops all the way to the Yalu and later replacing them with South Koreans, if possible.

On November 25, the Chinese began attacking in strength. Although it took several days before the picture became clear, the Chinese moved through a gap between the Eighth Army and the X Corps. United Nations forces rolled groggily with the punch, and a full-scale retreat was ordered.

In the same period, the United Nations was seized with the problem of Chinese intervention in Korea. On November 5, General MacArthur had referred to the intervention as a "grave" matter. The next day, he called the intervention to the attention of the United Nations. Warren Austin requested a special session of the Security Council to consider the matter. Delegate Carlos Romulo of the Philippines cautioned that Chinese intervention may have been occasioned by concern over the Korean-Manchurian frontier; he urged an immediate declaration to reassure China on that matter.

The Security Council met to consider the matter on November 8. Jacob Malik of the Soviet Union opposed placing MacArthur's special report on Chinese intervention on the Security Council agenda. The Soviet effort was defeated 10–1. Malik then proposed that a representative of the People's Republic of China be invited to participate in the discussion of all aspects of the Korean matter. This was rejected 3–2, with 6 abstentions. Great Britain then offered a resolution inviting a representative of China to attend a Council discussion of MacArthur's special report. Representative Austin objected that China ought to be summoned rather than invited, but he did not offer to amend the resolution and eventually voted for it.

On November 10, Cuba, Ecuador, France, Great Britain, Norway, and the United States introduced a joint resolution calling upon China to withdraw its forces from Korea while giving assurances that "it is the policy of the United Nations to hold the Chinese frontier with Korea inviolate and fully to protect legitimate Chinese and Korean interests in the frontier zone." The resolution also called attention "to the grave danger which continued intervention by Chinese forces in Korea would entail for the maintenance of such a policy."

The next day, China rejected the proposed invitation "because according to the contents of the resolution this invitation deprives the representative of the Central People's Government of the People's Republic of China of the right to discuss in the Security Council the most pressing question of the Chinese people, namely, the question of armed intervention in Korea and aggression against China by the United States Government, and limits the right of the Chinese representative to the discussion of the special report of the so-called United Nations Command." Malik stated that, if necessary, he would veto the resolution extending this invitation.

On November 15, Secretary of State Acheson stated: "[Chinese intervention] presents a very difficult problem for everyone. [If the Chinese] believe, as their propaganda states, that the United Nations or the United States have any ulterior designs in Manchuria, everything possible must be done to disabuse them of such an illusion because it is not true."

The next day, President Truman said, "Speaking for the United States government and the people, I can give assurance that we support and are acting within the limits of United Nations policy in Korea, and that we have never at any time entertained any intention to carry hostilities into China." This message was considered so important by the Department of State that Representative Ernest Gross read it to the Security Council the same day it was issued by the president.

On November 17, China replied to the Truman statement through the Peiping radio. According to the broadcast: "Observers here noted the pretended surprise evinced by American spokesmen that anyone could think for one moment that the Americans harbor aggressive intentions against China. . . . America has lied and smashed her way across the world to Chinese territory and into it, has seized Chinese Taiwan and is threatening another neighbor, Vietnam."

At the Security Council meeting that day, none of the representatives of the member states cared to speak on the subject of the proposed six-power resolution inviting China to participate in the discussion of the special report. On November 19, *Izvestia* charged that the United States was seeking to establish in the Security Council a formal basis for an attack against China and possibly against the Soviet Union.

Meanwhile, rumors were spreading in the United States that the administration, to appease the Communists, was going to establish a buffer zone between China and Korea along the Yalu and would possibly agree to admit the People's Republic of China to the United Nations. Compromises of this type had been bruited about United Nations corridors by representatives of states associated with or friendly to the United States in the Korean matter. Influential spokesmen in Congress denounced such attempted compromises. To stifle the rising clamor, Secretary of State Acheson announced on November 22 that no agreement had been reached by the Western nations to establish a buffer zone along the Yalu River.

In September, the General Assembly of the United Nations had invited representatives of the People's Republic of China to attend its sessions in connection with a Soviet-sponsored resolution accusing the United States of aggression against China. On November 24, a nine-member delegation arrived in New York and appeared before the United Nations Security Council on November 27. The provisional agenda for that session consisted of a single item of two parts. The first part consisted of a complaint of armed American invasion of Taiwan, and the second consisted of a complaint of aggression against Korea.

In the Council meeting, United States Representative Austin asked the Chinese delegates whether their intervention in Korea was in the interests of the Chinese people or that of the Soviet Union; whether it was still maintained that the Chinese forces in Korea were volunteers; why the Chinese had ignored United Nations statements that Chinese interests were not threatened by United Nations action; whether or not the Chinese would refrain from assisting North Korea as specified in the draft resolution before the Security Council, and whether there would be peace or war in the Far East.

Chinese representative Wu Hsui-chuan stated that the hostilities in Korea vitally affected China's security, and the United States concern was based on flimsy pretexts. In a public statement, Secretary of State Acheson claimed that by the words of the Chinese representatives, "the cloak of pretense has been thrown off.... these acts of aggression in Korea ... must be seen as part of the world-wide operations of the international Communist movement.... No one can guarantee that war will not come."

On November 30, President Truman told a press conference, "We have committed ourselves to the cause of a just and peaceful world order through the United Nations. We stand by the commitment.... We shall intensify our efforts to help other free nations strengthen their defenses in order to meet the threat of aggression elsewhere. We shall rapidly increase our own military strength." Truman charged that the Chinese people had been "forced or deceived into serving the ends of Russian colonial policy in Asia." Whether or not the scope of hostilities would be extended to Manchuria, he said, would depend upon the United Nations. Use of the atomic bomb was always under consideration. According to President Truman, it would not be necessary to wait for specific authority from the United Nations before using it. The next day, the White

House announced that consideration of use did not imply an intention to use, and that only the president had the authority to order the use of the atomic bomb.

At the Security Council meeting, the Communist-sponsored resolution was beaten 9–1. India refrained from voting because the delegation lacked instructions from New Delhi. The six-power resolution received 9 affirmative to 1 negative vote, but the Soviet vote had sufficed to veto it.

On November 29 British Foreign Minister Ernest Bevin told the House of Commons that it would be possible to localize the hostilities in Korea. Within the last twenty-four hours, he said, he had been assured by the United States that its policy was identical with that of Great Britain, namely, "to restrict aggression, to localize the hostilities, and to settle the Korean problem on a basis satisfactory to the United Nations." French Premier André Pleven made a similar statement on December 1.

On November 30, Winston Churchill advised the House of Commons that the fate of mankind would ultimately be decided in Europe. He urged the Western powers to avoid the strategic trap of falling into a sapping war with China. The Soviet Union, he said, was not yet ready to move in Europe, and the West still had sufficient time to increase its strength to prevent such a move. Although the Western powers would not be able within the next two or three years to overcome Soviet superiority in conventional weapons, Churchill thought that the atomic superiority of the West would deter the Soviet Union from attack.

British Prime Minister Attlee announced his decision to fly to Washington to confer with President Truman. It was widely believed that the trip was made necessary by British concern over Truman's suggestion that use of the atomic bomb in Korea was under consideration. On December 8, Attlee and Truman issued a joint communique informing the public of the broad results of their conference. Britain and the United States agreed to differ on the question of recognizing the People's Republic of China and granting that government China's seat in the United Nations.

With regard to Formosa, Truman and Attlee recognized that both the People's Republic and the Nationalists took the view that the United States and British Cairo Declaration of 1943, which Stalin accepted at Yalta and which specified the return of Formosa to China, remained valid and that they were reluctant to permit the United Nations to consider the status of Formosa. However, the president and the prime minister agreed that United Nations consideration of the matter represented the best solution. For his part, President Truman attempted to quiet fears concerning possible use of the atomic bomb by expressing the hope that it would never be necessary to use it.

Prime Minister Nehru of India and Sir Robert Gordon Menzies of Australia gave public support to the Truman-Attlee statements. However, the talks came in for sharp criticism in the United States. Republican Senator William Knowland of California said he was "shocked" by the communique. He regarded the expression of willingness "to seek an end to the hostilities by means of negotiations" as evidence of a "Far Eastern Munich" in the making. President Syngman Rhee of South Korea expressed his grave disappointment.

If it was impossible to please everyone, it did seem possible to displease everyone. On December 11, *Pravda* jumped into the fray and announced: "The [Truman-Attlee] comminique does not testify that the United States government wants to put an end to the aggression it undertook in Korea. On the contrary, Truman and Attlee have come to agreement to continue this hopeless action."[21]

On December 12, 1950, Prime Minister Attlee reported to the House of Commons on his talks in Washington. In an apparent reference to the atomic bomb,[22] he stated that agreement had been reached that no military action with political implications would be taken in Korea by the United Nations Command on orders from the Joint Chiefs in Washington without consultation with other governments. This reference also may have been to the possibility of air action over Manchuria.

Winston Churchill replied for the Conservatives that the atomic bomb was the only deterrent the West had, and that it was dangerous to state that it would never be used. On the other hand, he pointed out that Truman had promised only to keep Attlee informed of military decisions having political implications, not to consult him. Churchill complained that the agreement was stated in most general and inexplicit terms.[23]

On December 3, the United States took steps to restrict China's war-making potential by placing all shipping from the United States to the mainland of China, Hong Kong, and Macao under license. It was explained that licenses would be so difficult to obtain that the order virtually amounted to an embargo. On December 9, Canada took similar action. By December 28, China had ordered the retaliatory seizure of United States property and all United States private and commercial bank deposits within the territory of China.

Meanwhile, military events were going poorly. On December 4, a communique from the headquarters of the Supreme Commander announced that 268,000 Communist troops were opposing American forces and that to the rear, to the Yalu and beyond, 550,000 more troops were in reserve. MacArthur noted that the use of these troops was not "the result of a sudden impulse, but must have been preceded by a long period of planning, followed by a considerable time necessary for troop movement...." Nor did the Chinese claim they had acted on impulse.

On December 5, United Nations forces withdrew from Pyongyang. On December 6, a headquarters communique stated: "The probability that many North Koreans are training and regrouping in Manchuria must not be overlooked for, in that *privileged sanctuary* [italics added], they would be safe from United Nations air attack." Unofficial observers noted that the Communists had refrained from bombing United States bases in Japan, as well as debarkation points in Korea.[24] The opinion was widely held that unofficial ground rules were being observed by both sides.

By December 27, Communist troops had pushed south of the 38th parallel. General MacArthur's headquarters estimated that Communist forces at the front totalled 450,000 men, of whom two-thirds were Chinese, and that 900,000 troops were in reserve.

General MacArthur protested vigorously against the limitations placed upon his use of armed force. In a message to *United States News and World Report*, the Supreme Commander complained that the limits imposed upon his pursuit of Chinese forces and attacks on their bases constituted an "enormous handicap without precedent in military history."[25] On December 4, he informed General J. Lawton Collins and Admiral Forrest P. Sherman, who had gone to Tokyo, that, under the prevailing conditions, the evacuation of Korea might prove necessary.

On December 6, JCS warned all commanders, including CINCFE, that the situation in Korea had greatly increased the danger of general war. In a cable to CINCFE on December 29, JCS informed CINCFE that, in view of the danger of general war, more troops could not be spared for Korea; if war was to be fought, Korea was not the place.

MacArthur replied by urging the removal of limitations in fighting the enemy in Korea. He argued that this would not increase the likelihood of Russian intervention, for Russia will "act on [the] basis of [its] own estimate with little regard for outside factors." Later, he told the Joint Committee investigating the Military Situation in the Far East that he did not think the measures he advocated would "necessarily confine the area of the conflict to Korea; but it will give you an opportunity to hit the enemy where he is assembling to hit you."

The message of the Joint Chiefs to MacArthur stressed the prestige value of inflicting a defeat on the Chinese Communists. It also noted that, from the estimates available, the Chinese were capable of forcing United Nations evacuation of Korea. "Therefore in light of present situation, your basic directive, to furnish to ROK assistance as necessary to repel armed attack and restore to the area peace and security, is modified. Your directive now is to defend in successive positions, subject to safety of your troops as the primary consideration, inflicting as much damage to hostile forces in Korea as is possible. In view of continued threat to safety of Japan and possibility of forced withdrawal from Korea, it is important to make advance determination of last reasonable opportunity for orderly evacuation."

In his reply on December 30, MacArthur advocated blockading the coast of China, destroying China's industrial capacity by air and naval bombardment, securing reinforcements from Formosa, and permitting the Nationalists on Formosa to engage in diversionary attacks against the mainland. MacArthur recognized the superior importance of Europe, but stated that accepting defeat in Asia would insure defeat in Europe. If the proposed measures were not taken, he felt evacuation was the only alternative.

On January 9, the Joint Chiefs informed the Supreme Commander that the measures advocated by him would not be practicable. Strengthening armed efforts in Korea could not be considered in view of American global commitments. Moreover, United Nations concurrence would be necessary for some of the proposed measures; in particular, negotiations with the British would be necessary in order to establish a blockade of the China coast. The decision on air and naval attack on "objectives in Communist China must await attack outside of Korea on United Nations forces by Chinese Communists, ..." The Chinese Nationalists could be used better elsewhere, and they would not make for a decisive effect on events in Korea. If events in Korea could be stabilized, the security of Japan would have to be protected by the evacuated troops. If the position in Korea could be stabilized, two partly-trained National Guard divisions would be sent to help. Intensification of the economic blockade of China was being pressed.

In his reply on January 10, 1951, General MacArthur stated that, under the restrictions imposed upon him by the Joint Chiefs, the military position of the United Nations Command in Korea was untenable. He recommended that in "the absence of overriding political considerations under these conditions, the command should be withdrawn from the peninsula just as rapidly as it is feasible technically to do. If, on the other hand, the primary political interest of the United States in the Far East lies in holding a position in Korea and thus pinning down a large segment of the Chinese military potential, the military course is implicit in the political policy, and we should be prepared to accept any attendant hazard to Japan's security and whatever casualties result. ... if overriding political considerations so dictate, [the United Nations forces can hold] for any length of time up to [their] complete destruction."

On January 12, the Secretary of Defense forwarded to CINCFE sixteen possible courses of action that might prove undesirable under the worsening circumstances. According to a paraphrase of the cable:

> The Joint Chiefs of Staff have tentatively agreed upon the following objectives—A. With the preservation of the combat effectiveness of our forces as an overriding consideration, stabilize the situation in Korea, or evacuate to Japan, if forced out of Korea. ... E. Continue and intensify now an economic blockade of trade with Japan. F. Prepare now to impose a naval blockade of China and place it into effect as soon as our position in Korea is stabilized, or when we have evacuated Korea, and depending upon the circumstances then obtaining. G. Remove now restrictions on air reconnaissance of China coastal areas and of Manchuria. H. Remove now the restrictions on operations of the Chinese Nationalist forces and give such logistic support to those forces as will contribute to effective operations against the Communists. I. Continue to bomb military targets in Korea. J. Press now for United Nations action branding Communist China as an aggressor. Send a military mission and increase MDAP to Chinese Nationalists in Formosa. Initiate damaging naval and air attacks on objectives in Communist China at same time as the Chinese Communists attack any of our forces outside of Korea.

By the time of the National Security Council meeting on January 17, 1951, the report of General Collins from the Far East was encouraging; according to General Marshall, it was now felt, because of the improvement in the situation, that some of the measures tentatively approved were no longer necessary.[26]

Attempts to Negotiate a Solution

Meanwhile, parallel efforts were being made to seek a political solution to the Korean problem. On December 5, thirteen Middle and Far Eastern nations requested Chinese Communist representative Wu Hsui-chuan to transmit to Chinese and North Korean authorities an appeal that they declare their intention not to cross the 38th parallel. According to this Asian bloc, such moderation would provide a breathing spell in which the conflict could be resolved. The next day, UNCURK called for the immediate withdrawal from Korean soil of Chinese troops and an end to the unnecessary slaughter. Britain called the Asian appeal useful. Yugoslavia extended support to it. But Vyshinski ridiculed it and claimed that it would only provide a breathing spell for MacArthur's hard-pressed forces. Apparently, neither side was prepared to exercise moderation when it thought it held the upper hand.

On December 5, the General Committee of the General Assembly voted to consider the six-power plan that had been vetoed in the Security Council. The Assembly confirmed the decision of its committee and referred the resolution to the Political and Security Committee. The Political Committee gave priority to the resolution and also voted to invite representatives of the Republic of Korea to participate in the proceedings.

In the discussion, Warren Austin attacked the fiction of the "Chinese volunteers." He called the device part of a pattern to support Communist uprisings, "a new and dangerous weapon in the arsenal of Soviet imperialism." He said that the United Nations should have five objectives: (1) to assure the security of the United Nations forces in Korea; (2) to cause the withdrawal of the armed forces assisting the North Korean aggressors; (3) to localize the Korean conflict; (4) to bring about a speedy conclusion to the fighting on a basis satisfactory to the United Nations; and (5) to make assurances that the United Nations had no purposes hostile to the security or threatening to the interest of Korea's neighbors.

On December 9, Andrei Vyshinsky proposed the withdrawal of all foreign troops from Korea; it was not clear at the time whether or not this was intended to apply to the Chinese "volunteers." Three days later, with the backing of Middle Eastern and Asian powers, India proposed two draft resolutions designed to investigate the possibility of a cease-fire and to mediate terms of settlement. India's delegate, Sir Benegal Rau, suggested that the People's Republic of China was moving toward an Asian Monroe Doctrine and that China desired peace. Despite Soviet claims that the measures proposed by India only gave a breathing spell to MacArthur's forces, the General Assembly gave priority to India's proposals by a vote of 48–5, with 4 abstentions. It then approved both resolutions 51–5, with 1 abstention.

In accordance with one of the resolutions, Assembly president Nas-rollah Entezam of Iran appointed himself, Lester Pearson of Canada, and Sir Benegal Rau of India to a committee of three to determine a basis for a cease-fire. The Cease-Fire Committee met with UNCURK on December 15 and agreed: (1) to a general cease-fire; (2) to a demilitarized zone of approximately twenty miles depth across Korea, with the southern limit of the zone generally following the line of the 38th parallel; (3) that all ground forces would remain in position or withdraw to the rear of the zone, including guerrillas; (4) that the keeping of the agreement would be supervised by UNCURK, which would have free and unlimited access to all of Korea; (5) that all governments would cease sending personnel reinforcements or equipment to Korea; and (6) that prisoners would be exchanged on a man-to-man basis pending a final settlement.

The Chinese Communist delegation refused to meet with the Cease-Fire Committee on the grounds that the Chinese government had not authorized it to conduct cease-fire negotiations. In a statement that expressed China's desire to solve the Korean conflict by peaceful means, however, it hinted that the recognition of the People's Republic would be the price of peaceful settlement. The Soviet Union's Jacob Malik implied that a cease-fire would not be sufficient. He indicated that a final termination of the fighting and the withdrawal of foreign troops were required for this purpose. On December 16, the Chinese Communist delegation stated that it would leave for China on December 19. Four messages from the Cease-Fire Committee were met with silence on the part of China. The rejection by the Chinese of United Nations efforts seemed clear; Chinese Premier Chou En-lai stated that he regarded the cease-fire group as illegal.

On January 1, 1951, forces of the People's Republic of China invaded Tibet. One week later, the United States resumed arms shipment to Formosa. On January 3, the Cease-Fire Committee recorded its inability to recommend cease-fire terms usefully at that time. Representative Austin stated that the failure of the cease-fire efforts did not reflect upon the work of the committee. Austin said:

> The Chinese Communist regime by rejecting any cease-fire proposal, by refusing even to discuss one, has closed a channel for peaceful settlement.... The objective in Korea continues to be what it was before the Chinese Communist aggression: that is, the repulsing of aggression and the establishment of a unified, independent, and democratic Korea.... My Government believes, of course, that the position of the United Nations should continue to be one of seeking to achieve

its objectives in Korea by peaceful means. Accordingly, my Government remains ready to engage in discussions with the Chinese Communist regime at an appropriate time and in an appropriate form.

On January 5, Lester Pearson of Canada informed the Political and Security Committee that the cease-fire group was still trying to state a set of principles that would lay the groundwork for a satisfactory settlement. Abba Eban of Israel suggested that the following principles would achieve the desired objectives of the United Nations: (1) an immediate cease-fire; (2) an affirmation by all concerned states that they accepted the United Nations objective of a unified and independent Korea established by free nationwide elections supervised by the United Nations; (3) participation by the states bordering Korea in the work of UN-CURK; (4) agreement for the progressive withdrawal of non-Korean forces from Korea within a defined period of time; (5) the rehabilitation and reconstruction of Korea; (6) a guarantee of the status of Korea by the United Nations to which the People's Republic of China would subscribe; and (7) that upon the successful implementation of points 1 to 6, all questions affecting the relations of China to the United Nations would receive urgent consideration.

On January 6, 1951, the Department of State confirmed that it had sent telegrams to thirty countries, setting forth the United States' views concerning possible United Nations action to meet Communist aggression in Korea. Alternative courses of action were suggested, including an economic blockade, sanctions, an embargo, severance of diplomatic relations, and other collective measures. It was pointed out that no specific course of action had been suggested because the decision properly would be made by the United Nations. It was proposed that the newly established Collective Measures Committee recommend the type of action to be taken against Communist China. Reliable sources indicated that the United States opinion would be influenced by the decision of the United Nations, and that the question of American support for the United Nations was at stake.

On January 8, Nationalist China's representative, Tsiang, recommended condemnation and punishment of Communist China as an aggressor and a restatement of United Nations principles. Two days later, Sir Gladwyn Jebb of Great Britain stated the view of his government that a cease-fire be negotiated only on an honorable basis. He objected to the Communist proposal that the negotiation of terms must precede a cease-fire. Moreover, the terms would have to conform to

United Nations principles. Nevertheless, he urged fullest consideration of the Israeli proposals before "thinking in more drastic terms." The United States apparently was no longer in a mood to wait.[27] Speaking in Atlantic City the next day, Warren Austin urged that the United Nations convict China of aggression and that the Collective Measures Committee be called to consider steps against that aggression.

The actions of the United Nations delegations, except the American and Soviet delegations, largely were unrelated to the military expectations of both sides. Pearson, speaking for the Cease-Fire Committee, urged an immediate cease-fire; the unification of Korea; free elections; and the establishment by the United Nations of an appropriate body, including among its members the United States, Great Britain, the Soviet Union, and the People's Republic of China, whose purpose would be to achieve a settlement of Far Eastern problems including Formosa and the representation of China in the United Nations in conformity with existing international obligations and the United Nations Charter. Warren Austin supported the proposals for the United States, but made it clear that he was doing so only because of the wide support they commanded. Jacob Malik, representative of the Soviet Union, called the proposals "foggy and deliberately vague"; he complained that they had been presented on a take-it-or-leave-it basis.

On January 12, Abba Eban of Israel submitted a draft resolution embodying the principles set forth by the cease-fire group. After some amendments, the resolution was approved by the General Assembly the next day by a vote of 50–7, with 1 abstention. Two days later, Secretary-General Lie transmitted them to China.

Senator Robert A. Taft, Ohio Republican, called the resolution a "shocking step" toward appeasement. Taft took the position that it would be better for the United States to retire from Korea than to discuss the questions of Formosa and Chinese representation in the United Nations. New Jersey's Republican Senator H. Alexander Smith stated that the resolution signified "bluntly that the United Nations has sacrificed moral principle for expediency." Democrat Tom Connally of Texas, Chairman of the Senate Committee on Foreign Relations, indicated that he had reservations about the justice of the proposals.

Secretary of State Acheson replied that American support of the resolution did not represent any policy change. The United States did not share the belief that China could be prevailed upon to cease its "defiance" of the United Nations, but it had to take account of the fact that this belief was widely and sincerely held by other nations. Moreover,

Acheson said, no stone should be left unturned in seeking a peaceful solution of the Korean hostilities. Although the United States was prepared to discuss Far Eastern questions, Secretary Acheson pointed out that "obviously we have not committed ourselves on any questions which might be discussed."

On January 17, China rejected the terms embodied in the United Nations resolution. China claimed that negotiations for a peaceful settlement could take place only if they were conducted by the parties concerned, if American forces were withdrawn from Formosa, and if China were admitted to the United Nations. Moreover, terms would have to be negotiated before a cease-fire; otherwise, a cease-fire would only present the United States forces in Korea with a breathing spell. The basis of negotiations, China said, would have to be the withdrawal of all foreign troops from Korea. A committee of seven nations, including China, the Soviet Union, the United Kingdom, the United States, France, India, and Egypt, should conduct the negotiations.

Secretary of State Acheson called China's terms "unacceptable" and "contemptuous." Although Nehru advised against taking the Chinese statement as a flat rejection and warned against precipitous steps, President Truman told a press conference the next day that the United States would press vigorously for United Nations action. United Nations Representative Austin stated that aggression in Korea "is part of the worldwide pattern of centrally directed Soviet imperialism."

On January 20, 1951, the United States submitted a draft resolution to the General Assembly of the United Nations noting that the Security Council had failed to exercise its primary responsibility for the maintenance of international peace and security because of lack of unanimity among the major powers on the Council, and that China had rejected United Nations efforts to bring about a cessation of the hostilities. The resolution found that China had engaged in aggression in Korea and called upon it to cease hostilities and withdraw its forces. It affirmed the determination of the United Nations to continue its actions in meeting aggression and called upon other states to lend assistance to the United Nations activities in Korea and refrain from giving assistance to the aggressors. The resolution urgently requested a meeting of the Collective Measures Committee to consider additional measures to meet aggression and to set up a good offices committee of two, to be appointed by the President of the General Assembly, to bring about a cessation of hostilities by peaceful means.

The Indian representative, Sir Benegal Rau, argued against the proposed resolution on the grounds that the Chinese reply was not an outright rejection. There was still room for bargaining, he said. Branding China as an "aggressor" would serve no useful purpose. Sir Benegal Rau said, "To pass a resolution of aggression, even if the charge were fully justified, would hardly redound to the prestige of the United Nations, unless it was intended to be followed by other steps. As far as I am aware, the feasibility of these further steps has not yet been examined. In these circumstances, the only result of such a resolution would be to leave all the problems in the Far East not only unsolved, but also make them insoluble." Such a course, he said, would be "disastrous."

The next day, American Representative Ernest Gross strongly stated the American government's unwillingness to modify its position. However, on January 22, Sir Benegal was able to inform the General Assembly that the Indian government had been advised by the Chinese government that it was willing to assume full responsibility to advise the Chinese volunteers in Korea to return to China if an agreement were reached and if a limited cease-fire preceded the political negotiations. The Chinese government was insistent, however, that Far Eastern problems generally be discussed and that China be assured of its seat in the United Nations.

American delegate Warren Austin denounced the Chinese offer as a "transparent attempt to divide the free world" and to delay "the peacemaking functions of the United Nations." Nevertheless, the Political and Security Committee voted 27–23, with 6 abstentions, to give priority to a twelve-nation Arab-Asian bloc resolution calling for a meeting of the seven nations named in the Chinese communication to elucidate China's reply and make arrangements leading toward a peaceful settlement of the Korean dispute.

Moreover, Prime Minister Attlee had obtained the same clarifications of the Chinese position from the British *chargé d'affaires* in Peiping, and he felt that a negotiated solution was still possible. He declared, "The time has come to take further measures. Not to do so implies that we have given up all hope of reaching a peaceful settlement, and this we have not done."

The United States Senate, however, voted two resolutions unanimously on January 23, 1951. The first stated that "it is the sense of the Senate that the United Nations should immediately declare Communist China an aggressor in Korea." The second stated "that it is the sense of the Senate that the Communist China Government should not be admitted to membership in the United Nations as the representative of China." A third resolution, also introduced that day by Democratic Senator John L. McClellan, of Arkansas, called on the United Nations to take all necessary measures, including economic sanctions, blockade, and full-scale military action, to halt Chinese Communist aggression. It was referred to the Senate Committee on Foreign Relations for further study. Senate action left the State Department no room to maneuver, had it even desired to do so, and ended any genuine possibility of a compromise settlement at that time.

On January 24, Prime Minister Nehru of India stated that the United States draft resolution would not lead to peace. American Secretary of State Dean Acheson praised the Senate for endorsing his views on Korea and refused to comment on the Nehru statement. The Arab and Asian bloc of nations continued its efforts to mediate the matter and to delay precipitate action. The United States, on the other hand, did not desire further delay. The next day, President Truman said, "For my part, I believe in calling an aggressor an aggressor."

Sir Gladwyn Jebb announced Britain's approval of those portions of the American resolution calling upon China to withdraw its forces from Korea. He also called attention to Prime Minister Attlee's concern that precipitate action be delayed until all possibilities of negotiation had been exhausted. Moreover, he stressed the right of the Chinese mainland regime to representation in the United Nations.

M. Tsarapkin, of the Soviet Union, called the twelve-nation Arab-Asian resolution inadequate, but announced that in the interests of a peaceful settlement, he would not take exception to it. On January 28, Sir Benegal Rau stated that the American draft resolution, which first condemned China and then in a later paragraph set up a good offices committee to negotiate with China, demonstrated a lack of seriousness about either objective. Moreover, he said, he felt bound to mention that the Indian government "has been informed on the highest authority that once there is a condemnatory resolution, there is no hope of a peaceful settlement."

On January 29 and 30, 1952, President Truman and French Premier Andre Pleven met in Washington and found themselves in agreement on the necessity of resisting aggression in the Far East. The Political and Security Committee of the General Assembly defeated the twelve-nation Arab-Asian resolution in a closely contested vote.

On January 30, the American resolution was adopted by 44–7, with 8 abstentions, after some minor amendments had been made. On the last day of the month, the Security Council removed the Korean item from its agenda in order to pave the way for the vote on the resolution at the plenary session of the General Assembly. The Soviet delegate voted to support this move on the ground that all Security Council action on Korea had been illegal.

The Decision to Attack Korea

The Republicans have asserted that North Korea attacked South Korea because Secretary of State Acheson placed Korea outside the American defense perimeter in a public speech early in 1950. Under the best of circumstances, it is more difficult to determine why Communist nations make decisions than in the case of other nations. They rarely open their highest deliberations to public examination. Therefore, greater caution than Republicans have been prone to exhibit should be exercised before making such charges.

Further, upon examination, the charge has little substance. The decision to place Korea outside the American defense perimeter was primarily a military decision made because the United States was unwilling to support its defensive forces adequately. The Soviet Union was completely informed, for all practical purposes, of the withdrawal of American troops. If South Korea had not been removed from the American defense perimeter, American troops would not have withdrawn completely.

The only new information contained in the controversial speech of 1950 by the Secretary of State was the information that an invasion of South Korea would be brought to the attention of the United Nations. This may not have been a substantial deterrent to the Communists, but it hardly reinforced the information they had already obtained from the troop withdrawal.

The Republicans also ignore the fact that the Communists may have been encouraged in their belief that the United States would not intervene by the reluctance of the House of Representatives to appropriate money for military aid to Korea. Originally, the House—with Republicans in the vanguard—defeated the administration bill for military appropriations. Only strong action by the president and the secretary of state secured a reversal of this position. The Communists may have figured—wrongly, if they did—that the House would again become reluctant at the first sign of danger.

It is difficult to escape the conclusion that American lack of military preparedness also may have encouraged the Communists. Certainly the Congress was not conspicuous for its efforts in this direction. Nor could the Soviet Union have overlooked the reluctance of Congress to sanction foreign assignments for American forces. The charges against Acheson—on this score—came with ill grace from those who issued them.

The Decision to Defend Korea

There is little point in attempting to discover the rationale behind American policy in the fateful days following June 25, 1950. According to the best available evidence, the American decision to defend Korea had not been made in advance.

Although a skeleton version of the resolution that was submitted to the Security Council of the United Nations on June 25 lay locked in the vaults of the Department of State for at least several months before that date, the decision to use available but scant American military forces in defense of Korea was made as a consequence of day-to-day pressures resulting from the course of events. Each succeeding move seemed logically to give rise to the next. There was no master plan, no prepared pattern of action for various alternative possibilities.

It makes better sense to analyze the grounds on which the decision to intervene may have been rationalized later. Korea had been placed outside the American defense perimeter by a considered decision. This decision was based, in part at least, on the paucity of American military force. The United States could not afford to commit its scant military resources to a defense of Korea. Beyond that, however, General Wedemeyer had testified that Korea was without strategic importance.

Perhaps the remarks of the general should not be taken too literally. If South Korea were in the hands of the Communists, the encirclement of Japan by Communist elements would be accelerated. In all likelihood, the general meant to say that Korea was not of vital or decisive importance, that the defense of Korea did not warrant great expenditure or risks—on military grounds, at least.

Therefore, if the decision to defend Korea is to be rationalized *post facto*, the rationalization has to be phrased in political terms.

Within a few weeks of the decision, such a rationalization had already gained considerable headway in Washington. With one phase of the rationalization, few could disagree. If the North Korean aggression succeeded—particularly if it succeeded without any American effort to defend South Korea—other Asian nations would draw an unavoidable inference.

What happened in Korea sooner or later would happen elsewhere in Asia. The pressures toward making a "deal" with the Communist powers then would become irresistible. Despite their later fears that the United States might become too entangled in Asia, some European countries also would have been likely to make the same inference. Unless the United States had acted in Korea, its entire defense system might have collapsed.

The rationalization, however, went past the evident and entered the realm of the speculative and doubtful. It was assumed without question that the Soviet Union ordered the North Korean attack and that the attack represented something more than an isolated outbreak of violence.

If these interpretations had been entertained as possibilities—or even as probabilities—it would be impossible to quarrel with them. It was unlikely that the North Korean attack had been launched without a green light from the Kremlin. Dissenters might point out that the Greek revolution had been launched and sustained over the objections of the Kremlin and that the absence of the Soviet delegate from the Security Council might possibly have indicated that the Russians had been caught unawares by the outbreak of war.

However, it is also plausible that the Russians had been caught unawares by the vigor and swiftness of the American response. Perhaps they had failed to note Acheson's qualification that, although Korea was outside the defense perimeter of the United States, it could count on action by the United Nations. Or perhaps Stalin was in one of his stubborn moods and refused to recognize that things might not go precisely according to plan.

Official Washington is little given to tentative judgments. Attempts are usually made to discover the "real" objectives of the Soviet Union. When one view gains official predominance, it then becomes dogma. If questioned at lower echelons of the government, the very loyalty of the official becomes subject to doubt.

In the early stages of the Korean War, competing factions in Washington vied with each other in an attempt to present an interpretation of Soviet policy that would be adopted as the "official view."

The two major points of view were the "soft spot" and the "diversionary" points of view. The first position held that the Soviet Union was taking an opportunity to expand in the area in which American power was weakest. If the Soviet Union succeeded in Korea, there would be additional Koreas around the periphery of the Communist empire.

The "soft-spot" view had one advantage as a hypothesis. The North Korean attack might have been launched for many reasons. If it succeeded, however, the Soviet Union would have discovered a cheap method of expansion and would be likely to use that method in the future.

The "soft-spot" hypothesis was also safe from a bureaucratic point of view. It would be very difficult to disprove it. If North Korean efforts were opposed, the failure of the Soviet Union or of its satellites to engage in future acts of aggression would prove that American counteraction had been effective.

If, on the other hand, a satellite of the Soviet Union did strike in the future, one could then conclude that the Soviet Union believed it had found a new "soft spot." The "soft-spot" hypothesis predicted only that the Soviet Union did not intend to launch a major war. Thus, the absence of major war was sufficient to confirm it. If, on the other hand, the Soviet Union did launch a major war, that action could be called an act of desperation, chosen only because other possibilities had been closed off by effective and prompt American counteraction.

The second point of view—namely, that Korea was a diversionary move designed to engage American strength while the first Soviet team remained free to strike in Europe—appears to have gained credence in the minds of American policy planners. Perhaps the shock of the Korean venture and the fear arising in the minds of American officials upon the realization that they were completely unprepared to meet a major Soviet military effort combined to give credence to the diversionary hypothesis.

The diversionary hypothesis—rather than any fundamental desire to limit the Korean conflict to Korea—may account best for the decision of top American officials not to widen the war in Korea.

According to this view—although it was important to use force to oppose Communist aggression in Korea—American forces should not be so deployed in Korea that they could not be sent to the defense of Europe in case of a major Soviet military action.

From a strategic point of view, the foregoing considerations would have been sound if based upon possibilities rather than certainties. The exhaustion of American resources in Korea would open Europe to Soviet attack and might indeed have precipitated such an attack even if the original Soviet intentions had not included that aim.

The decision to cross the parallel partly may be accounted for by an effort to free American forces for transshipment to Germany. However, the two major decisions to which the belief in the certainty of Soviet attack in Europe led—namely the decision to cross the parallel and the decision to rearm Germany—reflected a schizophrenic paralysis of policy rather than an intelligent attempt to cope with the more dangerous possibilities to which the United States might have been exposed.

The interposition of the Seventh Fleet in the Formosa Strait may have looked to some Americans like an implementation of the announced aim, namely the protection of American transport lines to Korea, but this hardly seems plausible from a strategic point of view.

The decision was taken on the spur of the moment, and one must be careful not to read into the decision motivations that were not present. But whatever the motivations at the time of decision, the decision served three major purposes. The first was to serve as a warning to China not to intervene in Korea. The second was to prepare for the possibility of a general Far Eastern war by securing a strong anchor line in the Pacific. The third was to gain support from domestic supporters of Nationalist China for the military steps that were being taken.

The action also had the advantage of disarming Nationalist supporters and thereby of frustrating demands for a large-scale involvement in Asia that would have undermined the ability of the United States to defend Europe.

One must speculate about the decision of the United States to handle the Korean war as a United Nations venture. The United States knew that the military support it would get from other nations for the Korean conflict was hardly worth the costs of consultation. Although the costs of consultation were minimized by command arrangements that placed Korean operations directly under the American Chiefs of Staff, purely military considerations would have led to a different decision.

Partly, the appeal to the United Nations gave moral sanction to the American effort. But surely the American effort was not dependent upon the decisions of the United Nations. This seems to be indicated by the fact that the Blair House decisions were made without reference to possible disapproval by the United Nations.

The suspicion must persist that the United States was engaged in building an alliance for something more than the Korean venture. I must suspect that the United States did not expect Korea to be an isolated venture and that it was building its grand alliance.

Certainly other interpretations are possible and, on the basis of complete evidence, may yet prove correct. But American handling of United Nations resolutions in the first few critical days makes one wonder whether American representatives on the Security Council were even attempting to explore other possibilities.

From the first, the American representatives insisted on a wording that condemned North Korea. As matters developed, it soon became evident that the North Korean operations were too well-planned to constitute a retaliatory action against South Korean border raids.

Yet, that evidence was not in on June 25. Beyond that, Delegate Austin misrepresented to the Security Council the telegram he received from the U.S. ambassador in Seoul, John Muccio. Contrary to what Warren Austin told the Council, Muccio reported the North Korean action on the basis of South Korean Army reports rather than as confirmed information.

Certainly, the American representatives knew that Rhee had threatened major military operations against the north, and also that South Korean forces had at times initiated raids against the north. In fact, this was precisely why heavy military equipment was not supplied to South Korea by the United States.

It is true that the North Koreans could have halted their military operations against the south unless they were attempting a fast conquest before intervention by other parties could take place. On the other hand, the resolution of June 25—as the Yugoslav representative pointed out—convicted North Korea of aggression without even giving that nation a chance to state its case. In fact, a Yugoslav resolution that would have invited North Korea to state its case even after condemnation was defeated at the request of the United States. Although the North Koreans could have halted their military operations, the resolution of the Security Council was not stated in a manner likely to maximize this possibility.

The United States evidently wanted a formal condemnation on the record. Possibly it wanted this condemnation before the Soviet representative could return. But the resolution then could have automatically condemned North Korea if it did not halt military operations and state its case before the United Nations. Or the Yugoslav resolution could have been accepted even after condemnation.

The suspicion must persist that the United States wanted the United Nations firmly on record. Any invitation to the North Koreans to discuss their case would have interfered with efforts to construct an effective military alliance. Perhaps the very absence of the Soviet representative from the Council was viewed not as a blunder or even as indicative of lack of knowledge of the North Korean action, but as a sign that the Soviet Union was prepared to launch a major war effort in Europe.

In any event, military aid from other nations for the Korean effort was slight. This aid could not have been the focus of American concern.

Rather, it must have been the commitment of other nations to the American side that was so desirable.

However, much of the foregoing is extremely speculative and may legitimately be rejected by the reader. What is beyond doubt is that high American leaders were—during this first phase—extremely fearful that the Soviet Union would strike elsewhere while the United States was engaged in Korea. This fear in some ways must have influenced some of the decisions taken in the period.

A deep veil of pessimism overlay American policy-making in this period. Even when the North Korean forces were fractured by the American military effort, the gloom did not lift. Orders were given to General MacArthur not to cross the thirty-eighth parallel if Chinese or Soviet forces occupied North Korea and to resist as best he could if such forces were to attack him south of the parallel. However, under these circumstances, the United States believed that it would be forced to evacuate the peninsula.

General MacArthur's statement referring to Formosa as an unsinkable aircraft carrier caused dismay in Washington. Any incident that seemed to justify Chinese intervention would have threatened the American alliances and increased the possibility that major American forces would be tied down indefinitely in Asia. Gloom deepened in Washington.

Crossing the Thirty-Eighth Parallel

The decision to cross the thirty-eighth parallel probably was based upon a number of factors. In many ways, it is a remarkable decision that is easier to describe than to explain.

When the parallel was reached, the original American objectives apparently were attained. As Secretary of State Acheson told the American Newspaper Guild on June 29: "This action pursuant to the Security Council Resolutions is solely for the purpose of restoring the Republic of Korea to its status prior to the invasion from the north and of re-establishing the peace broken by that aggression."

If that were the American aim, it was accomplished brilliantly by the time the parallel was reached. The North Korean armies were shattered and in headlong retreat. Halting at the parallel would have been regarded as an act of magnanimous self-restraint.

On the other hand, continued pursuit of the North Koreans might invoke the already-threatened intervention of the Chinese Communists. In this event, the United States might become engaged in the Asian land war it hoped to avoid.

The argument that the North Koreans would strike again unless they were wiped out made little sense. True, they could hardly strike again if they were wiped out. But would they be likely to risk American intervention a second time? One could hardly maintain this position without contending that the original act of aggression was designed to achieve American intervention, i.e., to tie the United States down while the Soviet Union was free to strike elsewhere.

But if the Soviet Union were prepared to launch world war, it could strike a unified Korea from Siberia. Or did the United States fear satellite aggression in Europe rather than direct Soviet action on either continent? This possibility was remote. Soviet satellites did not strike at Yugoslavia in 1948 although Western retaliation would have been quite doubtful.

Was it likely that East Germany would attack Western Germany? This was hardly likely if NATO forces were stationed in Western Germany. Surely East Germany would not attack under these circumstances.

Only full Soviet participation in a European war effort would make the success of such efforts likely. In such an event, however, it would make little difference whether or not North Korea were occupied.

The more one examines the decision to cross the thirty-eighth parallel, the more incomprehensible it becomes. Unable to suggest any plausible reasons, I will suggest two contradictory reasons, both of which, I suspect, lay behind the decision.

First, the State Department was pessimistically convinced that either the Chinese or the Russians would occupy North Korea. It was considered quite possible that the Communists would intervene south of the parallel and drive American forces off the peninsula. The State Department became convinced—once the Communists passed up this opportunity and instead resorted to verbal threats—that American action had frightened the Communist countries.

Therefore, neither the Soviet Union nor China would dare to intervene. The United States could proceed to teach the Communist bloc a lesson it would never forget. Moreover, this lesson would destroy Communist prestige in Asia.

That the Communist powers might have strategic reasons for intervention under these conditions or that they were not prepared to suffer such a loss of prestige apparently did not worry official Washington. I have personal knowledge that State Department representatives told foreign delegates to the United Nations that they had secret information that "proved that there was no possibility of Chinese intervention." Apparently, the Department of State—except for a few of its officials—really believed this incredible estimate.

Secondly, the Chiefs of Staff wanted to transfer American forces from Korea to Germany and felt that this troop transfer could not be afforded unless North Korea were first occupied. The desire to move American troops to Europe was based on several reasons. In the first place, the United States feared a major Soviet effort in Europe. As Europe was the more important theater in official opinion, it was desirable to get American forces to Europe as quickly as possible. However, this reason implied that the Communists were "feeling their oats" rather than that they were frightened by American intervention in Korea.

A second reason for transferring American troops to Germany had greater validity. Apparently, the French were unwilling to increase their army commitments to NATO, and the British were unwilling to make such a commitment until the United States made a token commitment of manpower. However, it hardly seems plausible that this reason alone can account for the decision to cross the thirty-eighth parallel.

A third reason also may have underlain the decision. Secretary Acheson —who was getting rough treatment from Republican Senators—was able, by this decision, to prove that he also was "hard" toward Communism.

But make this decision, Washington did. Contrary to common belief, General MacArthur did not jump the gun and force the hand of Washington. MacArthur had permission to cross the parallel before the resolution to the same effect had been submitted to the General Assembly of the United Nations. Moreover, his permission was not dependent upon passage of the resolution.

The lack of consistency in American objectives and opinions was so striking in this period that it is difficult to account for American policy. The United States had already refused a Nationalist offer of troops for the Korean campaign, ostensibly because they were needed to defend Formosa, but actually because it wanted neither to provoke an engagement with China nor to create the impression among its allies that it was provoking retaliation.

Yet, by advancing past the thirty-eighth parallel, it was taking the very action that, by threatening legitimate Chinese strategic interests, was most likely to provoke China.

Perhaps one explanation for this seeming contradiction may be available if top administration officials really believed that they were not threatening Chinese strategic interests by the march to the Yalu River. Some substance for this hypothesis may be found in a statement by Secretary of State Acheson on September 9, 1950.

According to Acheson, Chinese intervention would be "sheer madness" because China faced "a great cloud from the north, Russian penetration," the aim of which was to dominate the areas of China bordering the Soviet Union. "We still believe that the Chinese are going to be Chinese before they are going to be Communists."

Secretary Acheson was right in one respect. The Chinese were having trouble with the Soviet Union and were on the verge of a split. He may even have been right in thinking that the Soviet Union and not China instigated the Korean War. However, the conclusion he drew, namely, that China would not have any interest in preventing American penetration to the Yalu River, was remarkable.

Under any circumstances, the propensity of official Washington to draw strong conclusions from slender evidence is shattering. If one is certain of what others have in mind, strategic decision-making under conditions of uncertainty is irrelevant. But such certainty is unwarranted, and the decisions which flow from it may be tragic.

The Narrow Waist of Korea

As United Nations forces approached the Chinese border, the threats from China became more pronounced. America's allies became dubious of the wisdom of driving all the way to the Yalu, and neutral or third-force nations began to exert considerable pressure to compromise the Korean conflict.

Many alternatives were under consideration. There is some reason to believe that Washington was paying considerable heed to a British suggestion that a buffer zone be established in North Korea. By the middle of November, Secretary of State Acheson and President Truman were broadcasting appeals to the Chinese enunciating that the United States lacked "any ulterior designs in Manchuria."

However, the United States had ignored its own previous declarations that it would be satisfied with the restoration of the prewar status quo. The Chinese might well be doubtful of a new statement that American objectives were limited. But, even had this not been the case, great nations are hardly likely to allow their military security to depend upon the self-restraint of other great nations.

Did the top American officials really expect China to depend upon the sincerity of American protestations? If so, they were guilty of gross naiveté. Or was the temper in Congress so high that the administration had no choice but to plunge headlong into disaster? By November 22, the Congressional storm had risen so high that Secretary of State Acheson was forced to deny the possibility that a buffer zone would be established in North Korea.

During this period, the strident voices of American representatives filled the diplomatic air with a crescendo of noise. On November 27, after the Chinese intervention, Chinese delegates in New York argued their case before the United Nations. Austin asked the Chinese representative whether Chinese intervention in Korea was in the interests of the Chinese people or in the interests of the Soviet Union. It is difficult to view Austin's remarks as indicative of a desire to negotiate.

When—in the midst of an equally unyielding reply—the Chinese representative pointed out that hostilities in Korea vitally affected the security of China, Secretary of State Acheson roared: "The cloak of pretense has been thrown off. . . . these acts of aggression in Korea . . . must be seen as part of the world-wide operations of the international Communist movement. . . . No one can guarantee that war will not come."

On November 26, President Truman charged: "The Chinese people have been forced or deceived into serving the ends of Russian colonial policy in Asia." Of course, as we now know, the Chinese had been on the verge of splitting with the Soviet Union when, in this period, American policy forced the Chinese into a close dependence upon the Soviet Union.

Nor had this curious interpretation of history been modified by the time of the Far East Hearings. Secretary of Defense Marshall claimed: "[China] you might say is a Russian protectorate in a sense. . . . I have gone on the assumption that [China] was operating not only in conjunction with but literally under the direction of the Soviet Union." Acheson turned the Chinese Communists into Rover boys, loyally eager to carry out the orders of Stalin: "[They are] Moscow-trained loyal Communists who are glad, very glad indeed, to carry out the Moscow line."

General MacArthur displayed much greater acuity. According to the general: "I never said the Chinese were under the control of the Kremlin. I believe there is an interlocking of interests. . . . The degree of control that the Kremlin may have in China is quite problematical. . . . there is a point that might well be reached where the interests of Red China and the interests of the Red Soviet did not run parallel, that they started to traverse and become antagonistic." Having displayed such great insight, one wonders why the general favored a course of action designed to drive China and the Soviet Union even closer together.

Of course, many of these remarks were for public consumption and do not necessarily indicate genuine private opinions.[28] Yet, one familiar with the atmosphere in Washington in this period must come to the conclusion that many high officials in the Department of State fully believed that the Chinese Communists were taking orders directly from Moscow.

Apparently, the administration assumed originally that the Soviet Union ordered the North Korean attack. From this, top officials drew the inference that China lacked strategic interests in North Korea. From this, they drew the inference that the Chinese would not intervene. Therefore, when the Chinese did intervene, American officials came to the conclusion that the Chinese were acting to protect Soviet rather than Chinese interests, and that they would not do this unless they took orders directly from Moscow. The conclusions in this paragraph may be wrong, but they seem to fit in best with the publicly available evidence. Any comment on the inferences themselves would be completely superfluous.

Limitation of Hostilities

Many Republicans, dissatisfied with the attitude of the administration during this period, subscribe to the myth that the administration was holding back, that it wanted to negotiate with the Chinese, and that it was making untoward concessions to allies who were making little contribution to the fighting in Korea.

More careful examination discloses that the administration usually compromised with its allies when preferred courses of action could not be carried out without their cooperation, as for instance, during the contemplated naval blockade of China. However, Washington tried as much as possible to commit its allies to courses of action those allies regarded as wrong-headed, and, on many occasions, succeeded. The march to the Yalu River is one example.

Other limitations on hostilities were enforced not as concessions to allies, but in an effort to avoid engagement in a prolonged land war in Asia. "Hot pursuit" appears to be one exception to this generalization but one possible reason for the decision to drop "hot pursuit" may have stemmed from the massive Chinese commitment to land war in Korea. If "hot pursuit," which, incidentally, despite Washington comments to the contrary, had no foundation in international law,[29] had the objective of scaring the Chinese in order to prevent their commitment to land warfare in Korea, it could no longer serve that purpose once the Chinese commitment had become irrevocable.

One gets the feeling that Washington was torn between irreconcilable objectives. It was unwilling to take a course of action that would have avoided Chinese intervention. But, having forced Chinese intervention by its disregard for Chinese strategic interests, it was unwilling to follow a military course of action that would have been effective in defeating the Chinese. Undoubtedly, the reasons for refusing to extend hostilities further in Asia were sound. But then, the decision to occupy North Korea was unsound.

Apart from their own private beliefs, President Truman and Secretary of State Acheson had strong political motives for pursuing this schizophrenic policy. But the results were catastrophic, and these results were also predictable at the time.

The United States squandered its resources for years in a secondary theater of action. It brought dismay to its friends and allies. It engaged itself in an unrealistic drive for German rearmament that threatened the unity of the Atlantic powers. It lost prestige in Asia and laid the foundation for a series of defeats on that continent.

Moreover, rather than relieving the administration from political pressures, the indecisive warfare to which it committed itself only increased those pressures. Finally, the United States, under the Democratic administration, had got itself into such a mess that it could not end the Korean War either by political or military means.

Negotiations with the Chinese

The United States, for all practical purposes, ignored the Chinese in their march to the Yalu River. No serious effort was made to negotiate differences, or even directly to take soundings on the Chinese position.

After Chinese intervention and the rout of American forces in Korea, the Chinese became extremely stiff in their attitudes. Apparently believing that American forces could be forced off the peninsula, the Chinese were unwilling to negotiate on terms that would not guarantee them a seat in the United Nations. Perhaps the Chinese interpretation of American motivation was as extreme as American interpretation of Soviet motivation.

However, the Americans became even more adamant in defeat—although the extent of American military reverses and the virtual decision to evacuate Korea were unknown to most members of the United Nations.

Many interpretations of American policy in this period are possible.

Republican sources evidently believed that the administration was ready to "appease" and would perhaps even have given up the defense of Formosa.

However, the decision to label China an aggressor was taken by the administration in December. By the same date, it was also decided to give extended support to Formosa.

It is possible to regard the equivocal American attitude in the United Nations as evidence of an intention to retreat from these decisions under pressure from other nations. However, I believe that the United States instead had the intention only of giving sufficient "lip service" to allied and neutralist positions to appear reasonable.

If the United States flatly opposed efforts to negotiate, it would be overridden in the General Assembly. If, however, it reluctantly appeared willing to go along with negotiations, although under pressure from Congress to oppose negotiations, other United Nations members would be eager to so word the resolutions that American cooperation would be possible. But, in this case, the United States might be able to place into the resolutions conditions unacceptable to China.

I realize that this is a Machiavellian interpretation of American policy. But, although others are free to disagree, it is the interpretation that seems most reasonable to me.

Unless China was condemned before the United States evacuated the Korean peninsula, other nations might prove unwilling to pursue the struggle. The pressure for peace on terms acceptable to China would then become irresistible.

Therefore, the American strategy was to appear willing to negotiate while enunciating terms and taking positions that made negotiation impossible. As Sir Benegal Rau pointed out, a resolution first condemning China and then establishing a good offices committee to negotiate with China demonstrated a lack of seriousness.

The portion of the resolution calling upon China to withdraw its forces from Korea before negotiations was unrealistic. Negotiations would depend upon the military situation. If China withdrew its forces from Korea, the United States would be able, if it desired, to enforce settlement terms without regard for China's strategic interests. The Chinese could hardly be expected to permit the United States to make decisions affecting China's strategic position unilaterally. China could not afford to relinquish its bargaining position. Regardless of the real reasons for China's actions—and we may never know them—the practical consideration just mentioned is sufficient to account for Chinese rejection of the terms of the United Nations resolution.

The American attitude continued unchanged even after the tide of battle turned late in January, and it became clear that the United States could maintain itself on the Korean peninsula. Domestic politics accounts partly for the unchanged American position. But one must also suspect that high American officials believed that peace in Korea without condemnation of China would weaken American strategic interests in the Pacific by undercutting America's new policy of supporting Formosa.

If, on the one hand, China and the Soviet Union were viewed as inseparably united in a determination to engage in a major war effort, a "phony peace" that weakened America's strategic position in the Orient would give the Communist powers an unconscionable advantage. On the other hand, if peace were made after China was condemned as an aggressor, some justification for maintaining the American position in Formosa would be available.

This line of argument, it must be pointed out, is tenuous and speculative. It accounts rationally for some positions difficult to account for on a different basis.

On the other hand, domestic political pressures and an "ideological" point of view may also account for the same sequence of events. If American leaders really saw the condemnatory resolution as a moral necessity, their actions may also be explained. Such thinking, however, would have been extremely fuzzy.

American intervention logically rested upon the strategic necessity of encouraging other nations to believe that the United States would aid them in case of attack. Otherwise, American intervention would have been a strategic and political monstrosity.

On moral grounds, the American decision to unify Korea by force had little justification. Moreover, it has never been recognized as immoral for a great nation to protect its own strategic interests by force if necessary. China had given full warning that she intended to do so, and the United States had no one else to blame if it ignored this warning.

Nevertheless, it must be admitted, such fuzzy thinking is a possibility, especially when those who make the decisions completely insulate themselves from alternate points of view. Particularly given the nature of the Republican attack upon the secretary of state, Acheson may have been eager to demonstrate his "Americanism."

Finally, the condemnation of China by the UN weakened rather than strengthened that organization. Ultimately, it was a humiliation for the world organization to negotiate an armistice from a position of equality with a nation it had condemned as an aggressor.

VII

The Big Scare
(1955)

The North Korean aggression touched off a big scare in official Washington. Chinese intervention in November convinced administration leaders that China was a willing puppet of the Soviet Union. The unreasonable fear that the Communist powers were prepared to launch world war grew to tremendous proportions, surpassing the war scare of March 1948, following the Communist coup in Czechoslovakia.

Consequently, the United States began to reassess its global strategy. Two of the major items reassessed were military policy in the North Atlantic Treaty Organization (NATO) and German rearmament. As the discussion will demonstrate, these items were closely interlinked. Moreover, it would be inaccurate to assert that the conclusions to which the United States came in the latter portion of 1950 represented a complete break with previous thinking on the subjects.

The policies adopted with regard to NATO and German rearmament had been advocated previously by important sources within the administration and by important sources in the opposition party. These policies did not represent a complete break with past policy. Nevertheless—foreshadowed though they may have been—these policies would not have been adopted at the time, or perhaps ever, had it not been for the big scare of 1950.

The Military Build-up

Military aid to Western nations, the North Atlantic Treaty Organization, rearmament efforts, and the enlistment of uncommitted nations in the free-world bloc were objectives of American foreign policy predating the Korean hostilities. The war scare of March 1948, following the Czechoslovakian coup, convinced Western strategic planners of the need for an organization such as the North Atlantic Treaty Organization, which, when activated, would serve to defend Western Europe against external Communist attack, internal Communist coups, and lack of morale resulting from European military weakness in relation to Communist military strength.

Nevertheless, the scope of these efforts, the timetable according to which they were implemented, the development of a unified military command for the North Atlantic Treaty Organization, and American ground force commitments to the unified command were all affected by the outbreak of hostilities in Korea. Except for the aggression in Korea or a similar event, it is probable that the scope of these efforts would not have been as great, and that particular important elements, such as the unified command in the North Atlantic Treaty Organization, probably would not have been adopted.

The North Atlantic Treaty Organization's military committee and standing group began discussions in Washington in October 1949.[1] As early as December 1, 1949, the twelve nations signatory to the North Atlantic pact reached unanimous agreement on a general plan to defend themselves against possible Soviet aggression.[2]

If approved by President Truman, it was announced, more than a billion dollars of American military aid would be released for Europe in addition to $900 million distributed under other provisions. It was not disclosed whether the five Brussels pact signatories—Great Britain, France, Holland, Belgium, and Luxembourg—would have the final say on European strategy, as Great Britain wanted, or whether this authority would be given to the twelve states joined in the North Atlantic Treaty Organization, as the United States, supported by France, desired. Underlying Great Britain's concern was the fact that the Brussels pact pledged its signators to military action if one of them were attacked, while the North Atlantic pact only provided that each of the signators would "take such actions as it deems necessary" under the circumstances.[3] Since the Brussels pact powers bore the more onerous commitment, Great Britain felt they should have the greater influence upon the disposition of forces.

According to reports, military planners did not feel that there was a definite time by which their plans would have to be completed. The plan took account of the possibility of aggression at any time. It was also influenced by the consideration that American atomic superiority was becoming less decisive as the Soviet stockpile of atomic bombs grew, and that it would be necessary to overcome the existing superiority of Soviet ground forces. It was stated that the question of a high command was deferred for later consideration.

Although not confirmed officially, it was believed that the general strategic plan that was adopted rested upon four propositions: (1) the United States would assume responsibility, in case of hostilities, to use the atomic bomb in an air offensive against the aggressor and that it would possibly have an obligation to aid the ground campaign; (2) continental Europe, France in particular, would be obliged to supply the ground forces to blunt the enemy offensive; (3) the United States, British, and French fleets would secure control of the seas; and (4) Western Europe would supply the aircraft for short-range attack bombardment and air defense. Pierre Montel, the French representative to NATO, estimated that the West would need sixty to eighty divisions for defense purposes, half of which would have to be armored.

During December, the military aid agreements circulated by the United States were reported to have as one of their objectives that of governing the shipment of war materiel or war potential to a country outside the pact. Although not named, it was understood that the Soviet Union was the object of this policy.

In addition, other American conditions were: (1) that in return for military aid, the receiving countries would aid the United States in stockpiling strategic materiel; (2) that the receiving countries would pledge themselves to make the most effective use of the equipment and supplies and would permit an American mission to observe their use of the aid; (3) that the receiving countries would pledge not to use the aid for any purpose other than that of the North Atlantic pact, unless such purpose was agreed to by the United States; (4) that aid items would not be exported from recipient countries without American agreement; and, (5) that the receiving countries would pledge not to pass on to other countries any secret weapons supplied by the United States.

On December 19, 1949, the United States, Great Britain, and Canada made arrangements to consider the standardization of military items used by their armed forces to insure, in time of necessity, that there would be no material or technical obstacles to armed cooperation. There were also reasons of economy for this decision. It was understood that standardization would not include atomic bombs or other specialized weapons.

Toward the end of December, the United States reached agreement with eight of its allies, including France, Belgium, the Netherlands, Great Britain, Luxembourg, Norway, Denmark, and Italy, for the distribution of Mutual Defense aid. Great Britain won the right to send its own equipment outside the North Atlantic Treaty area while receiving United States arms for the common defense of the North Atlantic area. British commitments in Asia and Brussels Pact matters were understood to be responsible for the concession.

The first Mutual Defense Assistance Program agreement, however, was not signed by a North Atlantic Treaty Organization member. On January 26, 1950, the Republic of Korea signed a bilateral pact under terms of an appropriation bill extending $27 million to Iran, Korea, and the Philippines. Not until January 27, after additional details were ironed out, did the eight specified North Atlantic Treaty Organization signatories sign bilateral aid agreements. The United States announced that military aid to these European nations would be speeded, and it was expected that the bulk of the material would begin to move by March. Three hundred million dollars of the aid was to be given to the French army. Submarines and various types of aircraft were included among the aid items. During March, an Iranian mission came to Washington to negotiate a bilateral aid agreement.

By late March, the Military Committee of the North Atlantic Treaty Organization had turned the general strategic concept of December into a detailed plan.[4] Veteran military officers declared they were amazed by the speed of the progress. It was believed, however, that the proposed defense system would require greater financial outlays by most of the twelve participants and that the heaviest burden would fall upon the United States. On the last day of March, it was reported that the United States was seeking Spanish air bases. Meanwhile, it was learned that the United States was resisting European pressure to establish an overall military command with an American in charge.

In early April, controversy broke out over John Strachey, the formerly radical British secretary for war, whom the United States did not trust with defense secrets. As a result of the controversy, it was learned that elaborate plans had been made by the North Atlantic Treaty Organization to screen personnel and to withhold information. Only the United States had complete information on Atlantic pact defense; Britain had somewhat less; France still less; and other countries only as much as they needed to carry out their roles in the plans. Steps had also been taken to remove secret information from the files of member governments if Communists entered the government, either as the result of a coup or through electoral victory.

On April 14, General Omar Bradley stated that the United States might have to scrap its historic theory of balanced military forces to concentrate on a greater air force and navy as a consequence of its assigned role in North Atlantic Treaty Organization strategic plans. He noted that closer military integration in the North Atlantic Treaty Organization would require relinquishment of a small bit of American sovereignty. General Bradley described the proposed 1951 defense budget of $13 billion as a proper base on which to build, and stated that he did not believe the Soviet Union would initiate a war unless the United States was so weak that it invited attack.

During mid-April, the Brussels-pact countries held meetings and agreed upon tentative steps for the pooling of resources, but they had difficulty in finding a formula for the joint financing of defense. They presented a list of their deficiencies to Lewis Douglas, the American ambassador to England and head of the United States mission for the coordination of military aid to Europe. It was understood that the Brussels powers hoped American aid would eliminate the difficulties of joint financing. Meanwhile, Washington was reported to be cool to France's Georges Bidault's plan for an Atlantic High Council to unify the defense, political, and economic policies of the North Atlantic Treaty nations. The United States felt that economic and political integration should be handled separately, and, in any event, they felt that the United States should not be bound.

On April 26, Defense Secretary Louis Johnson proposed that the 1950 defense budget be increased by $350 million because of Soviet atomic progress.

On May 3, 1950, it was reported that France would inform the United States that only immediate American aid to Indochina would save that country from the Communists, that France would make a proposal for the unification of basic European industries, and that the North Atlantic Treaty Organization should be reinforced by creating a permanent directing body with broad powers for coordinating the military and economic aspects of defense.

On May 11, Turkey expressed the hope that its request for inclusion in the North Atlantic Treaty Organization would be considered at the forthcoming London Foreign Ministers conference (United States, Britain, and France) . On May 14, the North Atlantic Treaty Organization Foreign Ministers meetings got under way. Reports from London showed that the Atlantic Pact countries were spending $20 billion yearly on defense, 75 percent of which was being borne by the United States.

The Atlantic Council meeting of Foreign Ministers established a permanent council of deputies to translate decisions into detailed plans for action, agreed on the functions of the organization, issued directives for future committee work, agreed on mutual assistance for integrated defense activities, made plans for the economic utilization of available forces and materiel, and established an ocean-shipping planning board.

Secretary of State Acheson stated that these accomplishments demonstrated great progress by the North Atlantic Treaty Organization. It was understood that the twelve nations also agreed to the principle of balanced collective forces rather than balanced national forces. A permanent board of strategy to correlate economic and defense activities of the member states, was established. It was to be headed by an American, according to the reports.

On May 19, Secretary Dean Acheson and Foreign Minister Ernest Bevin assured Greece, Turkey, and Iran that aggressive action against any of the three would be viewed gravely by the Western powers. It was doubted, however, that they would be included in the North Atlantic Treaty Organization for obvious geographic reasons. Secretary Acheson gave a specific pledge to help the associated states of Laos, Cambodia, Vietnam, and France "in their efforts to meet the threats to security of the region." On May 26, the United States announced that it would station jet fighters in England and would also set up permanent bomber bases in that country.

In May, the North Atlantic Treaty Organization powers had fourteen divisions stationed on the continent and fewer than 1,000 planes of various categories. There was no unified command for these forces. The Soviet Union had twenty-five divisions stationed in occupied or satellite territory. These were supported by more than 6,000 aircraft and the bulk of the Russian war machine in the Soviet Union. According to Field Marshall Montgomery, Commander-in-Chief of the Western Union forces: "As things stand today and in the foreseeable future, there would be scenes of appalling and indescribable confusion in Western Europe if we were ever attacked by the Russians."

On June 1, 1950, President Truman asked Congress to authorize the expenditure of $1.2 billion for the second year of the Mutual Defense Assistance Program (for the year beginning July 1, 1950). These requests included $1 billion for the North Atlantic Treaty area; $120 million for

Greece and Turkey; $27.5 million for Iran, the Philippines, and Korea; and $75 million for the general use of Nationalist China.

Nevertheless, Truman stated at his news conference that the world was closer to peace than it had been for the last five years. On the other hand, Secretary of State Acheson told the Senate Committees on Foreign Relations and the Armed Services that the cost of assistance to the North Atlantic Treaty Organization powers might rise above the $1 billion requested unless there was "a very considerable change in the international climate and actions of certain other powers."

Early in June, it was reported from Washington that the North Atlantic Treaty powers based their defense plans for Western Europe upon two assumptions: (1) that Western superiority in atomic weapons would deter the Soviet Union from engaging in acts of aggression for several years; and (2) that by the time the Russian stockpile of atomic weapons was sufficient for a major war, the West would have developed defensive weapons of such scope that the Soviet Union would not dare to attack. These weapons, it was hoped, would nullify the superiority of the Soviet Union in tanks and artillery.

On June 22, the Senate Committees on Foreign Relations and Armed Services issued a joint report declaring that the day of neutrality, anywhere in the world, had passed. They declared that "the Mutual Defense Assistance Program must be carried to a successful conclusion if the world is to maintain peace under conditions which will permit men to live free."

As a result of the Korean hostilities, the Mutual Defense Assistance Program requested by the administration was passed unanimously by the United States Senate on June 30. Some former opponents of the measure even criticized it as inadequate. On July 11, the House Committee on Foreign Affairs approved the program unanimously[5] and prepared a report calling for the formation of a Pacific pact similar in design and intent to the North Atlantic Treaty Organization.

As a consequence of the action in Korea, it was announced on July 14 that Secretary of State Acheson would ask the other members of the North Atlantic Treaty Organization to increase the size and pace of their rearmament program. On July 23, it was reported from London that the Korean hostilities were responsible for a prompt shift in the policy of the Atlantic community from economic recovery to military defense.

British War Secretary Strachey declared that such acts of aggression inevitably compelled the Western nations to consider increasing military preparations by diverting resources from reconstruction tasks. President

Truman asked Congress for an additional $10 billion in arms expenditures, making defense expenditures total about 10 percent of the American national income. It was understood that President Truman would supplement his new $10-billion program with a program of conditional dollar aid to finance arms production in British, French, and other European factories.

On July 24, 1950, following the outbreak of war in Korea, the North Atlantic deputies met to map an intensive armament effort. It was stated that the assumption that the West would have at least five years to arm to meet the Soviet threat had been invalidated by the aggression in Korea, and that the rearmament timetable would have to be speeded up greatly. Manpower requirements would also have to be raised. On July 25, France proposed a common defense fund to which each Atlantic pact nation would contribute in proportion to its income.

On July 26, it was reported that the task of the deputies was to find some way to raise, train, and equip a Western allied force of thirty-six divisions by 1952 or 1953. It was thought that the force should include 20 armored divisions and sixteen mechanized infantry and infantry divisions. The next day, Turkey repeated its request for inclusion in the North Atlantic Treaty Organization. On July 29, United States officials stated that some way would have to be found to fuse Marshall Plan funds and machinery with the military aid of the United States to Europe.

The French agreed to increase their arms budget by 800 million francs, but this increase was not to take effect until the following year. Britain proposed a £100 million increase in its arms budget and also a diversion of manpower and resources from civilian to military needs. Nevertheless, suspicions were expressed in Washington that European countries were not making their best efforts. It was stated that the American government required proof that the Western European governments really believed that armament should have priority over recovery. Meanwhile, European countries were reported to be hoping that American military aid would approach the lend-lease scale.

On August 1, President Truman asked Congress for $4 billion more in Mutual Defense Assistance Program funds. $3.5 billion was requested for the North Atlantic area; $193 million for Greece, Turkey, and Iran; and $303 million for the Philippines and southeastern Asia.

On August 1, it was announced that creation of a full-time high command was being considered by the North Atlantic Treaty Organization planners to integrate the various activities of the alliance's many military agencies.

The same day, it was announced that Turkey would make a formal request for inclusion in the Atlantic pact. It was understood that the Turkish plea would receive more favorable consideration in the United States than it had in the past because of the Turkish contribution to the United Nations' efforts in Korea.

Also on August 1, France asked for a troop pool, containing proportionate contributions from Atlantic pact states, for the defense of Western Europe. It was understood that one implication of the French plan involved an increase in American forces on the continent. On August 2, Secretary of Defense Johnson disclosed that $2 billion of tanks, planes, and artillery would be sent to Europe by the United States to guard against a "mechanized assault" by the Soviet Union.

On August 3, the British government announced that defense spending would total £3.4 billion over the next three years, compared with £780 million the year preceding the Korean War. It was stated that heavy dollar expenditures would make the program impossible without American aid. On August 4, North Atlantic Treaty Organization deputies decided to ask the member states to raise forty divisions for the North Atlantic Treaty Organization.

On August 5, Greece informed France of its desire to join the North Atlantic Treaty Organization.

During August, North Atlantic Treaty Organization members increased their projected defense expenditures in varying amounts. On August 7, France agreed to raise fifteen divisions. On August 8, France suggested an international loan to be given to help finance France's armament efforts. The same day, John Sherman Cooper, consultant to the State Department, called the measures taken by the other Atlantic pact countries "cautious and inadequate."

Also on that day, French Premier André Pleven stated that fifty divisions would be needed to defend Western Europe, and he asked that the United States and Great Britain contribute their proportionate share. On August 12, NATO military planners stated that six American divisions were a minimum requirement for the defense of Western Europe. On August 12, two American destroyers were turned over to France. On August 16, the military chiefs of the ten Atlantic pact nations met in Washington to plan naval defense in the event of war.

By August 20, it was reported that the United States was still dissatisfied with European defense efforts and would press for more urgent action. The question of the use of German manpower was beginning to receive greater emphasis in American thinking. During the second series of meetings of the Atlantic deputies in London, it was reported that there was a wide discrepancy between what the military planners thought necessary for defense and what the various nations were prepared to pledge.

On August 27, three days of Atlantic pact maneuvers ended amid reports of successful defense against the "invading" forces. On September 2, France lengthened the period of its universal military service from twelve to eighteen months. The same day, it was indicated in London that an American would be sought as commander-in-chief of the Atlantic pact forces. On September 3, Massachusetts Republican Senator Henry Cabot Lodge proposed that the United States offer to send more troops to Europe on the condition that the Atlantic pact allies take realistic steps to increase their armed forces. He suggested that one additional American division be sent to Europe for each ten divisions raised by the European nations. On September 4 the Atlantic Pact deputies approved a program granting top priority to the production of fifty critical defense items.

On September 9, President Truman approved "substantial" increases in American forces in Europe in the "sincere expectation" that other North Atlantic Treaty powers would "keep full step." This commitment greatly increased confidence in Western European capitals. The next day, Secretary of State Acheson declared that the major American effort would be in Europe. If strong Atlantic pact forces were created, he said, and if those forces were "united, balanced, collective forces—strong, well-equipped, able, and ready to deter aggression, then problems all over the world take on a different shape. Such forces alone will change problems in Greece, in Turkey, in Yugoslavia, in the Middle East and the Far East."

The secretary went on to state that he doubted that the Chinese would intervene in the Korean war and warned China that such intervention would be "sheer madness" because China faced "a great cloud from the north, Russian penetration," the aim of which was to dominate the areas of China bordering the Soviet Union. He stated that his emphasis upon Europe did not imply the "writing off" of Asia. "We do not think that any part of Asia is lost to the free world. We still believe that the Chinese are going to be Chinese before they are going to be Communists. We still believe that the people of Indochina will see this menace [of Soviet Russia] which is coming toward them. We think that the people of the Philippines, and the people of Indonesia, and the people of Japan, and the people of Korea see that menace. We are helping all those countries."

On September 13, Australian Minister of External Affairs Percy Spender proposed to President Truman the formation of a Pacific pact similar to the North Atlantic pact. The same day in New York, the Council of Foreign Ministers of the North Atlantic pact agreed on the urgent necessity of creating a unified Western force to meet the menace of Russian invasion. On September 18, it was reported that Turkey was disappointed because the foreign ministers had not accepted Turkey's bid for membership in the North Atlantic Treaty Organization.

On September 24, formal agreement on a unified army was reached amid reports that the post would be offered to General Dwight Eisenhower. A force of fifty divisions was suggested, according to reports. It was agreed: (1) that the integrated force would be organized under the North Atlantic Council; (2) that it would be under a supreme commander with wide, delegated authority for the training of national contingents in peace and war; (3) that the supreme commander would be supported by an international staff representing all contributing nations; (4) that pending the appointment of the supreme commander there should be a chief of staff with responsibility for training and organization; and (5) that the standing group of the Atlantic Treaty—the United States, Great Britain, and France—would be responsible for higher strategic direction.

On October 3, Premier Sofoklis Venizelos of Greece said that, as a consequence of the refusal of the North Atlantic Treaty Organization to accept Turkey's bid for membership, an effort was being made, with Western support, to create a Mediterranean pact, including as members Greece, Turkey, and other nations in the Mediterranean area. Nevertheless, there was to be some degree of association between Greece and Turkey and the North Atlantic Treaty Organization. The North Atlantic Council had suggested to Turkey in a verbal note on September 19 that it associate itself with such phases of North Atlantic Treaty Organization military planning as affected the Mediterranean area. It was understood on October 4 that a similar suggestion had been made to Greece. Both nations accepted early in October.

On October 8, the Defense Department announced that its expenditures for tanks, guns, and other major equipment items had increased 500 percent since the outbreak of hostilities in Korea, and that the outlay for the North Atlantic Treaty Organization had gone up 400 percent in the same period.

On October 19, former President Herbert Hoover urged cessation of aid to Europe until Europe demonstrated its will to oppose Communist aggression. To send ten American divisions to Europe was to send them to slaughter, he said, unless Europe first provided ten times that number of divisions.

In late October, links between NATO and the Organization for European Economic Cooperation (OEEC) were created, thus strengthening defense efforts in Europe. It was expected later that month that a unified army for the West would be in existence by May 1951. Because of disagreements with France over the utilization of German manpower, however, President Truman refused to name the Supreme Commander of the unified force until the issues were resolved.

On November 1, in an effort to submerge the issue of German manpower, the French pledged to supply twenty divisions for the North Atlantic Treaty Organization. On December 6, the French decided to compromise with the American position on the utilization of German manpower. The same day, it was reported that President Truman would ask the new Congress for $5 billion more in arms aid for other free nations resisting Communist aggression.

On December 13, the military committee of NATO completed agreement on the details of the unified defense force. Four days later, Secretary of State Acheson enplaned for Brussels for NATO meetings designed to complete arrangements for an integrated Western defense force. It was reported that he would also prod the other Western nations on their armament efforts and confer with Britain and France to discuss methods of opposing Communist pressures in Asia. These arrangements were completed on December 18, and the Council requested the president of the United States to appoint an American officer as supreme commander. The president appointed General Eisenhower the same day.

The next day, it was announced that key units of the American and Canadian armies would remain in North America, that the North American continent would not be weakened in reinforcing the command in Europe. In Washington, President Truman announced that more men would be sent to Europe as soon as possible. The next day steps were taken to merge Western Union (Brussels) defense forces with North Atlantic Treaty Organization forces. On December 21, General J. Lawton Collins stated that additional American troops would be sent to Europe before July 1. Early in January 1951, General Eisenhower said that sacrifices would be the price of freedom, and he urged European nations to match the sincerity of the United States in devoting their resources to the common defense.

At the same time, several prominent senators began to question the legal power of the president to send troops to Europe under North Atlantic Treaty commitments without the consent of Congress. A vigorous debate continued for several months. The president insisted upon his authority as commander-in-chief to send American forces where he chose, but did agree to consult Congress in the future. Moreover, administration supporters backed a Senate resolution extending approval to the troops already promised, although denying that this imposed any obligation by the president to consult.

On January 15, Great Britain promised to double its forces on the continent, raising the total to four infantry divisions by July 1. As a result of Eisenhower's visits to the capitals of the North Atlantic Treaty Organization powers, it was reported that he would be provided with six additional divisions by the end of the year, raising the divisions at his command to a total of eighteen (including four additional American divisions). On January 29, General Eisenhower appointed Field Marshal Sir Bernard Montgomery as deputy supreme commander and General Alphonse Pierre Juin, of France, as commander of the Central European Command, the two highest posts as his disposal.

The shifts in American policy with respect to NATO, rearmament, military aid to friendly governments, and the expansion of American commitments to Formosa and other Asian areas after the outbreak of the Korean hostilities can be viewed as merely changes in the pace of a foreign policy that predated this event. Nevertheless, they reflected profound changes with respect to American conceptions of the urgency of the Soviet threat, the risks involved in the measures being taken to meet that threat, the scope of the defensive measures required, and the diversion of resources necessitated.

Despite the virtually unanimous support given to some of the defense measures, a bitter partisan debate attended others. Herbert Hoover advocated a hemisphere defense policy because of the "unwillingness" of European countries to take adequate measures for their own defense. Ohio Republican leader Taft accused the president of the usurpation of authority in sending troops to Korea and Western Europe without Congressional approval. Moreover, Taft claimed that plans for a unified Western army would only provoke the Russians:

> If [the Russians] think the allies are gaining on them too rapidly, they can always begin the war. However defensive and pacific our intentions, to them the building up of this force must look like aggression when it is completed. Someone has invented the theory that the

Russians have a particular time-table under which they were at one
time looking to attack in 1955, then in 1952 and now perhaps in 1951.
I know of no evidence for any such conclusion. If they have an intention to attack, they will obviously attack before the Atlantic Pact forces
are built up, and it will take at least three years to build them up. Why
should they wait? If they have no intention to attack, then we don't
need the armed forces, at least in such coordinated form and in such
close proximity to Russia as to seem to threaten an attack.

Senator Taft also objected vigorously to the commitment to fight a land
war in Europe for which the United States did not have sufficient manpower resources. He favored reliance upon the navy and air force to deter
the Soviet Union.

Nevertheless, the opposition could only harass the administration
in the determination of the major lines of foreign policy, particularly
because influential members of the opposition party, such as senators
Lodge and Knowland, often supported the administration on crucial
issues.

From Washington, it was reported early in 1951 that military plans
were not being based on the assumption that general war would break
out in 1951. If that assumption were accepted, it was pointed out, a military budget of $150 billion and the mobilization of 15 million men
would be called for. The major debate within the administration was
over the question of whether a 3.5 million- or a 6 million-man armed
force should be called for in the fiscal year of 1951. Later in 1951, the
lower figure was accepted by the administration. The danger believed
most serious by administration planners was that the Kremlin would decide, through China, to launch a drive to eliminate the Western powers
from their remaining footholds in the continent of Asia, particularly in
Indochina and other southeast Asian areas.

To meet this threat, military aid was given to Formosa. Over $300
million in ECA aid for a two-year period was earmarked for French Indochina in November 1950. Moreover, the French were encouraged by the
United States government to enlist nationalist sentiment in Indochina
by granting greater internal autonomy to the associated states of Vietnam, Laos, and Cambodia. American activity was stepped up throughout
the southeast Asian area in 1950 and 1951; by April 1951, President Truman had become convinced of the need for a Pacific pact similar to the
Atlantic pact and proved receptive to the overtures in that direction by
Australia and New Zealand that led to the ANZUS Pact, which included
Australia, New Zealand, and the United States.

In his message to Congress on January 15, 1951, President Truman proposed a $72-billion preparedness budget. This was an increase of 78 percent over the previous fiscal year. The president asked for $222.8 billion in new contractual authority and $92.4 billion in future spending authority. The defense budget of $13 billion for 1950 was increased to $54 billion for 1951. Defense officials wanted to provide for a 3.5 million-man armed force, the build-up of the air force to more than eighty-four groups, and the operation of more than 500 combat navy vessels. In terms of obligational authority, it was the largest military budget since the wartime year of 1944. It was estimated that there would be a deficit of $16.5 billion, and the president stated his intention to ask for new taxes to absorb the gap.

By far the greatest revolution in American policy, however, was the commitment of American military manpower in peacetime to the ground defense of Europe and within a unified military command on the continent of Europe. Moreover, the Mutual Defense Assistance Program aid was comparable only to lend-lease aid previous to American entry into World War II. But then, the war had been raging in Europe before the measure had been adopted. Although the Mutual Defense Assistance Program aid, unlike the unified command, predated the Korean War, its scope and size increased greatly as a result of that incident.

This policy of unifying and building up the armed strength of Europe undoubtedly carried the risk of provoking the Soviet Union, as pointed out by Senator Taft. However, the administration considered the risk a calculated and acceptable one. This was brought out by New Hampshire Republican Senator Styles Bridges' questioning of General Marshall:

> *Senator Bridges:* ... if Russia needs the skills and resources and industry of Europe, and we are not going to be fully prepared until 1953, is Russia therefore going to permit us to arm Europe, and in light of the facts, isn't our present program for Europe much more provocative than, for instance, the bombing of the bases in Red China?
>
> *Secretary of Defense Marshall:* I agree with you as to the hazards we have accepted in Western Europe. The hazards were inescapable there unless we just abandoned Germany and let the other part go. We had to take them.
>
> There is ... Soviet concern as to the situation in Western Europe, but I don't think for a minute their advisers consider that we are preparing for an offensive campaign against them.... The situation ... is different in Korea, because there it is not Soviet ground that is occupied, but territory to which they attach undoubtedly great importance.

For whatever reason, the strengthening of Western defenses did not impel the Soviet Union to take action of a military nature.

American policy also influenced the policies of the other North Atlantic Treaty Organization signatories. As a consequence of the Korean hostilities, the American aid program was revised to give priority to military rather than reconstruction aid. Loans for armament production and the later policy of off-shore procurement undoubtedly had economic effects in Europe, but these may very well have been deflationary effects.

Moreover, American pressure was applied strongly to persuade the other NATO powers to devote higher percentages of their national incomes to military efforts. These policies had political and economic consequences for the countries involved that cannot be summarized briefly. Because European nations had smaller national incomes than the United States, the diversion of roughly similar percentages of the national product to the military program represented greater deprivations in terms of their standards of living. Little attention was given to the political and economic consequences of this fact by the Washington planners because of their conception of the urgency of the situation, and also because it would have been difficult politically for them to extend full American support for European defense if the American public were not convinced that Western European countries were making a maximum effort to help themselves.

German Rearmament

No American objective was more closely related to the Korean "police action" than the decision to rearm Germany. Although German rearmament was advocated by some in official positions before the outbreak of hostilities in Korea, the compelling reasons responsible for the decision were connected organically to that event and illustrate the global interlocking of foreign policy problems.

The importance of Western Germany in NATO defense preparations has long been realized. Without that area, the strategic plans of NATO planners would lack sufficient depth for defensive maneuver. Original Western plans, however, were for the NATO planners to use German territory but not German armed forces.

Although General Lucius Clay advocated the use of German troops, Field Marshal Sir William J. Slim, chief of the Imperial staff of the British Army, took a more cautious attitude. In December 1949, he characterized Germany as "the most valuable and the most dangerous" nation in Western Europe. He said that whether Germany should be rearmed was a matter for the politicians and statesmen, but that, if he were instructed to rearm Germany, he could do an effective job of it.

Although not advocating the rearmament of Germany, Pierre Montel, chairman of the Committee of National Defense of the French General Assembly, estimated that the Soviet Union had 150 divisions on an active footing. But because of defense needs elsewhere, it would not be able to use more than 80 divisions in an attack upon the West. Montel thought that a Soviet attack could be repelled by a defense force of 60 to 80 divisions provided that half of these were armored. A force of that magnitude would not have been easy to provide.

American Secretary of State Dean Acheson insisted that American policy had not undergone any change with respect to the arming of Western Germany and stressed continued official opposition to such a course. On December 20, 1949, the West German government asked the Western Allied High Commissioners to inform it officially what plans, if any, were being made by the NATO powers to defend Germany in the event of war with the Soviet Union. The Bonn regime expressed fear that only a holding operation would be made on the Elbe and that a serious Western defense effort would not be made short of the Rhine. The Bonn government, however, did not indicate that it desired to rearm in order to defend its territory. Such a suggestion, of course, would have been explosive politically.

By March 1950, General Pierre Billotte, who had recently resigned as French representative on the Military Committee of the United Nations said: "[In the event of war with the Soviet Union] we wish to fight as far as possible to the east. We cannot do this without a certain rearmament of Germany. But France and the other signatories of the Atlantic Pact must be provided for first." However, his statement did not reflect official French thinking. The same month, opposition leader Winston Churchill stated in Parliament: "I say without hesitation that the effective defense of European frontiers cannot be achieved if the German contribution is excluded from the thoughts of those who are responsible."

Nevertheless, at a meeting of the Chiefs of Staff of the NATO powers in March, N. E. Halaby, assistant for military affairs to Secretary of Defense Louis Johnson, said that any initiative for discussion of the German problem must come from the nations bordering on Germany. It was understood that the chiefs had agreed tacitly not to discuss the German problem, and that, if the defense ministers did discuss the issue, the discussions would be only informal. Johnson later implied that the issue never arose at the meetings.

Early in April 1950, Secretary of State Acheson proclaimed that the American position on the rearming of Germany and the dismantling of German plants was unchanged. He did express the hope, however, that the Western German Federal Republic would accept the invitation to become a member of the Council of Europe.

Shortly before the May meetings of the Three Powers and the Atlantic Treaty Powers, Acheson, when asked whether it was true that proposals for the inclusion of Germany in the political and economic machinery of NATO were being studied, replied that all kinds of ideas are being studied. Reports were emphasized from France, which indicated that if Germany were brought within the Atlantic Council, it must not be included within the military framework of NATO. France feared that a European organization, not including Britain, would be dominated by Germany.

Meanwhile, pressure from Washington for the integration of Western Germany with other Western European countries, short of the rearmament of Germany, was increasing according to reports. On May 2, 1950, State Department official Francis H. Russell stated: "The [North Atlantic Foreign Ministers] who will meet at London know that Germany cannot be kept weak and in quarantine without gravely impairing the health and strength of all Western Europe. They know, too, that Germany's neighbors are too close to the painful past to be able to view with calm the prospect of uncontrolled and renewed German strength. We are faced, more urgently than ever, with the task of making plans to foster the growth of true democracy in Germany and progressively taking the free German peoples into partnership."

However, at the meeting of the Atlantic Powers, the Foreign Ministers agreed to postpone discussion of Germany. It was felt that, if German rearmament were desired, it would be better to invite Germany to join a strong functioning organization at a time when selective use of the German potential could be made by that organization.

Early in June, General Omar Bradley expressed the view that Western Germany was strongly anti-Soviet and said he regarded this as a source of strength for the Western democratic nations in their dealings with the Soviet Union. He also refused to discuss a recent request of the Bonn government for a police force on the ground that the subject was a political one.

In late July, just prior to the first meetings of the North Atlantic Council deputies, a French spokesman, referring to reports that the

United States would like to discuss the subject of German rearmament, stated that he did not see how the subject could be placed upon the agenda. He declared: "The position of France has not changed either with respect to the impossibility of reconstituting, in any form whatsoever, a German army, or with respect to the necessity of maintaining international control on the Ruhr and the limitations and interdictions imposed on heavy German industry."

An American briefing officer outlined the assumptions underlying American strategic reasoning during the preparatory conferences before the formal meetings of the North Atlantic Council. He stated that, when the Foreign Ministers of the Atlantic pact powers had met in May, it was assumed that the Western nations would have at least five years to organize their defenses against a Communist assault, that the Soviet Union and its satellites would not attack until they thought themselves fully prepared to gain an assured victory. That assumption had been negated by the attack of the North Korean forces. Korea convinced Western strategists that aggression could be expected at any time, and that, therefore, the Western powers must revise their strategic timetable.

On July 25, French spokesmen indicated a revision of their earlier position that German industry must not be permitted to manufacture materiel of war. They now proposed that Germany manufacture arms that would be used by the North Atlantic powers to defend the West.

Meanwhile, an anonymous American spokesman pointed out that the real job facing the Council was to raise thirty-six divisions by 1952 or 1953, at the latest, to defend Western Europe. The Korean fighting, he said, had emphasized the importance of ground troops; Europe's defense could no longer be viewed as a question of American dollars and increased arms production in Europe. Manpower was the crucial item. The critical defense area was West Germany. The Western Allies, he said, had only 7 understrength divisions facing an estimated 200,000 Russian-armed and trained East German "policemen," backed by a potential Russian strength of 175 combat divisions. Larger forces were needed in West Germany to guard against a German "civil war." France was tied down in Indochina, but might increase her European strength from 5 to 20 divisions. The Scandinavian countries might provide a small number of divisions. But the 40 million people in West Germany might some day provide up to 25 divisions for European defense. He noted, however, that there were still no plans to use that manpower in the foreseeable future.

Meanwhile, in response to domestic murmurings, Jules Moch,

French Defense Minister, was telling the National Assembly that there could be no question of a French infantry, British navy, and American air force to defend Europe. France expected Britain and the United States also to make ground force commitments for the defense of Europe. Nevertheless, by early August 1950, France indicated her resolution by promising to equip fifteen divisions, with American aid, as her share of the Western rearmament program. It was pointed out that this effort would not have been possible except for the firmness America was showing in Korea and the confidence this created in France concerning the intentions of the United States.

However, the effort did not appear sufficient to John Sherman Cooper of the American delegation, who warned that European plans for rearmament were "cautious and inadequate." On August 11, the Consultative Assembly of the Council of Europe recommended the creation of a European army on a motion by Winston Churchill, ex-prime minister of Great Britain, thus introducing a novel element into proposals for Western defense.

On August 15, an American spokesman gave qualified approval to French rearmament suggestions. He noted, however, that France's raising of fifteen divisions was contingent upon Britain and the United States each stationing five divisions in Europe. He pointed out that, while the United States was fighting a war in Korea, it could not promise to divert that much manpower to the continent of Europe, particularly given the limited size of the American army.

On August 19, John Sherman Cooper said that the United States must show firmly its intentions to take part in the defense of Europe in the initial stage of the assault, should one occur. "This means that the United States and Great Britain must commit men and equipment before such an assault begins. . . ." Although he did not make any recommendations for the rearming of Germany, he did state, "It is inevitable and moral that Germany be given the opportunity to defend herself."

Thus, the United States felt that it had to commit its ground forces to Europe for successful defense and for morale purposes, even though it was short of troops in Korea. Moreover, the United States was evidently beginning to believe that successful ground defense implied a German manpower contribution and was beginning to hint that its commitment to European defense was contingent upon European acceptance of the German contribution.

Meanwhile, an American spokesman in Western Germany stated flatly that Germany would play a role in the defense plans of the West and added that the Germans would take part in the decision as to what their role should be. He also stated that the three Western Allied High Commissioners were studying the proposal of German Chancellor Conrad Adenauer that a West German defense force, equal in size, training, and equipment to that of the "police force" in the Soviet Zone of Germany, be created.

In Washington, it was reported that the possibility of permitting German volunteers to serve in the coordinated Western defense forces was being considered. In Germany, the Social Democratic Party leaders attacked the Adenauer proposals for armed forces.

On September 6, Secretary of State Acheson stated that it was important to find an appropriate way in which Germany could contribute to the defense of Western Europe. However, the United States took steps to indicate its interest in European defense. On September 9, 1950, President Truman approved "substantial" increases in American forces in Europe in the "sincere expectation" that other North Atlantic Treaty powers would "keep in step." How the bulk of these troops could come from any place but Korea was not stated.

It was reported from London that this step would encourage the West European governments who had been anxious as a result of American reverses in Korea and who had wondered what would happen if the East Germans embarked on a war of aggression against the West Germans. Henry Cabot Lodge spoke of a plan to raise and equip thirty American divisions, twenty of which would be stationed in Europe.

General Mark Clark said that the first troops promised by the president would arrive in about four months, although the bulk of them could not arrive before spring. Acheson emphasized that the major American effort would be in Europe. A less reassuring note was sounded by Texas Senator Tom Connally, chairman of the Senate Committee on Foreign Relations, who urged that additional American troops not be sent to Europe until the Korean War was won.

At the New York meeting of the Foreign Ministers, prior to the NATO meetings, informants stated that the creation of a German national army was not an objective of the meetings. The planners were concerned with initiating West German participation in a West European armed force, not with creating an army like the People's Police of East Germany. This was designed to still French fears and objections. Nevertheless, Robert Schuman, Foreign Minister of France, said that the question of West German rearming could not be considered until other Western troops had been equipped.

At the NATO meetings, the role of Western Germany in the increased defense effort of Western Europe constituted the third item on the agenda. This item caused intense disagreement in the talks, and the United States considered meeting British and French objections by giving assurances that British and French units would have equipment priorities in case of shortages. The French asked for delay, however, and complained that Acheson had given too little advance notice for the item.[6] Schuman claimed that the item had never been received officially before.

Jules Moch, the French Defense Minister, flew over to support Schuman and stated that France would agree to a larger role for a West German police force, but it would not agree to the creation of German divisions. The United States tried to secure agreement in principle to the future creation of West German divisions but met opposition. It was claimed that the United States was risking Western European unity by pressing this demand.

On September 19, to reassure Germany, which was increasingly disturbed by the debate over the German role on Western defense, the Foreign Ministers of Great Britain, France, and the United States declared that their occupation forces in Germany were also "security forces for the defense of the free world and that they would treat any attack against the Federal Republic or Berlin as an attack upon themselves." Meanwhile, as the Atlantic Council recessed reports circulated that the English Foreign Minister, Ernest Bevin, had received instructions to support in principle the arming of Western Germany.

On September 23, 1950, the United States pressed the issue again in a meeting of the Big Three Foreign Ministers, claiming that the rising volume of Western arms production could be absorbed only if West German units were created. American spokesmen emphasized for their French listeners that these forces would not be under the control of the Bonn government and would take orders from the unified command.

On September 25, the Atlantic Council resumed meetings and discussion of the German issue continued unabated. The communique of September 26 noted only the agreement in principle that "Germany should be enabled to contribute to the build-up of the defense of Western Europe" and that the manner in which the contribution would be made was under study.

French circles argued that the pressure of Acheson conflicted with his earlier assurances that France should take the lead on matters concerned with the continent of Europe. French spokesmen maintained that only on the basis of French leadership and a Franco-German understanding could the issue be settled in a manner consistent with European unity. The Schuman plan should be permitted to establish the framework of unity before the armament program for Germany was pushed. The French felt that the pressure placed upon them that led to the agreement in principle had not been constructive.

By early October, criticism of the American secretary of state was increasing in responsible French circles. He was accused of delaying efforts to achieve the defense of Europe, of creating the first important deadlock of a major issue in the Western camp, of jeopardizing final agreement on the Schuman plan to pool Western Europe's coal and steel resources, of upsetting relations between France and Germany, and of arousing suspicion in pro-American French circles where none had existed previously. Meanwhile, High Commissioner John J. McCloy was reassuring anxious Germans that they would not be rearmed without their consent.

On October 19, it was reported in Paris that Foreign Minister Robert Schuman would propose to the French cabinet that the question of German rearmament be solved by merging the continental European forces in a single army and unifying the armament production of the western part of the continent. Finally, such a plan was proposed on October 24 by Premier Pleven.

Early British reactions labeled the plan impracticable. Reports from Germany were negative at first. It was argued that, by going from the Schuman plan to the Schuman army, France would run the risk of reducing the political and economic importance of the former while delaying European defense longer than was desirable. Moreover, it was doubted whether German rearmament would be effective if it were limited as France desired. However, it was stressed that Germany did not desire a national army of her own and desired only to contribute a contingent to a European army.

On October 29, there were reports that the Atlantic Treaty Conference of Defense Ministers might break up without agreement on German rearmament. To still reports of serious disagreement among the Western powers, Secretary of Defense George Marshall gave military personnel strict orders against discussing the results of the conference. It was understood that the government of Premier Pleven refused to budge from its opposition to the creation of German units of divisional strength.

It was reported in high American circles that if the government of Premier Rene Pleven would not permit German rearmament, another French government might.[7] American authorities complained that the

French refusal to accept the British and American position jeopardized the whole concept of balanced collective forces. On October 31, the Defense Ministers adjourned without reaching agreement, although General Marshall expressed the hope that agreement would be reached soon.

It was reported that the Atlantic pact countries were studying a series of American guarantees, which predated the Pleven plan for a European army and were designed to still fears connected with German rearmament. American assurances were understood to include a restriction of the German force to 20 percent of the Atlantic force, or a maximum of ten of the projected fifty divisions; the German units were to remain under civilian control; the German contingents were to be severely restricted with respect to the use of heavy armor and materiel; there would be no German general staff; new officers would be trained rather than recruited from the old officer class. Acheson meanwhile emphasized that disagreement over the use of German contingents would not be permitted to delay the establishment of a unified Western defense force.

Reports from France began to emphasize that the Ruhr must be europeanized before France could agree to German armed units. Complaints were made that Germany had been delaying agreement on the Schuman plan because its bargaining power had been increased by the emphasis on arming Germany.

In despair, France offered to supply twenty divisions to Western defense and to compromise on other elements of its plan for a European army provided only that German contingents of divisional size were not permitted. Defense Minister Moch pointed out that German units could be integrated into Western defense efforts faster under the French plan than under that proposed by Acheson. The United States was then understood to have sent a "stiff" note to the French, explaining that small German units would be useless. It was stated privately in official American circles that if the French were realistic, they would recognize that their defense efforts were completely dependent upon American aid.

On November 8, Chancellor Konrad Adenauer stated that Western Germany would make an adequate contribution to the defense of Western Europe so long as it enjoyed equal rights and was part of a coalition sufficiently strong to deter Soviet aggression. He, thus, warned against plans imposing limits upon Germany not placed upon the NATO powers, and at the same time, he indicated an unwillingness to provoke the Soviet Union by arming Germany until the West was strong enough to discourage Soviet aggression.

On November 9, it was reported that the United States would refuse to name a commander for the unified forces or to commit additional American forces to Europe until France changed its position on German rearmament. At the opening of the meetings of the Atlantic Council deputies on November 13, 1950, M. Moch reiterated the French position that the German contribution should be at the battalion level.

However, the same day it was reported that France and the United States had reached agreement on German combat teams of 6,000-man strength. These reports turned out to be premature. Meanwhile, Soviet proposals for a four-power conference on Germany were also creating difficulties between France and the United States.

Early in December, it was reported from France that the Chinese intervention in the Korean War had modified the attitude of Paris with respect to German rearmament. The French feared that the United States might neglect Europe for its concerns in the Pacific; therefore, the French felt they would have to modify their opposition sufficiently to permit organization of the Atlantic pact forces. They could do this only by meeting some of the conditions of the United States with respect to German rearmament.

On December 6, an American compromise was accepted by the French because of the urgency resulting from the Korean situation. It was tentatively agreed to permit German combat teams the size of a third of a division, without the equipment of a heavy division or a divisional staff. France would be permitted to go ahead with the organization of a European army provided that it could get the other concerned states to agree. German strength was not to exceed 20 percent of the total or about twenty combat teams in an army of thirty-five divisions. There was to be no German ministry of war or armaments. German recruiting was to be handled by civilian agencies. Priority in matters of equipment would be given to non-German nations. A civilian high commissioner would supervise continental military affairs. These provisions were to be subject to West German agreement.

American thinking at Frankfort still favored the creation of a German national army, however, although it was not supported in this objective by the government in Washington. Bonn authorities also called the compromise plan unacceptable. Bonn demanded units of divisional strength and a defense ministry.

Meanwhile, to still senatorial objections to American troop commitments in Europe, General J. Lawton Collins, Army Chief of Staff, warned a group of senators that loss of Western Germany to the Soviet Union would prolong for years a war with the Soviet Union and might make it impossible for the United States to win such a war.

On December 12, the Chiefs of Staff of the Atlantic pact nations reached agreement on the compromise proposals. On December 17, the Soviet Union informed Great Britain and France that the rearming of Western Germany would violate their alliances with the Soviet Union.

The same day, the Brussels conference of the Foreign and Defense Ministers of the Atlantic pact countries began. It was agreed at the meetings that the compromise proposals should serve as a basis for negotiations with the Bonn government. It was understood that the combat team limitation was only a provisional solution for a transitional period.

The Bonn government was to be offered a plan that authorized German tank forces and supporting aircraft and that did not exclude the formation in the future of infantry divisions. The Germans were now becoming a force to be bargained with, rather than ordered about.

General Eisenhower, just appointed chief of the Unified Western forces, stated on December 20 that Germans would be included in his forces "if they came in voluntarily."

On December 21, Great Britain, France, and the United States informed Chancellor Adenauer of their readiness to place allied-German relations on a contractual basis. The High Commissioners informed the chancellor that the form of the German contribution to Western defense was still a matter for negotiation, that the Germans were not being confronted by a *fait accompli*. Reports from Paris stressed the fear that the Bonn government was now in the driver's seat and could name its own terms for cooperation.

Talks with Germany began in January 1951. On January 15, as a result of German nonreceptiveness to the compromise, reports circulated that political uncertainties in Western Germany would force the West to base its defense on the Rhine. This did not mean the abandonment of Western Germany, it was said, as it was hoped that other deterrents would keep the Communists behind the Elbe.

On January 30, Sir Ivone Kirkpatrick, British High Commissioner for Germany, stated that German participation in Western defense efforts was a secondary issue that could be delayed until a partnership had been established between the Western powers and the Federal Republic, and until the North Atlantic Treaty powers themselves became a source of strength. After the West was strengthened, German difficulties would be automatically resolved, he said.

American policy with respect to the rearmament of Germany—in a sense, a startling reversal of American objectives that were pursued during and shortly after World War II—was based upon certain critical assumptions. The first of these assumptions—and one upon which there was general agreement—was that Germany for all practical purposes had ceased to be a serious present or potential menace to the peace of the world. The second assumption—and there was general agreement here also—was that the place of Germany in the role of menace had been usurped by the Soviet Union and the Communist bloc of powers. Other assumptions on which the policy rested by no means attained the same degree of general agreement.

It was assumed that Europe was the key or vital area that had to be safeguarded from Soviet aggression, and that the primary means of defense or deterrence would be the availability of infantry manpower and conventional or tactical atomic weapons. Initial NATO planning established 1954 as the key date by which Western defensive efforts would have to be completed.

By that target date, Western strategic planners believed that the Soviet Union would be prepared for aggressive war. The outbreak of the Korean hostilities indicated to American strategic planners that their timetable would have to be revised; they believed that the Soviet Union had indicated her readiness to strike by 1951 or 1952, even though her capabilities were not yet developed to an optimal degree.

West Germany was a strategic area of importance, if Western planners were to have defensive maneuverability and a chance to absorb the initial Soviet blow. And because manpower was a Western strategic need, some official quarters had contemplated the use of German manpower from the earliest days of NATO. But the change in the strategic timetable of the West made the matter urgent and convinced officials, who otherwise might have opposed German rearmament, either on principle or because they feared the political difficulties the proposal would raise.

If the timetable were to be shortened appreciably, and if Soviet ground capabilities in Europe were to be counterbalanced to any degree, it was believed that German ground contributions would prove essential, given American commitments in Korea and the political difficulties confronting any expansion of the American armed forces greater than that called for by current plans.

To secure German cooperation, American leaders—and soon leaders of the Christian Democratic Party in West Germany—began to stress that German reunification could be expected only if Germany were strong. German integration in Western military plans, it was said, would provide Germany with strength.

Conclusions

The lack of military preparedness of the Western nations in 1950 was beyond question. Therefore, efforts to improve the military position of the West *vis-à-vis* the Soviet bloc can hardly be quarreled with by sensible people. Efforts to organize NATO into a more coherent and unified organization integrated the military systems of NATO members and permitted more efficient use of existing resources. The appointment of an American Supreme Commander and the commitment of American ground forces to Europe did much to improve the morale of Western European nations and to stiffen their resistance to Communism.

On the other hand, the emphasis on military—as contrasted with political or economic—integration and the decision to rearm Germany were blunders comparable to the decision to cross the thirty-eighth parallel in Korea. They also seem to have stemmed from the same estimates and the same psychology.

The emphasis on increased military commitments from America's partners in NATO was probably unavoidable from a political point of view. Influential members of the Senate opposed American troop commitments to Europe—especially in view of the gravity of the course of events in Korea and the paucity of aid from America's allies in that venture[8]— unless other NATO members stepped up their troop commitments to NATO and increased the proportions of their national budgets devoted to military expenditures.

American lawmakers were not prepared to listen to reasons for alternative policies when their mail was filled with complaints from voting parents concerning sons who were participating in combat in Korea. American lawmakers were hardly likely to worry about the problems of French lawmakers when they had their own pressing problems. For this reason the administration had little choice but to place tremendous pressure on its NATO allies and to insist upon heavier military contributions from them. If—given their lower standards of living and other economic problems—military contributions became too much of a drain on the economies of NATO members, a reassessment could be made later when the political climate had changed. The important thing in 1950 was to commit Congress to American participation in a unified NATO ground command.

Many of the same political pressures were operating with respect to German rearmament. However, this decision apparently was based more upon military considerations than upon domestic political considerations. Moreover, these military considerations were invalid and their international political consequences extremely unfortunate. The decision to rearm Germany may be ranked as one of the major blunders of postwar statecraft.

From a military point of view, the commitment of American manpower to Korea increased the urgency of a German troop commitment to NATO. The possibility that other Koreas—or even a major war—might break out seemed only to add strength to this consideration.

American expectations that the Soviet timetable for war in Europe had been moved up to 1951 or 1952 became the binder. But if the Soviet Union did strike in 1951 or in 1952, there could not possibly have been a German contingent in the field, even had the French been completely willing to cooperate with the goals of German rearmament. American security in Europe in this period rested primarily on the strategic air force.

The decision to rearm Germany was oriented to a contingency about which nothing could be done. Meanwhile, a policy about which something could be done—namely, integrating Germany into Western Europe in an economic or political sense—was either neglected or inhibited by the pressure for rearmament.

Moreover, the United States was so committed to this course of action that it became virtually impossible to substitute alternative policies under different political conditions. In short, the United States set off a chain reaction in Europe and so tied its own hands that it later could do nothing about it even had it wanted to.

It is difficult to know for sure whether France could have been won to full cooperation with Germany in political and economic matters. But officials less blinded by their own genius should have recognized that France was unlikely to cooperate with German rearmament.

The tremendous pressure placed upon France and the French desire to commit the United States to a unified command in NATO sufficed to produce a French plan for German rearmament. But it did not suffice to secure French implementation of the plan once American troops were on European soil and an American was appointed Supreme Commander of NATO forces.

A German army contingent had not joined NATO as late as 1955. Nor was it certain how effectively Germany would cooperate with NATO if it did rearm. But it was certain that the urgent need that led to the decision could not have been satisfied by the consequences of the decision.

And, in the meantime, prolonged negotiations over the form of the German contribution to NATO embittered intra-NATO relations and impeded political cooperation among NATO members.

These consequences could hardly be called "calculated risks." There was not the slightest chance that American policy on German rearmament could have satisfied the objectives it was designed to satisfy. Nor could there have been reasonable doubt concerning the real consequence of that policy.

In the meantime, the failure to unify Germany within a Western European alliance or to rearm Germany led to increasing demands within Germany that Germany be neutralized in order to secure Soviet consent to German unification.

Rearmament had been sold to the Germans on the specious thesis that the Soviet Union would agree to reunification as soon as Germany was a member of a strong Western bloc. It has since become clear, however, that the Soviet Union would not permit its strategic position to deteriorate in that fashion, and that the West was not prepared or able to make the Soviet Union concede on the issue of German unification. This should have been obvious in 1950.

It may be quite dubious whether or not the Soviet Union would agree to the unification of a neutralized Germany if genuinely free elections were part of the bargain. Nevertheless, the demonstrated failure of the reunification-through-strength argument and the hope that the Soviet Union would permit unification on these terms paralyzed efforts to integrate German efforts with those of other members of NATO. Germany would not contribute economically to expenses, and it was dragging its heels on the army issue. It could yet withdraw from NATO. But, even if it did not, it was unlikely to be an effective member of NATO.

Thus, Germany had no strong ties to the West. The military emphasis of the 1950 decisions inhibited the growth of political and economic ties among NATO members and it did not strengthen the military ties, except for the unified command decision.

VIII

United States Foreign Policy in a Revolutionary Age (1961)

The following essay is necessarily oversimplified. In the first place, it attempts to deal briefly with many broad-ranging topics of foreign policy. The complexities of the problems involved in American foreign policy can barely be adumbrated. In the second place, the general line of policy recommended represents a striking departure in many respects from general postwar policy as practiced under both the Truman and Eisenhower administrations. The effort to outline the nature of the policy and to relate it to the structural features of contemporary world politics can best be carried out if the policy is presented in its most stark and simple form.

Of course, no policy can be implemented in this simple fashion, for it is not possible to obtain sufficient domestic or allied agreement. In addition, particular features of individual situations almost always require qualification of generalized prescriptions, regardless of the nature of the prescriptions, unless they are so general as to be meaningless or inapplicable. General formulations are better for establishing frameworks of attitudinal responses than for deriving detailed policy. This essay is intended primarily to indicate the changes in attitudes toward foreign policy that are desirable in today's revolutionary world.

There are many difficulties with the pursuit of American foreign policy, and it is, of course, much easier to criticize than to undertake the responsibility for formulating and executing national policy. If I were to single out, however, two general criticisms, they would be: (1) that the policy of the recent past has been more appropriate to a "balance of power" system than to a bipolar system; and (2) that policy has been more appropriate to an era in which society is static than to one in which there is rapid and revolutionary social change.

Bipolarity and Revolutionary Change

With respect to the first criticism, that past policy has been more appropriate to a "balance of power" system, several brief observations may be made. The "balance of power" system operates on the basis of short-term alignments of a flexible nature. It is a system in which alignment preferences are based on specific and limited interests. Thus, the enemy of today may be the ally of tomorrow. The nature of regimes and of internal social conditions are indifferent to alignment decisions. And, hence, morality or sentiment, as contrasted with "interest," plays a subordinate role in the decision process. Although the system can tolerate neutrals, neutrals as such do not play an essential role in the system. Indeed, if important states essayed such a role as permanent, their decision might be quite inconsistent with the stability of the system and with their own long-range interests.

The loose bipolar system, on the other hand, depends upon the formation of blocs based upon considerations of long-term interest. The closer the value patterns of the bloc members, the easier it is to maintain the solidarity of the bloc. Clearly democratic nations could not easily function as members of the Soviet bloc. Although the converse proposition has less force, it still has some validity. NATO solidarity is strong because there are many shared values and institutional practices among most members of the organization. In addition, in the bipolar system, it is not desirable to have all nations within the bloc structures. The uncommitted nations play a stabilizing role that, in a nuclear age, is of value to the blocs. The United Nations may also play a mediating role that, within limits, merits the support of the blocs.

For the reasons just enumerated, the policy of building blocs has definite limits in a bipolar age. Also, the distinction between "interest" and "sentiment" is not as compelling as in the "balance of power" age. The kinds of nations one aligns with, and the policies one pursues internationally, ought to be more closely oriented to value—or moral— considerations than was the case in the past.

If we take into consideration that the present age is also a revolutionary one in which change sweeps from nation to nation, sometimes without respect to alignment pattern, the preceding conclusion is strengthened. Blocs cannot obtain generalized support from uncommitted nations, and specific support may very well depend upon what values the bloc stands for and attempts to propagate. The solidarity of the bloc and the willingness of the populace within a nation to take those risks necessary for long-term stability in a nuclear age may depend upon the pursuit of policies that accord with basic ideals.

If we move from the confines of the model of international politics, this conclusion becomes even more compelling. The West, in particular, the United States, is on the defensive. We have become modern Canutes, attempting to hold back the tides, unresponsive to the currents of our time. In an age when new nations have been proliferating and old nations undergoing revolutionary changes, the United States has been implementing a policy designed in general to discourage radical change and to aid governments in power, regardless of the nature of their regimes, provided they are avowedly anti-Communist. The two aspects of the policy, of course, are related, for often the most anti-Communist governments are those that fear radical change at home and are willing to join American military alliances to receive support that may bolster them against the forces making for internal change. As a consequence, in many areas of the world, the United States seems to represent reaction and a barrier to the hopes and aspirations of large masses of people. It seems to stand for corruption, inefficiency, and maintenance of the status quo. And, at least to many, the alliances it espouses raise the danger of local war for causes not understandable to large masses of the local populations.

The United States has so defined the issues that, for many revolutionary social movements, to pursue what they desire both nationally and internationally is to oppose the United States. This, of course, gives the Soviet Union great leverage. This also makes the bipolar system even more unstable than it otherwise would be. Since, in addition, many Westerners are opposed to the policies that produce these results, the bipolar system weakens the ability of the United States to counter the Soviet offensive. Coalition problems increase, and elements within the United States become disaffected.

The Soviet Union is an active and disturbing foe. Supported by its belief in the historic inevitability of Communism, it challenges the present structure of world politics. The Soviet Union is little inhibited by domestic opinion or by bloc dissidence. The Soviet Union is not associated with colonialism by the new nations, and it can support, almost without qualifications, actions designed to change the status quo radically. It holds forth the threat of nuclear war and, because it seems impervious to change or to influence, drives those who fear war to put pressure upon the West to make concessions. Along with the threat of war, the Soviet Union advocates disarmament under conditions that are not genuinely acceptable to the West.

Under pressure from the Soviet and Chinese threats, and faced by revolutionary changes in the world, the West retreats. Its alliances become fragile. Compromise and temporization are the order of the day. And, even in the United States, there is difficulty in mobilizing domestic opinion behind policies involving risks. The effort to halt Communism hardly seems worth the risk of nuclear war to many, particularly if a stand must be made in a remote and seemingly unimportant area of the world. It is much easier to postpone risks and to enjoy the luxuries of contemporary American life or to seek scapegoats either on the left or right of the political spectrum. After all, the hard choices can also be avoided by blaming the United States' problems on Communist subversives or on warmongering generals. The witch hunt and the peace march are both symptoms of the breakdown and rejection of political life. They are both symptoms of an essential malaise in the West—of the absence of a unifying political ideal.

Western societies are no longer politically vigorous. Large segments of the public are complacent and desire to preserve what they have rather than to lead crusades that will transform the world. Their attitudes are largely defensive, and even the protests against these attitudes are fed more by a gnawing discontent or by impotent anger than by a vision of the future. The bright hopes of the past are transformed into disillusion and bitterness.

There was a day—not far past in the history of the world—when political democratization held forth to most the hopes of redress of past grievances. It was thought that democracy shattered the chains of tradiion, made people masters of their fate, vanquished ignorance and poverty, and permitted a race of Prometheans to rule the world. Vain hope! It is not that democracy is worse than other forms of government. However futile the hope of self-government, and thus of individual dignity, democracy comes closer to reaching these goals than any other form of government. It is consistent with economic vigor, with a standard of living and health higher than any the world has ever known, and with the freedom of an individual to pursue his own future as he wills rather than as the state dictates. The disillusion does not lie in the comparative lack of achievement of democracy as contrasted with other forms of government. The disillusion stems from the gap between the ideals of the democratic creed and the performance of democratic government.

The United States has explored the possibilities of democracy, and it knows that there are limitations on its ability to transform the world. It takes tremendous self-discipline to recognize these limitations as inherent in human organization and to work for limited but possible improvements. For most people, there is a tendency to become complacent about the achievements of democracy and to value personal satisfactions. Such people do not want to sacrifice in the name of an ideal that cannot be achieved. Others find their mission in fighting injustice in some abstract sense. These fasten onto the past and present "sins" of democracy; and, in their desire to punish democracy for its shortcomings, they ignore the immensely larger evils of a creed that still promises abstract justice at some future time if only it can conquer the world.

The essential difficulty of the democratic position is that it seems to deny to many, in democratic nations as well as to those elsewhere, goods that are legitimized by the democratic creed. Any political system must suffer defects. No system can be consistently true to its own ideals. Democracy is challenged in the present age in terms of its own ideals. The inability of democratic government to satisfy this challenge by present performance—and sometimes its indifference to real and pressing injustices—creates an internal opposition that cannot be suppressed consistently with the institutions and values it espouses.

Thus, within the democratic nations, there are articulate groups, with some political effectiveness, who are essentially disaffected and who are motivated to inhibit effective political action designed to maintain the security of the NATO bloc. These groups are at basis recriminatory; they are more inclined to view Western policy with suspicion because of its "sins" than they are to view Soviet policy with suspicion. They have a mistrust of capital, which they feel has alienated and exploited man; of military leaders, whom they suspect of warlike aims; and of politicians, who they believe desire to suppress movements for national freedom and independence. Because many of the articulate intelligentsia belong to these movements, they have a political effect disproportionate to their numerical strength. And, because the intelligentsia are citizens of democracies, their arguments convince many in other nations of the injustice of the democratic nations.

To describe what is necessary to rejuvenate American political life may be beyond the powers of any individual. That subject certainly cannot be considered within the scope of this paper. A few aspects of the problem as it affects the conduct of foreign policy can, however, be mentioned. The goals of American foreign policy must be derived from the basic ideals of the nation if they are to obtain sufficient support for a chance of effective implementation. The United States must begin to think not in terms of specific deals or outcomes but in terms of the kind of world in which American democracy can survive. *Realpolitik* and cynicism may once have been effective technique for the conduct of foreign policy. If they are resorted to today at the highest levels of policy-making, they will corrode the political faith required for an effective American policy and, if necessary, for the resort to force in support of that policy.

If the United States enunciates policies merely to gain support and not because it is convinced of their rightness, it encourages others to raise the price of their support. If it assumes a posture of strength in support of policies it is not really willing to run risks to implement, the Soviet Union is likely soon to call its bluff and expose the irresolution. If the United States is to act with hope of success, it must find a source of strength not merely in weapons, but also in values and ideals.

The United States can no longer afford to be a conservative nation. Conservatism is appropriate when change threatens desirable values *and* when these values can be defended best by defensive measures. There must be an ability to weather the storm. It made sense for Franklin Roosevelt to replace "Dr. New Deal" with "Dr. Win the War." But the United States is no longer faced with a military conflict of relatively short duration. It is confronted with a revolution of worldwide dimensions, a revolution that cannot be halted by military measures or by temporary defeats. The United States cannot—and should not attempt to—halt this revolution. It can attempt to influence the direction this revolution takes and the values that flourish as it progresses.

Although the "Free World-Communist" dichotomy is grossly over-simplified—witness the authoritarian satrapies of the United States, such as Spain—it points to an essential truth about the present world struggle. Imbedded in the American tradition as it has developed is a belief in the right of each individual to find his own truth, provided only that he respect the rights of others to find their truths. Just as the American political process encourages the enunciation and pursuit of any political goal compatible with the maintenance of a political system permitting such a pursuit for all, the American intellectual system permits an experimental attitude toward beliefs—permits the individual to pursue his thought as best he can. There is no official dogma that circumscribes this process, that must be accepted, that cannot be tested or denied. There is a distaste for official or governmental indoctrination and a belief that the only dignified beliefs worthy of free men are those that can withstand free and public challenge. There is the belief that the proper goal of society is the mature, free individual—and that it is the object of society to provide, or at least to permit, the conditions under which such people can flourish.

The democratic system is one that institutionalizes dissent and that encourages criticism, as long as they do not attack the fundamental principle that others also, even if members of a minority, possess the rights of dissent and criticism. These ideals are imbedded, even if imperfectly, in American institutions. But they are not otherwise related to class, race, religion, or nationality. If we believe in these values, we must believe in them for others as well. And, if we are moral people, within the limits of prudence, we shall not hold to these beliefs passively, but we shall encourage and support those who also subscribe to these values in other lands.

Before examining specific problems, we can summarize the three kinds of major problems facing the United States:

1. The uncommitted states are alienated and act in ways that increase the instability of the bipolar age.

2. The West has no positive set of ideals to generate a confident set of foreign policies. NATO is beset by divisions and fears. The individual member nations complacently desire to protect what they have, but lack an image of a world they desire that will induce bold and purposeful programs and policies.

3. The Soviet Union and the Communist bloc constitute an active set of foes. They take advantage of the divisions in the West, and of the fears and complacencies of individual Western nations, to increase the pressure on the West and to force concessions disadvantageous to it. The Communist leaders know the kind of world they want to build and are willing to take risks to achieve their goals. Despite some internal quarrels, they achieve reasonable cooperation and are able to induce reasonable domestic support. The United States must learn how to deal with the Soviet challenge and, to the extent possible, increase the problems facing the Soviet bloc both internally and externally.

There are no complete or easy solutions for these problems. But the United States must learn to cope with them in an adequate way if it is to preserve the values that underlie the American experiment.

The Uncommitted States and United States Policy

The passion for self-rule, for independence, applies both to groups and to individuals. Colonial existence, no matter how necessary it may seem at some times to promote still further development, is incompatible with human dignity. And although rule by a local dictatorship is far removed from the ideal, it at least extends to the group that which should also be extended to the individual. It is a necessary, if not a sufficient, condition for human dignity, and Americans ought not to be indifferent to the desire for independence, whether that desire be of the black man in Africa, the white man in Eastern Europe, or the yellow man in Asia.

Alliances with the Uncommitted States

Most of the new nations are weak and backward. Their leaders remember a period of colonial subjection. They are fearful that their new independence may be compromised and are dedicated to modernizing. The problems of these new nations are enormous, and their leaders desire to insulate them from quarrels they do not recognize as their own. Moreover, they have a genuine interest in attempting to shift the burden of defense against Soviet aggression to others. They will resent any effort to commit them to objectives that divert them from modernizing or that threaten to move them toward the center of the Cold War.

The United States has, fortunately, given up the idea of creating extensive chains of military alliances that depend on the adherence of uncommitted states. This attempt frightened the leaders of many of the new nations. It brought their nations to the center of the Cold War and subjected them to Soviet political attack. The leaders did not desire this—except where internal problems or national divisions, as in Korea or Vietnam, seemed to necessitate it. Where the populace knew of the commitment, it often misunderstood it. Counterelites opposed to the governments often used the commitments as weapons, as in Iraq. Those who thought the first problem of their nation was development viewed such alliances as a diversion of resources and effort. They much preferred an anticipated insulation from the Cold War and the opportunity to play the East and West off against each other both politically and in terms of access to investment funds.

Where conservative regimes desired alliances to support internal policies, the alliances identified the United States with the policies of these regimes. Where nationalist regimes existed, the attempt to induce them into alliances against their resistance appeared as a threat to their goals, as in Egypt.

In addition, the idea behind these alliances was unsound from the very start. Such nations had little to add in a military sense, although some of them were able to provide bases that temporarily were important. The military aid often unbalanced the economies of these states. In adidtion, the real and undervalued mediatory role these nations could play when uncommitted was neglected. Where they might have been bulwarks in upholding desirable principles of international law as uncommitted nations, they were instead weak, vulnerable, and temporary members of a Western alliance.

With few exceptions in the present period, military alliances with the new and largely uncommitted states will serve neither their interests nor ours. Alliances or even strong political coalitions are unlikely to work out well. We shall do best if we attempt to commit these nations to the support of universal principles of international law or norms of international behavior rather than to specific American interests. Economic aid and the political problems arising therefrom also will constitute an important problem area for American relations with the new and uncommitted nations. This last problem will now be considered.

Economic Dominance over the Uncommitted States

Many of the uncommitted nations believe that the United States, because of its economic power, represents an economic threat to their independence. This fear undoubtedly is greatly exaggerated, but it exists even in countries such as Canada. Whatever the economic arguments to the contrary, it would probably make good political sense to encourage at least some other countries, particularly in Latin America, to purchase controlling interests in large local corporations controlled from or owned abroad, especially those which dominate important natural resources such as oil. The United States government should attempt to facilitate the transfer of ownership and control by underwriting it to some extent.[1] This would help to circumvent extremist demands that might force nationalization under conditions that would cause political strains between particular foreign nations and the United States and that would lead to local, irrational economic decisions inconsistent with American efforts to support modernization and political liberalism. Moreover, transfers of ownership and control, freely offered, might do much to dampen the entire issue and to forestall extensions of the nationalization principle that would be economically harmful or that would interfere with needed access by developing nations to the American capital market.

Soviet Aid to the Uncommitted States

The United States has tended to view Soviet aid to uncommitted nations as a calamity, inconsistent with their independence and with American attempts to entice them into political or military alliances or ententes. This has reinforced the auction aspects of American relations with the uncommitted nations, and it has debased American generosity. Instead, the United States should welcome Soviet aid as a substitute or complement for American aid even where we may consider the specific forms of aid undesirable. The receiving nations should be depended upon to insist on conditions that preclude major political gains by the Soviet Union. The United States should be prepared to cooperate with such efforts on the part of the uncommitted states. It should insist that the major burden of maintaining independence rests with the uncommitted states; it should not permit these nations to exploit American fears that they might not want to maintain their independence.

American aid offered merely as an alternative to Soviet aid necessarily leads to an auction that cannot be won. The Soviet Union can pick and choose its aid targets. It was always able to breach the wall of aid containment, even at a time when it was relatively weak economically, and was able to force the United States to utilize its aid in ways that were not economically rational. As the Soviet Union grows stronger economically, the problem worsens. If the United States welcomes Soviet aid as an alternative and offers its own aid without regard to securing allies, this vicious cycle can be broken.

Principles of American Aid—General

We can now inquire into the principles that ought to govern the extension of American aid to the uncommitted nations. Although the United States may properly give preference to nations that cooperate with it politically and deliberately bail these nations out of political difficulties, it should not attempt to buy outright support and should even discourage such support on the part of those nations where there is no popular local basis for it. In these last cases, failure to follow the suggested principle makes the regimes vulnerable to criticism for forfeiting independence and drives the opposition into an anti-American position. In general, aid should be given because people desire to live in a world where they can look forward to better lives, not because we expect political support, or even because we believe that better conditions will make Communism less likely. Indeed there is little evidence that aid will accomplish these latter objectives.

The United States and the uncommitted states do not have the same community of values or institutions that the United States and Europe have. Except where there are quite specific and compelling common interests—as in the case of South Korea, for instance—we cannot expect the uncommitted states to share our foreign-policy burdens, whatever some abstract ethical system might seem to imply. It would be foolish, therefore, to use aid as a weapon in an attempt to gain foreign-policy support. Within broad limits, aid ought not to be dependent on the external policies of the aided state—unless, of course, that state goes so far as to become a member of the Communist bloc or unless that state acts in a manner consistently disruptive of desirable principles of international order rather than merely in a manner opposed to specific American interests. Attempts to condition aid on foreign-policy support confuse the purpose of the aid, injure the national pride of the aided nations, and eventually undercut the purposes of the aid either by identifying local regimes with the United States in ways that alienate them from their bases of local support, or by driving such regimes into anti-American positions.

However, we should attempt to convince the uncommitted nations that independence and lack of commitment do not imply that they attempt to compromise the differences whenever the United States and the Soviet Union differ. If they really essayed such a role, then it would be strategically advisable for the United States and the Soviet Union to exaggerate their demands and differences; otherwise, the suggested compromises would be disadvantageous to them. And if either failed, or was unable to do this, the other would gain a strategic advantage that might destabilize the international system. The uncommitted nations must be persuaded—but not coerced by aid policy—to the extent possible, to support universalistic normative rules of behavior consistent with the kind of international system in which their own best interests will be protected. It can be argued that opposition to some specific American objectives might be a small price to pay if the uncommitted states could be committed to certain stabilizing norms of international behavior.

In applying its aid, the United States should be concerned with building the kind of world it desires to live in. Modernization, regional cooperation, and democracy undoubtedly are features of the world the United States desires for the future.

Specific Principles of Aid—Modernization

The leaders of the new nations—in particular the educated elites—desire modernization and independence. These two goals are viewed as inseparable, for it is thought that independence cannot be maintained without modernization and that modernization can be carried out only by independent governments. The existence of dependent colonial areas or of nonmodernizing independent states is viewed as a threat to the modernizing regimes. American exhortations to act moderately, responsibly, or democratically seem to many modernizing leaders so irrelevant to their difficult tasks that some believe them to be hypocritical.

The disorder in the Congo and the authoritarian regimes in some of the uncommitted states shock American susceptibilities. But the United States may be judging these nations by the wrong standards. The historical plays of Shakespeare depict situations no better than those of the Congo; Tudor England was hardly democratic; the Spanish women treated Napoleon's soldiers more cruelly than the *Force Publique* behaved in the Congo; and the Nazi and Ustachi villainies are barely two decades old.

The nations of Europe were not built without bloodshed, corruption, villainy, and misery. But at least these nations did not have modern neighbors to set spectacular expectations for them. They could accept slow progress not only in economic development, but also in the development of a national consciousness and of a state apparatus. Their independence was not seemingly threatened by more developed and more powerful states. In the new nations, national consciousness does not exist, except perhaps in inchoate form. There is no state in the European sense. Tribal ties, illiteracy, low levels of resources, production, and skills are inconsistent with the entry into the modern world that their educated elites demand. Even though considerable assistance is available to them, their task is much harder than was the task of the European nations.

Most of the European nations had considerable governmental intervention when entering the modern world. Even in England, Tudor intervention preceded Manchesterian capitalism. Many of the new nations believe they require—and, in fact, they may be correct—more governmental intervention in the economy than seems proper to us. But we must remember that their economic development is dependent upon political and social revolutions that can be carried out only against the resistance of powerful vested interests. In some of these states, territorial loyalties must replace tribal loyalties. In some, land reform is required. In all, agricultural techniques must be modernized. In many, there is no entrepreneurial class and, even if there were, it could not be expected to take the huge risks required to establish industry, transportation, and communication—without which no contemporary state is viewed as modern. In most, the moneyed interests—where such exist—refuse to use their money productively. Education is essential, but only the state can insure an adequate educational program. These considerations could be multiplied, but that would not be profitable. It is necessary only to point out that these new nations cannot repeat the experience of the United States. If they are to succeed in modernizing at all[2]—and this may be in doubt—there must be considerable intervention in the economy by the state.

Economic aid should be related to the ability of the aided area to modernize, to solve its economic problems, and to build a viable and independent nation or areal grouping.

In many of the countries where American aid may be wanted, modernization cannot be carried out without radical social change. This does not mean that existing regimes are always opposed to modernization, any more than were the Shogunate in pre-Meiji Japan or the Nuri as-Said regime in Iraq. But these last two—perhaps unlike the present Thai regime, which is not based on a large landholding class—were unable to carry modernization through without undercutting their bases of political support. In these cases, political revolution was probably a necessary if not sufficient condition for modernization. In some of the Latin American nations, the requirements for radical social reform by existing regimes are not so formidable, but may still be sufficient to deter the regimes from taking political risks in order to modernize.[3] Where this is the case, American aid is likely to be used ineffectively, and the extension of large-scale aid may even identify the United States with antimodernist goals.

Intervention in internal affairs to induce modernization is a risky business that may well fail or backfire. Intervention should not be resorted to blithely. On the other hand, the failure of existing regimes to modernize may only insure radical and pro-Soviet revolutions. No specific answers to this problem can be attempted here. There will be cases where intervention may work and others where the risks are too great.

But the United States must avoid association with antimodernist goals. It must display sympathy with modernizing regimes even where specific American economic interests may be affected adversely.

Specific Principles of Aid—Regional Cooperation

Modernization and cultural independence may be aided by regional cooperation or even by regional integration. The Mahgreb, for instance, is possibly an area where cooperation crossing national boundaries may be feasible and desirable from the standpoint of building a new world order consistent with American principles. Oil-pooling in the Arab Middle East might also be encouraged. Although the Iraq claim to Kuwait could hardly be conceded, the defense of the sovereignty of what is essentially a nonviable political unit demonstrated lack of political foresight.[4]

The American government presently proposes to set up regional groups in Latin America and Africa with which aid negotiations would be carried on. Little study, however, has been made of the consequences of such a scheme for Africa, in particular, where the question of which states to include would have profound political effects both within the continent and elsewhere. It is at least worth asking whether the political consequences of regionwide economic planning would moderate the policies of the more forward African states, inflame the more moderate states, increase continental harmony, or make worse continental frictions. The inclusion of the United Arab Republic would, of course, have other consequences for American foreign policy.

The commitment of the United States to the OAS leaves little choice except to encourage some kind of regional cooperation in the use of American aid to Latin America. Yet, the program of the Kennedy administration is tied to land reform and to other social and economic reforms. It is doubtful that many of the existing regimes in these countries will, in fact, carry through reforms of a needed radical nature. For this reason, even within the OAS framework, the United States should consider concentrating its aid to those countries that have the desire and ability to modernize themselves. Brazil, Venezuela, Mexico, and Argentina may fall within this category. By committing the major portion of its aid to areas that do modernize economically and socially, the United States would identify itself with such progress. The nations so aided might serve as examples to still others that they need not go the way of the Castro regime in Cuba. On the other hand, by not entirely denying aid to other Latin American countries, the framework of hemispheric solidarity is maintained and American sympathy for the peoples of the hemisphere affirmed. Within this framework, smaller, specific aid programs oriented to other and shorter-term needs could be formulated and carried out. The case for picking and choosing may be even stronger in Africa where the United States lacks historic ties that demand continental solidarity and cooperation. In all cases, major American aid should be predicated on efforts by the nations involved to help themselves.

The United States should make clear to all that the major purpose of its aid is to help other countries to enter the modern world. Thus, in general, the United States should not commit itself to outworn social or political systems that cannot satisfy aspirations with which it, in terms of its own national values, must strongly sympathize.

Specific Principles of Aid—Internal Politics

For reasons specified previously, new nations, in the effort to modernize, must engage in considerable governmental intervention. Efforts to overcome tribalism or to carry through social revolutions necessary for modernization may lead to considerable authoritarianism. The democratic and humane values destroyed in the process may not be properly appreciated by the leaders of the new nations. Many may lack the sophistication of Attaturk, who used authoritarian forms in an effort to create the conditions under which democracy could maintain itself.

Moreover, many of the leaders of the new nations unfortunately have accepted Marxist myths concerning capitalism. Although, in fact, the socialism of the new states is more pragmatic and accommodates more capitalism than some Americans believe, there is a real danger that the new states may either stifle or fail quickly to create the middle class that stood as a bulwark against governmental despotism in the West (but that took more than a century to develop). Moreover, much of the human misery of the European economic revolution was the consequence of an impersonal market mechanism rather than of conscious governmental decision. The governments of the new nations, however, largely take responsibility for economic decisions. Resentment, therefore, may crystallize against these governments for the real or seeming failures of governmental policies. And, in their efforts to modernize rapidly and to maintain control of the situation until this is done, the governments may institutionalize repressive mechanisms resistant to change from below although possibly subject to *coup*.

The United States should leave no doubt concerning its sympathy for the efforts of the elites in the new nations to modernize, of its desire to aid them, and of its recognition that modernization cannot be carried through painlessly or according to its own model. On the other hand, it should not be indifferent to the internal politics of the countries that receive economic aid or assistance from it.[5] The effects on American institutions and values, if the United States becomes an isolated island in a totalitarian—even if non-Communist—world, are too complicated to describe here and, in any event, are moot. But surely Americans prefer not to live in a totalitarian world, and even more surely, they do not desire to permit their aid to modernizing nations to be diverted toward the maintenance of a totalitarian police state. (Even if the funds are not used directly for this purpose, they permit the diversion of other funds.) If the United States cannot police the world to maintain democracy everywhere—indeed even if it must recognize that the conditions for democracy are not everywhere present or that in some places democracy may be incompatible with modernization—it does not have to close its eyes to the human drama and to resolve political issues in favor of totalitarianism either through a failure of will, or in a fit of absent-mindedness.

In applying a criterion related to the nature of the regime, an effort must be made to make decisions in context rather than in the abstract. Thus, for instance, a distinction can be made between an area where the conditions for some degree of political liberalism are present but repressed by the government and an area where such conditions are not present. For instance, given the cultural and social background of Cuba, it is dubious that most of the totalitarian measures of the Castro regime are necessary for—or even consistent with—rapid modernization, although a mere return to the old constitution might have forfeited the possibilities for social revolution.

The situation is quite different in Ghana and Guinea—which, in any event, are authoritarian and not totalitarian—where tribalism must be overcome to create a national state where one did not properly exist previously. A distinction must also be drawn between a Guinea, which has had little experience in government and little time to create liberal institutions, and a Spain, which has made no effort to create such institutions and which seems determined to maintain a rigidly authoritarian regime indefinitely. Moreover, although Guinea or Ghana may be given the benefit of the doubt, because of their brief existence, it is possible to distinguish between those two cases and Nigeria, which seems more inclined, at present, to develop representative institutions.

African single-party systems, which seem to permit debate and consent within the single-party structure, must also be differentiated from

Communist-type single-party systems, which prevent national debate or dissent and which restrict debate to centralized and hierarchical party structures. Thus, whether a nation such as Yugoslavia is aided might be made to depend on whether the party structure is sufficiently loosened to permit genuine and general debate and political alternatives not decided on in advance by the party leadership.

Even if the only two criteria for aid were those previously discussed —modernization and regime character—the applications would be subject to some debate. Spain would clearly be excluded, for it is not modernizing, and it is committed to the maintenance of an authoritarian regime. Cuba would not receive aid because, although it is attempting to modernize, it is now doing so within the framework of a totalitarian regime, which applies terroristic methods in case of dissent. Nigeria and some of the French African states are modernizing, but not rapidly, in an effort to avoid harsh political methods. Even so, many of those French African states are one-party states. At this stage of their development, they should probably be given the benefit of the doubt on both counts. Ghana and Guinea are attempting to modernize rapidly, are following foreign policies that are unpalatable to the United States, are probably on balance pro-Soviet, and are employing quite harsh political methods. Even so, they are not totalitarian and, within the framework of African political experience, do permit political alternatives. They should probably receive the present benefit of doubt, but the decision might well be reevaluated after a reasonable period of time. So also should the Jagan regime in Guiana receive the benefit of the doubt, unless it shows signs of becoming totalitarian or of entering the Soviet bloc.

The difficult questions will involve the choice between the rapidly modernizing and less liberal and the more slowly modernizing and more liberal African regimes. No single criterion can be applied here, for policy decisions must rest on prognostications concerning the probable future course of development of these nations. If the judgment is that the more slowly modernizing nations have a reasonable chance to succeed in modernizing with external support, while maintaining relatively liberal institutions, preference should be given to them where emphasis in allocation is made. If, on the other hand, one comes to the conclusion that modern nationhood in any of these areas rests on rapid and forced evolution from tribalized relations to national solidarity or that political demands on the part of the younger, educated elite permit no good alternative, then despite dissatisfactions with their external policies and fears concerning their future political development, aid to the more radically modernizing African nations might have higher priority than would otherwise seem desirable.

In any event, although the United States may prefer a particular set of choices for developing nations, based on its own values and prognostications, and may legitimately allocate aid on the basis of these choices, the decisions on modernization affect it only indirectly. Advice may be offered. Attempts to encourage desirable values can and should be made. But in the last analysis, the developing nations must make their own independent choices, for it is their fate that is directly involved. Where the choice that is made involves a destruction of human dignity that offends the United States' most important values and degrades the human beings so manipulated, as in the case of Cuba, the United States has an obligation to make its opposition clear. But where the differences are based upon tolerable differences in basic values or prognostications concerning the consequences of particular policies, sympathetic understanding would be more appropriate than harsh rejection.

It is inevitable that particular American decisions, even within the framework of clear policy principles, will be misunderstood by some and resented by others. The United States does not always properly understand or appreciate the actions or intentions of other nations. The new nations require radical change, and the rich United States is not likely to be viewed sympathetically by the harassed leaders and uneducated masses of these nations. Their values, their goals, and their interpretations of policies differ from those of the United States. Popularity is not to be expected. If, however, there is a posture of disinterested support for modernization, social reform, and political liberalism, if American policy is not tied merely to anti-Communism or to attempts to build systems of alliances, there is some hope that American policy will command respect, and that it will invite support when it accords with the most important interests of the uncommitted developing nations.

It must be clear that the United States does not seek *direct* political benefits from its aid. Unlike Communism, which, despite its talk of many roads, has a relatively narrow doctrinal content and organizational form, American favoritism for democracy implies little with respect to the content of legislation—apart from support for modernization—and party and governmental structure. It implies support only for organizational forms that permit the institutionalization of dissent and the relatively free play of ideas. Indeed, the democracies do not possess political means by which control can be exercised over other countries, and, as long as the United States does not attempt to force uncommitted nations into pacts for which they are not prepared, it presents no political threat to their independence.

Mode of Aid

The question of whether aid should be given bilaterally or multilaterally is a difficult one to answer. However, proposals to siphon aid through the United Nations according to its normal constitutional procedures would almost surely be unfortunate. As long as the amount of aid handled through the United Nations is small, the temptation to assert the kind of political control that would be inconsistent with the objectives of the aid will be minimal. As soon, however, as large-scale contributions of aid money to be spent by the organization come to be viewed as a tax to be contributed regularly by the richer nations, the kinds of pork-barrel decisions that are often made in the United States Congress will be made in an even more exaggerated form in the United Nations General Assembly. Since economically irrational decisions are also likely to be made at the national level, this compounding of irrationality would be thoroughly inconsistent with the aims of the aid. Multilateral aid, however, might insulate the United States from criticism in the choice of aid recipients. It is true that the history of bilateral aid leaves little room for optimism. But it is at least easier to reform United States aid programs than to reform international political processes.

In sum, therefore, the question of policy, primarily including economic-aid policy, toward the uncommitted states is not susceptible to an easy answer that permits clear applications. The usual reasons given for aid, namely, that it will make friends, produce political stability, and halt Communism, have little evidence to support them. But, in the end, modernization is probably a good thing. It is doubtful if the demands for modernization can be halted in any event. To the extent that modernization is carried through successfully by non-Communist governments, the expansion of the Communist world system will be halted. Political instability is probably inevitable as rising expectations, new organizations, and political counterelites produce accentuated demands on the governments of the underdeveloped nations. The sooner modernization occurs, the fewer the barriers it must overcome. And the more support the West gives to it, the more successful and the less anti-Western it is likely to be. The more the West attempts either to halt modernization or to use it for ulterior purposes, the more radical and the more susceptible to Communist influence modernization is likely to be. The more disinterested the assistance policy of the West, the greater the control of the West over its allocations of resources and the less susceptible the West is to blackmail in various guises.

Undoubtedly, in nations that lack any democratic experience or tradition, some degree of strong political control—even of authoritarianism—will be needed to handle excessive demands on governmental allocations. In others, such as India, the democratic method may be made to work in modernizing the nation and may serve as a model for other nations, if not in the present, then at least with respect to the future. At present, however, democratic values have no appeal for the poor, the backward, the illiterate. They appear to be luxuries or even undesirable. Our best hope is to produce a period of relative stability during which these values can become appreciated. This will not happen until other and prior—even if less important from our viewpoint—values are first achieved. The present period is a crucial one, and the choices made by the West—and primarily by the United States—will play a critical role in determining the shape of world politics for some time to come.

Although specific choices of aid policy or allocations of funds may be responsive to highly particular circumstances, the philosophy that guides the program will be of major importance in determining its effectiveness and acceptability to the aided nations. This guiding spirit in the intermediate run will have more impact on the consciousness of the leaders and peoples of the developing nations than the details of policy. Mistakes will be made and can be overcome with respect to those details. But the failure of the general outlines of policy to accord disinterestedly with the requirement of modernization eventually will lead to major discord between the aims and accomplishments of policy. The aim of the United States must not be popularity or even instrumental alliances. The major aim of American policy must be a structure of world politics in which the most important Western interests can be protected and the democratic form of government survive. The status quo cannot be preserved. The question concerns the shape of the changes to come. It is here precisely that the West and the United States must take their stand as a matter or principle rather than as a matter of expediency.

UNITED STATES GENERAL ALLIANCE POLICY

The United States should begin to overhaul its alliance system along with its program of aid. Unfortunately, it is not always wise to scrap alliances that it was initially unwise to form. Withdrawal from an alliance may too easily be interpreted as withdrawal from an obligation to defend and, thus, may set in motion other undesirable events. For instance, withdrawal from the South East Asia Treaty Organization (SEATO) might encourage Chinese aggression and might also encourage political deals favorable to Communism by local political elites. Opportunistic political elites, convinced that withdrawal from the alliances signified withdrawal from an interest in the independence of the area, might then begin to make "hedging" internal political deals. Moreover, some areas literally require an overt United States military guarantee to forestall attack. Taiwan is a case in point.

Except, however, in the NATO area, the system of multilateral military pacts has been a failure. NATO, which so far has been relatively successful, is in serious and, likely, increasing trouble. Many Europeans are afraid of the risk involved in the nuclear age: some fear that the United States will not risk nuclear war to defend them if they remain in NATO and hope that the United States will come to their aid anyway, even if they do not contribute to or participate in the nuclear military forces of the free world. They desire not to become the locus of nuclear attack. If it is urged that a nuclear-armed NATO is a deterrent to attack, they hope that others will bear the burden of that deterrent. Necessary as a nuclear-armed NATO happens to be, the strains within NATO are bound to increase tremendously as long as it remains a purely military organization.

There is a human tendency to discount risks when the alternatives are especially unpleasant. A Russian military move, therefore, is apt to be discounted if the means of preventing it are nuclear, unless there are incentives additional to military ones for taking risks. If the only incentives are the military, the nation that calls attention to the Russian threat is apt to be disliked; such action forces the attention of other nations on unpleasant things—things they would rather deny or ignore.

It would be much better if NATO were a politically organized community with shared interests and values, and if the problem of shifting risks and responsibilities did not arise in the acute form presently apparent. Nationalism, at least in America and Western European nations, has outlived its usefulness. It is no longer a moral inspiration or a generator of efforts of vast magnitude. Europe has already discovered this in a political and economic sense and is making first efforts to develop larger associations in the form of the Common Market and the various European Communities.

The United States, which has encouraged these efforts so far, has remained aloof. This is unfortunate, for it is no longer viable politically as an independent political entity, though a case might still be made for military viability—at least in the foreseeable future. But even more important, the accession of the United States—and Britain—to the European Community would provide a psychological as well as a material inspiration of the greatest magnitude. A strong case can be made that economic measures, as the least difficult to secure agreement on, should precede political measures in order to prepare the way by establishing practices and habits of joint action. Conceivably, however, the urgency of the situation and the need to capture the imagination of people may require bold political measures, despite the risk that the attempt at this level might forestall action to construct a genuine Atlantic community. But it is hard to deny the conclusion that the NATO nations soon must face the world as an inseparable unit, dedicated to a common fate, and united by common policies and values.

The building of a viable Atlantic community is the most important task facing the West. This community must represent its best hopes and ideals. Present American relationships with Spain and Portugal are inconsistent with these ideals. These nations do not merely lack institutions that would permit them to participate constructively in such a community. The relationship the United States has with them presently is inconsistent with the appearance it is trying to present to the world.

It might be argued that Portugal is a valuable member of NATO, that the Spanish bases are important to the United States, and that it has cooperated without serious objection with many other authoritarian regimes. There is, however, a fundamental difference between a newly independent nation, such as Pakistan, which is trying to enter the modern world, and old nations, such as Spain and Portugal, whose leaders regard the modern world as evil. Some degree of authoritarianism may be essential in new nations, which are desperately trying to modernize and improve the lot of their people. Authoritarianism is much more difficult to justify in old nations that want only to preserve an oligarchic and backward society. The living standards in Spain and Portugal are Asian rather than European. No major efforts are being made to modernize—to improve standards, to educate the people, or to prepare the conditions under which democracy might develop. Instead, Franco and Salazar take pride in their rejection of democracy and have no desire to improve the conditions of their people.

U.S. bases in these countries may have some importance, but it is quite doubtful that they are worth the political price. Exhortations to the new nations to choose democracy and U.S. condemnation of totalitarianism in Cuba appear hypocritical. The United States also makes it difficult to take its own ideals seriously when it regards them this cheaply. No one desires another prolonged civil war in Spain. But surely Spain and Portugal need not be welcomed as allies and colleagues; surely some pressure can be brought upon the two governments to reform. If they are totally unresponsive, the United States can support the democrats in exile.

There is a risk that a Castro type of regime might succeed the present regimes if the United States pursues this course. But a failure to press for democratization and reform may also so discourage the real democrats that the totalitarians have a clear field in advocating change. And, if it opposes the Fascist regimes before they are kicked out, it at least helps to legitimize its opposition to a new authoritarianism should such a type of regime succeed the present regimes.

The attempt to institute idealistic principles in the formation of an Atlantic community undoubtedly will give rise to serious problems: the military services will resist the loss of bases; conservative groups will fear the political effects of the decisions. The alternative political costs, however, would be much greater.

This advice goes against most recognized principles of statecraft. But those principles are designed for stable international systems in which conservative policies are protective of existing interests. The United States must learn that it is precisely with respect to this issue that the character of its national response must change. It must learn to act in ways that generate support for constructive changes in the shape of world politics in a period when sufficient support cannot be mobilized to preserve the status quo. It must take some of the risks that all revolutionary movements must take, or it shall suffer the fate of all systems that fail either to adapt to their environment or to adapt their environment to them.

The United Nations

American policy toward the United Nations also requires drastic revision. American security—and world peace also—undoubtedly rest more on American military power and on the NATO alliance than on the United Nations. If the United States is ever confronted with a clear-cut, either-or choice—and, undoubtedly, this would be a tragedy—the United Nations would have to be subordinated to NATO. On the other hand, the United Nations has a real and important role to play in world politics. It would be a serious mistake—unfortunately, the United States has repeatedly made such mistakes—to attempt to make the United Nations merely an instrument of the Cold War or to attempt to use it to solve problems which it is not and cannot be equipped to solve given the present structure of world politics.

The postwar period has perhaps seen the United Nations misused in two different ways by the United States. The Truman administration attempted to use the United Nations as an instrument of American foreign policy. The Eisenhower administration attempted to use the United Nations as a substitute for American policy. It would be wrong to deny that convincing rationales for either course can be constructed. And, of course, both charges are greatly oversimplified. Yet, it is well to weigh the cost both policies have entailed.

It can be pointed out—and rightly so—that the Truman administration faced an intransigent Stalinist regime in Russia that finally supported—and in all probability ordered—the North Korean attempt to unify the Korean peninsula by force. Although an independent American action in Korea probably would have been preferable to the one followed, it was argued with some merit that an American action that bypassed the United Nations would have reduced the organization to impotence. Yet the United Nations' action in Korea did intrude that organization directly into the Cold—and, in this case, hot—War. The change in the goals of the operation, from defeating aggression to unifying the peninsula by force, clearly placed too great a burden on the organization. It thrust the organization into a war it could not win—at least under the terms the United States was willing to wage it—and made the United Nations a direct and continuing party to a dispute rather than a mediatory agency. Moreover, American efforts on many other issues to put the United Nations on record with respect to Cold War issues alienated many new and uncommitted nations. It again involved the United Nations as a party to Cold War disputes rather than as a mediator or an enunciator of universal rules of conduct formulated in advance of, and without specific reference to—until application became necessary—specific Cold War disputes.

General Dwight Eisenhower, on the other hand, evidently considered that the United Nations came closer to being a world governmental agency than most other observers of the organization would believe. Even within a national government such as the United States, some have questioned the ability of the government to act effectively in crisis situations without strong leadership from the executive. Nonetheless, General

Eisenhower apparently believed that the United Nations was an appropriate deliberative body, with respect to issues involving the use of force, and that support of its decisions by the United States was the method best calculated to build a peaceful world. This, of course, again shifts the function of the United Nations from mediation and places upon it a burden that some may suspect it is ill-prepared to bear. The crisis in the Congo indicated how, despite strong leadership from the Secretary-General, the United Nations can govern only with great difficulty when the interests of the Soviet and American blocs strongly conflict. The present temporary Secretary-General lacks Dag Hammarskjold's strength, and it is doubtful that any genuinely strong successor can be agreed to.

It is simply a fact of international life that the security of the West—and indeed of much of the uncommitted world—rests upon the military strength of the NATO nations. The United Nations is no substitute for NATO, and primarily military and security problems cannot be relegated now, or in the immediate future, to that organization. It is not prepared to move quickly or strongly where military matters are concerned; consequently, its resolutions, even when not compromises, lack a deterrent effect. It is the threat of American intervention that prevents more direct Soviet intervention in Laos and the Congo, not the possibility of a United Nations resolution. Undoubtedly, United Nations actions play a role, indirectly, by creating a political climate in which American intervention becomes politically feasible—because of the reactions of nations whose cooperation is desirable and because of the reactions of the American public. But the two different effects should not be confused.

It is necessary that the United States play a strong leading role in both NATO and the United Nations, but the nature of the leading role ought to differ with the nature and function of the two organizations. The proper function of NATO in a bipolar world is to provide a military deterrent to the Soviet bloc and to present a political image that facilitates unity of action and that at least does not arouse strong opposition from uncommitted nations. The proper function of the United Nations is to mediate in a way that reduces the possibility of thermonuclear war and that facilitates support for desirable and universal rules of international behavior.

With respect to these functions, there can—and will likely—be conflicts between short-term interests of American policy and the interests of the United Nations organization. Such a conflict occurred at the time of the decision to cross the thirty-eighth parallel in Korea. That decision could have been justified from the standpoint of United Nations interests only had the United States been prepared to carry matters with the Soviet bloc to a military decision at that time.

Another conflict arises with respect to the admission of Red China to the United Nations. Red China is a state within the meaning of the Charter; indeed, a very important state. At some point, the United States may have to decide whether keeping Red China out of the United Nations (this is not directly related to American recognition of Red China) is of such overriding importance that it is worth the cost in terms of committing the United Nations organization to universalistic rules of international law. And it must be remembered that it is only on the basis of commitment to such universalistic rules of law that the United States stands much chance of making effective use of the uncommitted nations in international bargaining procedures.

It is, of course, a grave error to fail to differentiate foreign policies according to the arenas in which they are pursued, for this would assume that the context of a policy decision did not affect the consequences of the policy. If the United Nations plays an important role in American objectives, other objectives—at least when pursued in the United Nations and perhaps also at other times—must be modified to take this objective into account. And as long as the mediatory function of the United Nations is important, or as long as the support of other nations who highly value the United Nations is important, American policies in the organization ought to be related to the nature and functions of the organization and not merely to other objectives of American foreign policy. Much of the opposition to past American policies stemmed from a desire of various nations not to get involved in the Cold War— a not inconsiderable factor to be taken into account—rather than from an understanding of the best way in which the United Nations could execute its functions. But this failure of understanding on the part of other nations does not make less grave the failure of the United States to pursue its own best interests in that organization.

In addition to the mediatory functions of the United Nations, the United States may wish to strengthen functions that isolate some areas or functions from the Cold War in a way that is desirable, or at least acceptable, to both the United States and the Soviet Union. Proposals of this kind ought to be strongly supported and presented in ways appealing to the popular understanding. The present Antarctic treaty, for instance, is not inconsistent with eventual United Nations administration, and such administration might serve as precedent for the moon.

Such administration ought to be proposed. The Suez crisis might have been avoided had the Western nations had sufficient foresight to turn international waterways over to international management. It may not be too late for such management, although the issue now would be doubtful at best. It is conceivable that the N-country nuclear problem and arms control may be solved by means of an international agency. In the process, some experience for handling the even more difficult problems that may arise in the future could be gained.

This is a far cry from world government. But there are many disadvantages to world government from the standpoint of human freedom and cultural and social diversity—even were such government feasible. Given the inconsistency of Communist and democratic forms of government and their diversity in cultural and economic standards, clearly such government is not feasible at the present time. To attempt it would be harmful, for such attempts would interfere with support for feasible proposals to control pressing problems.

Even the step toward an international police force, although part of avowed American policy, is unwise at present. *Ad hoc* forces secure, within reasonable limits, cease-fires between minor billigerents. But we must assume that the kind of police force advocated as a United Nations police force would be considerable in size and permanent in nature. If roughly equivalent to American or Russian forces, it might only be a source of additional instability. If superior to American or Russian forces, this force might itself engage in military adventures. Moreover, how could it be possible to agree on the composition and control of such a force? United Nations organs are not representative in a consensual sense.

Surely, the United States and the Soviet Union would not agree to a United Nations force responsive to United Nations organs, except possibly under conditions of veto. But this condition would undercut an essential function of such a force, namely, to control disputes among the major nations. Moreover, if such a force were controlled by the minor nations, what guarantee—or even reasonable presumption—is there that it would be used responsibly? If strong American or Russian units participated, we could expect resistance, sabotage, or other clandestine measures that would impair actions that displeased either of them. Reliance upon a force that might be crippled by internal strife might subvert the deterrent effect of national armed forces. Such a force under existing world conditions would increase rather than decrease uncertainties and would, thus, raise rather than lower the probability of war. And particularly if the United Nations force controlled atomic weapons, we would have problems arising from the increase in the number of nuclear powers. The world has enough uncertainties without increasing the number. Surely it is not a recent discovery that abstract constitutionalism is no substitute for political analysis.

The United States, however, should support the development and possible expansion of the *ad hoc* police-force procedures of the United Nations. It should attempt to demonstrate how these procedures enter into the stream of world politics in a manner supportive of existing law or even in a manner that leads to the growth of law. The independent functions of the Secretary-General ought to be supported and the civil-service status of the staff protected. There should be less hesitation to demonstrate the destructive consequences of present Soviet proposals to reorganize the United Nations. And, instead of agreeing to a larger Soviet quota of staff employees, the existence of any Soviet quota in the absence of independent recruitment should be attacked. The United States ought not to act defensively under Soviet attack. It ought to counterattack with a program designed to improve the level of the law and orderliness in the world.

The present organization of world politics does not provide a desirable level of security. Attempts either to demonstrate the dangers of the present international organization or the need, in at least some respects, for new modes of organizing consensus and the institutional means of exercising force are desirable. The belief, however, that radical changes can be implemented at the present time is dangerous, for such belief, unaccompanied by a host of other changes, might produce either an unworkable and dangerous constitutional experiment, or an eroding support for the only measures capable of maintaining even the low level of security the United States possesses under present conditions.

The United Nations is also the forum in which the United States can encourage the new and uncommitted states to support universal principles of law and behavior consistent with the kind of world order we desire to encourage. On specific issues, this may involve real costs. For instance, the conflict between American policy on China and universal standards for United Nations representation is one area in which costs may have to be paid. But, in general, the United States desires a world in which overt military intervention in foreign nations is minimized, in which the dangers of nuclear war are reduced, in which new nations are permitted to develop in independence, in which problems of outer space are organized appropriately, and so forth. Within limits too complicated to explain here, the new and uncommitted nations may well support such standards as generally—if not always—consistent with their own interests. As the imperialist or colonial issue vanishes and as political boundaries become more stable in the ex-colonial areas, the coincidence of interests should increase rather than decrease. Support, therefore, may well be won in these areas provided that matters are not confused by attempts to win support on specific issues, as opposed to general policy, and provided that military strength is maintained. If, however, the United States seeks support in the form of generalized alliances, because aid will be withheld if support is not forthcoming, or because it wishes to be the "good guy," or if it allows its military strength to dissipate, it will either frighten off or discourage support, and it will gain victories on specific individual votes rather than on the issues that count in the long run.

Support for a viable United Nations system may also serve as a positive ideal to disaffected groups in the Western nations; it may also appear as a desirable alternative to those who misunderstand the role and function of NATO. Thus, strong support for an expanded *but realistic* United Nations system may be an important implement in mobilizing the West by appealing to idealism, while many are still wrongly and unfortunately associating NATO only with "power politics."

POLICY TOWARD THE COMMUNIST BLOC

If the United States desires to encourage political liberalism in the uncommitted nations, it ought also to assert its belief in democracy as the proper way of life for those behind the iron curtain—not merely those in Eastern Europe, but also those in Russia and China. To this end, a reasonably democratic China in Taiwan is an important means. Unless the United States has as much faith in democracy as the Russians have in Communism, Communism will eventually sweep the world. Although the United States cannot encourage premature uprisings at times when it is unable or unwilling to extend aid, it must not come to terms with the status quo. No status quo ever endures, and if the United States recognizes only one mode of change—toward Communism and totalitarianism—it determines the fate of the future by that decision.

But there are other and stronger reasons why the United States must oppose not merely Communist expansion, but Communism itself. The world is an unsafe place in which to live, and it is becoming increasingly so. The measures required to control or to minimize the nuclear dangers are inconsistent with the organizational structure of Communism. The insulation of the Communist system from the outside world minimizes moderating influences on Communist leadership. It is relatively unresponsive to popular pressures as they arise spontaneously or as they are influenced by trends of opinion elsewhere in the world. High-ranking Russians who reported to outsiders on events in the Soviet Union—perhaps on the secretion of nuclear weapons after an arms control agreement—would lack the sanctuary within the Soviet state that American citizens would have in the American state under analogous conditions. In the Soviet Union, governmental leaks occur rarely and then usually as a consequence of a high-level decision to leak. Decisions to hide weapons or to engage in surprise attack can be made secretly by a small group of men who have no need to mobilize public opinion in favor of their move prior to it; neither is there within Soviet society a belief in a norm obligating them to do so or obligating citizens to inform on and oppose the government if it secretly violates solemn agreements, as there is in the West. As long as the Soviet Union remains the kind of nation it is, the dangers of nuclear war may be much higher than many people are willing to accept.

If the United States cannot induce major changes in the Soviet system, and if it is unwilling to live with the dangers of nuclear war, it has one other alternative: it can disarm unilaterally—in effect, it can surrender—and pass on to the Soviet Union the task of policing the world. One possible consequence is that the Soviet Union would effectively control the arms race—that it would prevent other nations from acquiring nuclear weapons. This contingency cannot be examined in detail, but it is unlikely that Soviet leaders would be able or willing to do this without considerable political interference in other nations. Evasions of Soviet arms regulations would have to be cruelly crushed. And a nation that has transported entire populations within its own territory may exact a tremendous price from other nations in this respect, in addition to exploiting them economically. The West would almost surely have to submit to political tyranny. Indeed, the immensity of the task would likely insure this. The physical, as well as the political, difficulty of maintaining control might lead to the development and use of behavior-control devices. Even if the worst of these consequences did not occur, life would be difficult and unpleasant.

However, the Soviet Union might not succeed in imposing arms control on the world. The United States might, as one possibility, enter a world of independent Communist states, many of which controlled effective nuclear systems. This would likely prove a more dangerous world than the present one. Even today there are important strains be-tween Russia and China, for instance. If the threat of the democracies was removed, the strains among the Communists would become much greater. Yet, these would be governments possessing nuclear systems shrouded in secrecy and capable of being employed without advance publicity. (Indeed, several hundred millions of excess Chinese might occupy the United States prior to a nuclear war between Red China and Red Russia.) This is a world that might end up both Red and dead.

Moreover, the policy of unilateral disarmament has even graver dis-advantages. If implemented, it is, as we saw, bad enough. But there would be much opposition to it. The advocacy of the policy might only pro-duce policy debates, delays, and compromises that weaken the Western posture and encourage the Soviet Union to take bold steps that only make war more likely. When the West finally resolved to stiffen its position and to make no further concessions, Soviet miscalculations concerning Western intentions might well precipitate a nuclear war. (A strong argument can be made that the Oxford peace movement in the 1930s made a major contribution to the development of World War II.) Thus, surrender to Communism is not likely to constitute an acceptable solution to the grave problems facing the world today. Attempts to change the Soviet system, or at least to mobilize world opinion against that system, would be preferable.

Therefore, the United States must make clear that the great imped-iment to arms control or disarmament lies in the nature of the Commu-nist political system. So far, most people speak of the concessions that must be made to the Soviet Union because one cannot expect to change its political system. Unfortunately, the concessions that can be made con-sistently, with reasonable security, are not sufficient to minimize the present dangers of the nuclear arms race. It has become necessary to emphasize that it is the Soviet system which must change if the world is to have reasonable security in a nuclear age. And it is the Soviet gov-ernment that must be thrown on the defensive for refusing to make changes consistent with international security. As nuclear technology im-proves and spreads to other nations, it may become necessary for the powers of the United Nations to be drastically increased. It is important that, long before this, the United States has stated the changes necessary in the Soviet system so that everyone will be familiar with the reasons for them.

This cannot be accomplished by shrinking from negotiations with the Russians as the United States has so often done in the past. It may be that the Russians misuse negotiations in an effort to impede the West from taking needed political measures or in an effort to change the political situation during the course of negotiations. For instance, political negotiations over Berlin might so alarm some people that political events might be set in motion to provide the Russians with what they want without the necessity of making counterconcessions.

These possibilities cannot be denied. The Russians are engaged in serious political warfare with us. Khrushchev has stated openly that coexistence means only a willingness to defeat democracy by means other than by military war and not a willingness to live indefinitely in the same world with democracy. Coexistence does not imply the absence of military threats. Nikita Khrushchev is a past master at the use of such threats, having learned much from the practices of the late Adolf Hitler. But even if one believes that Khrushchev really will not resort to overt military adventures—and there is no need for him to do so as long as things go well for him—coexistence on his terms means a struggle, without any real community of interest, in which deceit and subversion play major roles. Indeed, a failure to understand this is a failure to take the Russians seriously.

The answer, however, does not lie in a refusal to negotiate with the Russians; neither does it lie in bargaining as the Russians bargain, for those techniques are not appropriate to democracies and free associations of nations. But the United States can debate the issues on its own terms rather than on Russian terms. There is no reason why Russian demands on Berlin should not be countered by demands for UN-supervised elections in all of Germany—or even in the other satellites. There is no reason why the relationship of the totalitarian Russian system to the dangers of the arms race should not become the focus of debate. If these issues are linked to the broader issues of peace and war and disarmament and arms control that worry the peoples of the world, it may be possible to use them effectively against the Soviet Union.

It would be wrong to pretend that Communism alone is responsible for the troubles of our age. Indeed, in part, it is a response to even deeper problems. But it is legitimate to point out that Communist political organization increases existing dangers tremendously. It is the responsibility of the American government to publicize these dangers and how Communism increases them. The political organization of the Communist states is not merely an internal matter beyond the legitimate concern of other nations.

Apart from the fact that the Communist states themselves do not hesitate to interfere in other states and attempt to produce changes in their forms of political organization—itself reason to have interest in the internal organization of the Communist regimes—Communist political organization poses a security problem for other states; it increases tremendously the danger of nuclear war and of partial or total destruction. No nation can remain indifferent to this threat. The United States must call upon the Soviet Union to provide more freedom for its people, to permit political opposition, and to open up the country to inspection. Whatever merit there may have been to the Soviet fear that a freer society would have made the Soviet Union more vulnerable to external attack, that fear no longer can have any validity. The Soviet Union is now one of the two strongest nations on earth. It boasts that it is no longer encircled by capitalism and may soon encircle capitalism. It no longer has a right to behave like a weak nation and to plead fear, whether of attack or of espionage. And if, after forty years of Communist rule, the Russian people are unfit to govern themselves, surely that is an indictment of the regime and an additional reason to advocate change of the form of government.

The United States should make it quite clear that the objection to Communism lies not in its form of economic organization—although the United States may prefer a different form or even fear that centralized state control of the economy may make free government more difficult—but in its political organization. The United States must make clear that it does not desire to impose its own substantive views on Russia but desires a situation in which the peoples of the Soviet Union can influence Soviet policy and decide questions of political leadership—a situation in which differing points of view can be put forward and receive circulation.

The United States should no longer view the Soviet leaders as supermen in complete control of their internal environment. The Soviet bloc has its own strains and stresses. The United States should attempt to increase them. Potential conflicts between the members of the bloc should be encouraged by American policies designed to bring them into prominence. Internal stresses within the nations of the bloc should be increased where this can be done responsibly, although obviously the United States does not desire to encourage another "Hungary," where it is unwilling to come to the aid of the revolutionaries. And, most important, the United States should throw the Russians on the ideological defensive.

MILITARY POLICY

American security must continue to rest upon American and NATO arms, although, of course, a merely military policy is bound to fail. However, combined with a constructive diplomacy, the policy of armed resistance to military attempts to change the political map of the world is a sound one. As the United States approaches a situation, however, in which both East and West possess credible second-strike forces, the policy of massive retaliation loses credibility, although fear of an irrational massive retaliation may still deter military aggression. The United States might run great risks to deter future aggressions, but massive retaliation under the specified conditions would be suicidal, and, thus, would serve no useful purpose. Moreover, a military machine geared only to massive retaliation would likely grind to a halt if challenged and, thus, might encourage provocatory actions.[6]

The Russians surely would be clever enough in the future, as they have been in the past, to increase the ambiguity of the circumstances in which they acted and to create at least the pretext of legitimacy or legality. The United States has already seen them maneuver in this fashion in the Congo and Laos in recent years; and they would surely make their demands, each time they made them, relatively moderate. The crisis would be permitted to build slowly, and each time, American allies in Europe and much of the public at home would put pressure on the government to stand firm and inconsistently, at the same time, to compromise. The Laos incident is a good case in point. The most effective intervention the United States could make would be against North Vietnam, and for this, there is a reason in the extent of the Vietminh intervention. There is also strategic reason, for such retaliation would make of intervention something less than a one-way street. Yet clearly, in the present state of opinion, such a measure is not politically feasible.

Unfortunately, despite the inherent incredibility of the policy of massive retaliation, the threat of massive retaliation will have to play a deterrent role in the coming years. However, because of the lessening credibility of the policy, particularly in ambiguous situations, the United States, if it desires an effective foreign policy, will have to be prepared to intervene where necessary with appropriate nonnuclear forces. An inability to so intervene has reduced the bargaining power of the United States in the Laos case. Similar situations may arise elsewhere in Asia, or in Africa and Latin America, in the future. The lack of trained manpower in Europe, although undesirable, is not quite so dangerous because the tripwire theory, if not the best military doctrine, still possesses considerable deterrent power. Guerrilla warfare and internal subversion are not as effective in industrial Europe as they are in underdeveloped areas. Therefore, ambiguous measures are more difficult to find. A massive Soviet push across a clearly defined border would confront the United States with a head-on challenge that it could not afford to duck.

Reliance, however, upon local resistance forces is at best an uncertain expedient. Despite assertions about the superiority of defense over offense, with respect to nonnuclear forces, such a policy would probably only slow Soviet advances. There have been too many blitzkriegs in modern times to place much reliance in this defensive strategy.[7] The ability of the attacker to choose the place and time of attack is a considerable advantage. Perhaps, if the policy of nonnuclear defense were combined with a policy of nonnuclear counterattacks at other points of tension, the policy might have more to recommend it. But clearly this combination would meet with more political resistance than any other kind of strategy including limited strategic nuclear reprisals. There is much to be said for building nonnuclear forces that increase the probability that important areas can be held against nonnuclear attacks even without resort to nuclear reprisals, but there is little to be said for a strategy that depends almost entirely upon the workability of this arrangement for success. It would be as dangerous as a commitment to massive retaliation.

Unfortunately, democracies such as the United States find it politically difficult to develop a coherent and reasonably rational military policy. Regardless of which policy is resorted to, some aspect of it becomes politically infeasible, either through the inability of the United States to carry its allies, or because of domestic opposition within the United States. It is deplorable, not that different strategic doctrines are advocated outside the government, but that various groups place such pressure on government that no coherent doctrine can be adopted. Unfortunately, some vociferous sections of the public cannot distinguish between advice and coercion.

The United States faces one of the most curious and dreadful dilemmas that could be imposed upon a free people. There can be no doubt that democratic political organization is a severe handicap in the kind of world struggle in which the United States finds itself. Yet, the United States cannot win this struggle in a way consonant with its own values without maintaining democratic forms. It, thus, has the problem of presenting its military policy in ways least likely to arouse opposition while at the same time maintaining at least a minimally satisfactory military capability. At best, the means employed will arouse fears and opposition; for this reason, it is essential that public attention be directed to nonmilitary policy goals that arouse widespread enthusiasm. Attention must be diverted from risks to prospects.

It is as difficult to defend an adequate military policy as it was to answer the charges of the late Senator Joseph McCarthy. Such charges have the element of simplicity—answers, that of complexity and subtlety. This is particularly true in the nuclear age when weapons of mass destruction arouse feelings of both horror and fear. It is tempting to the public to believe that there are easy answers to these problems permitting complete avoidance of the dangers. Military strategies immediately frustrate such hopes. Military systems must envisage the possibility of use. It would be useless and wrong to argue that military systems eliminate the possibility of nuclear war. But to demonstrate that appropriate military systems and strategies minimize the probability of nuclear war—and the loss of other values as well—is impracticable, although the argument is correct; understanding the logic of the argument requires considerable knowledge, expertise, and emotional maturity. As is so often the case, the marketplace of ideas does not necessarily make truth popular. And just as Senator McCarthy was finally beaten, not by rational argument but by a change of public sentiment, the case for an adequate military policy rests with the ability of the government to create a climate of opinion in which its proposals will be given the benefit of doubt.

One of the more difficult problems stems from a misguided fear that the military want war or that war is likely unless civilian authorities have firm control. Undoubtedly, many military men resent the damper that the Kennedy administration has placed on their public utterances. But this new policy is necessary, for, given public stereotypes, the military are their own worst proponents. Confidence is much more important than clarity, and the new administration seems effectively to be restoring a confidence that was badly lacking.

The same persons arguing for a foreign policy that would direct public attention from military hazards to constructive tasks are also beginning to argue for the removal of overseas nuclear bases. The United States is reaching the stage at which the major deterrent to the Soviet Union can be based in the United States, the oceans, and perhaps also in the Australian desert. Although there would still be some advantages in having IRBM bases in Europe to insure accuracy in limited strategic retaliation, these reasons probably will be overbalanced by irrational fears that such bases would draw Soviet nuclear fire. A joint NATO deterrent—desirable for still other reasons—could be based in the seas. Thus, Europe would have less reason to fear that American or NATO nuclear bases in Europe would draw Soviet nuclear fire. On the other hand, nonnuclear bases, at least in Europe, would also reassure Europeans that they would not be abandoned by the United States. Although the question is difficult to answer on the basis of public information, serious consideration should be given to relinquishing bases entailing more political liability than military advantage. Bases in Spain, Cuba, Japan, and elsewhere may fall into this category. I do not want to argue that military considerations are unimportant or should be ignored or to deny that many public reactions to military policy are unwise and unfortunate. But decisions have to be related to the constraints that exist—not to those the United States would choose.

SOME SPECIFIC TROUBLE SPOTS

Berlin

A brief look at a few trouble spots in the world will force some qualifications in the more generalized guide-lines for policy that have been suggested earlier. However, this is inevitable whenever principles must be applied, and the seemingly anticlimactic nature of the discussion is a necessary price that is paid for greater specificity.

Perhaps the most vulnerable spot lies in Berlin. It is exceedingly unlikely that an airlift would overcome a similar blockade today. Moreover, the Russians or their East German satellites are unlikely to try anything so crude as the blockade, for such a move, although nonmilitary, might permit unified Western resistance. The Communists are much more likely to raise transit costs, to restrict transit routes, and to close off and "repair" facilities in such a way that the city is slowly strangled. There are really no good countermoves available to the West. The suggestion to move the city of Berlin to another location is hardly feasible and in any event would constitute a symbolic capitulation.

The Russians clearly have reasons to apply the squeeze in Berlin. Defeat in Berlin—even by means of a face-saving, free-city formula— would constitute a tremendous loss in prestige and would affect the credibility of Western protection elsewhere, including areas where feasible protective measures are available. But even were the Russians forebearing enough not to desire to inflict such a loss of prestige upon the West, they would have reason to apply pressure in Berlin. Berlin is in the heart of East Germany. It not only is an area through which skilled workers and professional people had been able to escape to freedom before the new barriers were imposed, but it also provides a direct contrast for East Germans between democracy and totalitarianism, between a life where joy is possible and a life of Communist drabness and puritanism. Even apart from charges that West Berlin is a spy and propaganda center, the existence of a democratic West Berlin subverts Communist tyranny in

East Germany. The East Germans will never accept Communism as a permanent fixture in their lives while they can observe, virtually in their midst, the life of free Germany.

If the issue of Berlin is isolated from other issues, or if the West refuses to consider aggressive action, the trumps are with the Communists. They can choose their moment and need only wait in order not to jeopardize other issues on which they desire negotiation with the West. Their strategic superiority is reinforced by the unwillingness of some Europeans —particularly the British—to take risks for the Germans. Yet, this is an issue on which the West cannot safely concede. It would be morally more indefensible than Munich to sell out the West Berliners, and the political and the military consequences might well be disastrous. If the Communists attempt to strangle Berlin, the West might send an armored column there. Or, alternatively, it might support active paramilitary and subversive actions in East Germany that both threaten the existence of the East German regime and involve a substantial risk of major and nuclear war in central Europe. And the Russians should privately be apprised of a decision to employ such measures before they commit themselves irrevocably with respect to West Berlin. Moreover, the United States should refuse to treat West Berlin as an isolated issue unrelated to freedom in East Berlin or East Germany. On the other hand, some compromise that genuinely protects the freedom of Berlin ought not to be excluded. However, the sooner the risks on action in Berlin are credibly raised for the Russians, the more likely they are to avoid entrapping themselves, and the less likely they are to confront the West with the alternatives of surrender or of policies involving a high risk of war. The issue here, as in China, should be presented clearly as one of human freedom. The United States may occasionally have to compromise this principle, but if the United States betrays it, it will destroy the moral basis of its policy. In this present dangerous and unstable bipolar world, the United States will destroy itself unless its policy is based on an idealism that can generate support.

China

Another major American problem is, of course, China, with its attendant problems of Taiwan, Quemoy, and Matsu. There may be indirect reasons, e.g. alliance pressures and United Nations relationships, to consider Chinese Communist membership in the United Nations, but it is difficult to discover any direct reasons, that is, reasons independent of the interests of third parties, that would establish any American interest in acceding to Chinese Communist representation in the United Nations. There is no substantial evidence that such membership would modify Chinese behavior in any desirable way. It is abundantly clear that such membership would restrict numerous American actions that make life difficult for the Red regime, that bolster non-Communist nations on the periphery, and keep open the possibility of radical change in the regime or of successful revolution.

It is often said that the Communist regime in China is so firmly established that the possibility of successful revolution is, in any event, no longer present. Certainly there is no present reason to predict success-ful revolution. But it is going much farther than the adequacy of either social science techniques or information warrant categorically to exclude the possibility. On similar grounds, many would have denied the possi-bility of the Hungarian revolution—certainly successful until the inter-vention of the Russian army. The Red Chinese regime is indigenous in a sense that the Hungarian regime was not, and this may make difficult a unified national uprising. Moreover, a small nation, with a single major center of national control, is easier to take in revolutionary action. In a large nation, troops can be stationed far from their home area and may not sympathize with revolutionary forces. Such techniques of troop dis-position were employed both under the czars and the dictators in Soviet Russia. And troops can be shifted to trouble spots before the revolution sweeps the entire nation. On the other hand, the Russians could not hope to intervene as they had in Hungary. China is too large. In the last analy-sis, the possibility of successful revolution cannot be excluded, and if this possibility is less probable than the alternatives, the consequences for the United States would be at least as desirable as the event is improbable.

The supposed changes in Chinese behavior that would accompany Red Chinese representation in the United Nations are as hypothetical as a Chinese revolution, and it is difficult to imagine any changes in be-havior that would be strongly supportive of American interests, even though such changes might have some desirability. It is not inconceiv-able that Communist China in the United Nations would be more in-transigent than Communist China outside the United Nations. Whether with American support or against American opposition, whether with an agreement that kept the Nationalist regime in Taiwan in the United Nations or not, the fact of United Nations recognition would confirm to many the Communist Chinese view of the United States as a paper tiger. It is likely that Red Chinese representation would have grave political and military repercussions through Asia.

There are two striking arguments, however, favoring it. One concerns the general qualifications of membership, which ought to apply universalistically. It is possible that the United States ought to support Red Chinese entry—at least on conditions of representation for the Taiwan regime also—on the grounds that interest in the norms governing membership outweighs other consequences of such representation.

A second consideration is that many other nations—some for reasons that are legitimate—believe such action appropriate or desirable and resent American efforts to prevent such representation. The arguments, however, that one must "recognize" reality or that membership in the United Nations will produce better behavior on the part of the Chinese Communists are not worth serious discussion.

It must be added that United Nations representation for the Chinese need not be determinative of American recognition policy. Of course, United Nations representation would remove a barrier to recognition and make more difficult the policy of nonrecognition, but the problems of different forums are themselves different, and the arguments that might weight a decision with respect to the United Nations need not be determinative of the decision in Washington. There is no point to United States recognition until it has more to gain from such recognition than to lose. And it is difficult to see what substantial present advantages would flow from such actions. The opportunity to have diplomatic representation, to observe directly, and to influence does not seem of prime importance and has been much exaggerated in discussion. On those issues that require negotiations with the Chinese, appropriate *ad hoc* means can be found in the future as they have in the past. They will be successful or unsuccessful depending upon the incentive for the Chinese to reach agreement. And at least the *ad hoc* means required by nonrecognition avoid the infelicities and dangers of negotiations at the level of either chief of state or government or high cabinet.

The problem of recognition of the Chinese Communists also directly involves American policy toward Taiwan. Much misinformation exists about the situation on Taiwan, and it is difficult to resolve it in a short space. However, a few remarks are in order. The regime on Taiwan is not fascist or totalitarian. Neither is it an exemplary democratic regime. The national, as opposed to the provincial, government is supposed to represent all of China, and Taiwan is represented only as one of the provinces of China. Along with other measures, including the control of the army and police, this preserves the control of the Kuomintang and of Chiang Kai-shek over Taiwan. Opposition and dissent are permitted but not to the point at which they would challenge the stability of the regime. Personal freedom is quite satisfactory. Economic conditions are improving rapidly despite one of the world's highest birthrates. The land reform is one of the best in the world and has produced a class of peasant entrepreneurs who are proud of their achievements and determined to defend them. Whether the Chiang regime would win a majority vote after freely conducted elections is difficult to determine, but it has at least the passive support of the immense majority of the population. There is no significant support on Taiwan for revolutionary action against the Chiang regime or for Communism. Any policy that permitted Communist conquest of Taiwan would constitute a betrayal not merely of the Kuomintang, but also of the ten million people on Taiwan who abhor Communism and all it stands for.

On the other hand, the Kuomintang is not the organization best endowed to exploit revolutionary possibilities on the China mainland. Although it has reformed considerably since its loss of the mainland, its reputation both in China and in other countries, without whose support aid to revolutionary forces would be difficult or impossible, is bad. A belief that successful revolution would succeed only in reestablishing the Kuomintang in control, although almost surely incorrect, would nonetheless inhibit successful development of the revolution. There are dangers involved in dissociating the United States from the Taiwan regime that should not be underestimated. Yet, in some fashion, a transition in support attitudes seems necessary.

The Quemoy and Matsu problems are exceptionally difficult. There is little sympathy in other countries for retention of these islands, and there seems little doubt that eventually they must be given up to the mainland regime. On the other hand, they do have considerable strategic importance. They block off the important ports of Amoy and Minhow, interdict coastal shipping, and make most difficult any move toward the Pescardores or Taiwan proper. They are quite defensible militarily and could be taken only at a most severe cost, considering the high morale and military ability of the defending forces. Moreover, loss of these islands would bring the active war much closer to Taiwan and have considerable psychological and political consequences on that island. The situation grows progressively more difficult; yet, there seems little reason for a change of policy at this time. Perhaps as part of a deal stabilizing many of the problems in Far Asia, the return of the islands to the mainland regime should be considered. That seems premature presently.

Japan

The problem of American policy toward Japan also is quite difficult. The United States has suffered through a period in which the American embassy cut itself off from the main currents of Japanese opinion and helped to place Japan in a position in which it appeared to have a satellite foreign policy. This has done grave harm to American interests in Japan. American military bases in Japan also do considerable political harm, primarily because their use is misunderstood by most Japanese. Such bases are not designed for offensive operations of either a conventional or nuclear kind. They are important primarily for tactical and logistic reasons. Without these bases, American ability to act rapidly in case of aggression or subversion in important Asian areas would be questionable. The bases also commit America to Japanese defense in a way not possible in their absence. They, thus, deter the use of nuclear threats or blackmail against Japan. There could be no good military reason to use nuclear weapons against these bases without also using them against the United States. Instead, the Japanese wrongly see these bases as increasing the nuclear danger for Japan. It is doubtful, however, whether argument, no matter how correct, will be persuasive on this matter. The United States may have to decide whether the bases are worth the political costs.[8]

Additionally, the United States must encourage Japan to play an independent role in Asia, a difficult proposition because of Japanese unpopularity in much of Asia. But Japanese political frustrations can best be satisfied when Japan has an independent political role that is satisfactory to its dignity as a great and progressive nation. Even though this may mean occasional differences in policy between Japan and the United States, even with respect to a China policy, the improvement of the political situation in Japan ought to be a far more important objective of American foreign policy than the elimination of policy differences. Indeed, it was a fault of American foreign policy under John Foster Dulles that America was too fearful of independent foreign policies on the part of associated nations. Since the United States did not have available Communist techniques for coordination of national policies, despite differences in specific interests, this produced dissatisfaction and malaise on the part of governments that felt they were unwisely or inconsistently coerced or on the part of publics who felt their governments lacked the independence of action consonant with pursuit of national interests and dignity.

Cuba

The ill-fated invasion of Cuba in April 1961 compounded military and political errors that need not be detailed here. In brief, however, the United States moved against Cuba before it moved against right-wing dictators; it supported the wrong elements from among the various anti-Castro groups. These political errors were most serious, for the United States cannot permit itself to appear to oppose Castro only because of his pro-Communism or to support certain Cuban groups because they would reestablish American economic interests in Cuba. Quite apart from the validity of the charges that would arise from such appearances—and I believe them to be false—the fact of the appearances cuts the United States off from the support it needs in a world in which it is not politically feasible to act merely according to the politics of force.

Intervention, as such, was undoubtedly a sound policy, for the present world is not a world in which nonintervention is possible. It is, however, the effectiveness of policy that is important, and it was with respect to this effectiveness that American policy in Cuba failed. Now that intervention has been attempted and has failed, it would be most difficult to resurrect it as a policy in the absence of acute provocation on the part of Cuba. The major American effort must be devoted to reform and modernization in Latin America exclusive of Cuba. This, plus the possible failure of the Cuban revolution to satisfy Cuban expectations concerning modernization, may lead to increased political dissidence and sabotage in Cuba. If the regime can be isolated by the OAS, it may then collapse, or some later intervention may be attempted under more favorable circumstances.

There is, however, another aspect to the problem: this concerns the political consequences for the United States of anti-Castro activities on the part of regimes in nations like Mexico and Venezuela, which the United States wishes to support. It is possible that too overt an effort by the United States to forge an anti-Castro alignment would produce consequences more undesirable than the ouster of Castro is desirable. Yet, Castro in power does pose a threat to the hemisphere. Moreover, failure to support the anti-Castro forces would constitute betrayal of the best and most democratic elements in Cuba. Thus, it would appear that some form of support for the anti-Castro forces is mandatory. The United States cannot afford merely to oppose Castro. It must stand for values it can defend to itself as well as to others. Otherwise, it will fail.

Israel

In the dispute between Israel and the Arab states, there is only one honorable course that the United States can take. Contemporary Arab demands on Israel do not have the function of adjusting a wrong; they have the function of destroying Israel. This is particularly true of the repatriation demand. This does not mean that the United States ought not to sympathize with the plight of the Arab refugees, or that it should approve of the more rambunctious actions of the stiff-necked David Ben-Gurion. Yet, Israel has a right to exist; the Israelis have as much right to self-government as the Arabs; Israel is a democratic state; and it represents most of the virtues in which America believes. Even if the latter were not true, the United States could hardly connive in efforts to destroy a state that is legitimate according to the standards of international law merely to win the favor of the Arabs.

It is a truism to call the Middle Eastern problem complex. To deny the Arab claims is not to underestimate the depth of Arab feelings or the difficulties Arab politicians would have in trying to make peace with Israel. Neither is it to deny that the existence of Israel imposes costs on the United States that would not exist had there never been an Israel; nor is it to deny that the venom the Arabs carry toward Israel helps to corrode their own political efforts individually and collectively. But Israel does exist, and one cannot create the conditions that would have existed had there never been an Israel by cooperating in its demise. Arab demands against Israel are of a nature that cannot be compromised and, therefore, they cannot be met in a way satisfactory to the Arabs short of the destruction of Israel. As much as the United States needs to reconcile the Arab states, destruction is an impossible policy. This is true not merely for internal political reasons, but primarily because a cold-blooded policy of this nature would corrupt U.S. decision processes, make the Arabs contemptuous rather than friendly, increase the demands of those who wish the United States ill, and destroy the confidence of those who wish it well. The United States cannot afford a Machiavellian policy. The United States would only disillusion itself if it behaved in that fashion.

The existence of Israel is due primarily to the desires and organizing skills of the Jews of Palestine. United Nations resolutions and American decisions did not create Israel. They only recognized an existing fact that the Arabs did not have the power to change without extensive outside aid. The United States can share neither the credit nor the blame for the existence of the state of Israel, and those in the Department of State who argued "realistically" for a policy opposed to the Israeli state had little genuine understanding of the world in which they lived. If there was any past mistake in American policy, it was in refusing to impose peace while the United States was strong in the Middle East and the Russians weak. Then, compromises of a durable nature might successfully have been imposed on both sides, and sheer duress might have produced adjustment. Clearly, a state of war would have been difficult to reestablish after the formalization of peace treaties. In the meantime, transactions between Israel and the Arab states, beneficial to both and difficult to sever, might have been established. But that opportunity— sacrificed as usual by the "realists"—is past and cannot be recalled. The present situation is most difficult and will remain so almost regardless of what the United States does.

Harsh as it may sound, the United States cannot gain from major efforts to reconcile the Arab states. It must depend upon their self-interest in maintaining independence from the Russians and in continuing the flow of oil. When and if the Arabs ever become ready, the United States ought to cooperate with them in endeavors or projects consonant with American values and Arab interests. Until such time, there is no point in wishing for a world that cannot be.

Conclusion

Any particular policy recommendation may, of course, prove inappropriate on the basis of more careful analysis or more thorough consideration of the relevant factors. But two general considerations emerge from the preceding analysis that, in my opinion, would constitute good guidelines for policy decisions. The United States needs to enunciate foreign-policy goals that are capable of arousing support and enthusiasm both within the United States and among our allies. Indeed, these goals would serve best if they became known behind the iron curtain and had subversive effects there. The status quo will no longer be sufficient for success. The United States must take its chances with change and attempt to promote those changes harmonious with its own values and with the best interests of peoples everywhere. Time is no longer with the United States. Holding the line and delaying actions will not do. The United

States is neither rich nor strong enough to be conservative or to ignore or to deny the aspirations of the great masses of mankind. It must choose, and only if it chooses rightly can it hope to preserve those values and institutions that it holds dear.

Positive goals must be backed by a sound military and diplomatic posture. Idealism in terms of objectives must not be confused with muddleheadedness in terms of means. The United States faces a strong foe, capable of resorting to military action and willing to employ threats of the most provocative type. This foe will use negotiations and conferences primarily, not to reach cooperative agreement but to destroy America's institutions and way of life. Unless and until the United States can force changes in the foe's mode of organization and operation—not necessarily by physical means—it also must regard the situation as a struggle. It must be ceaselessly alert, reasonably confident, and ready to defend what it stands for.

In its relations with its friends and allies, the United States must recognize that their interests and their goals are not identical with those of the United States. It must expect some disagreements with them and, if it respects their freedom and independence, it should also respect their right to disagree. Despite the desperate nature of the struggle, the United States cannot expect to dictate to other nations. It does and ought to expect general support from its friends. But it must earn this support in terms of policies that win their support. Where this is not feasible, and where the United States is certain that it is right, it must have the courage and moral fortitude to temporarily go it alone, without renouncing its interest in or friendship for other countries.

These are difficult demands to make in a democracy. To repeat what has become trite, but nonetheless remains true, this cannot be accomplished without strong presidential leadership, which takes the people into its confidence and builds the kind of public support, based on trust, that will permit ventures into the untried and the imaginative realms of statecraft. Beneath the layers of selfishness and self-centerednesss the ideals of the United States will still support policies oriented to vision and faith. There is still an American ideal that views democracy and the products of modern civilization as the heritage of all.

IX

American World Strategy and the Mediterranean Basin (1975)

The Mediterranean basin, although posing problems for American world strategy that are specific to its history, culture, and political, economic, and strategic characteristics, also encapsulates the central problem of that world strategy. The future of world politics will depend, at least for the next decade and probably for the next generation, upon the evolution of the area that radiates outward from the Mediterranean basin. The northwest quadrant—roughly that of Western Europe—contains the largest concentration of skilled manpower in the world and an economic capacity comparable to that of North America or the Soviet bloc. The southeast quadrant of the area possesses vast and cheap energy resources, the continuous flow of which for the next decade or two is essential to the economic and political health of the northwest quadrant.

The northeast quadrant contains the Soviet zone of Europe, including European Russia and Eastern Europe. With Asian Russia, it takes in most of what MacKinder called the heartland. If that zone dominated the northwest and southeast quadrants, its concentration of strength upon China might well become overwhelming, and the imputed Soviet goal of a *cordon sanitaire* around China, extending from Siberia through India and Southeast Asia, might create an environment in which China

This article was first presented as a paper to The Chicago Council on Foreign Relations as part of a seminar held on *Issues in the Mediterranean Basin* in the late winter of 1975.

would have no choice except to accommodate itself to a hegemonial Soviet system centered in Moscow. In this case, the Soviet Union would
dominate what MacKinder called the "world island," which, he said,
dominates the world. In any event, even if MacKinder's analysis is wrong,
the United States would effectively be encircled, and the Fortress America
that some groups proclaim and that others fear—a fortress that in my
opinion would be economically and militarily, but not politically or
socially, viable—would have come into being.

If this projected nightmare is not a certainty, or perhaps is not even
a high probability, neither is it an absurd projection from potentialities
that are already present in world politics and that are hoped for by at
least some in the Soviet hierarchy. The character of this potential threat
is masked by overreactions to the discredited cold-war hypotheses of Soviet military attack, and also by historical memories of Western Europe
as the locus of world politics and as the center of immense economic and
military capabilities.

The cold-war myths have always obscured the real character of the
Soviet threat to American interests. And the countermyths that have been
generated since then have helped to obscure the real problem of statecraft with respect to contemporary Europe. The extent to which nations
or other organized congeries of individuals can play effectively independent roles in world politics depends upon far more than economic potential and available military manpower. It depends also upon strategic
space: space that is measured in miles is a phenomenon almost totally
different from space measured in minutes of time. A military defensive
front that has open terrain within which to function is quite different
from one that is interpenetrated by huge masses of fleeing civilians. A
political system that can retreat intact to a hinterland while considerable
portions of its population lie within enemy control is far different from
one in which the front consists of the entire nation.

During World War II, some of the fronts in Eastern Europe had a
depth of over six hundred miles. The distance from the East German
border to Paris is less than three hundred miles or, to use an American
analogy, approximately the width of the state of Pennsylvania. In terms
of today's military technology, the northwest quadrant of the Mediterranean basin is not a surface but, rather, a skin on an Eurasian world
island. Conversely, just as certain optical illusions provide the appearance of contrasting pictures simultaneously, the northwest quadrant may
be viewed as a semi-autonomous skin on an Atlantic system. In this case,
the hinterland reappears, as does strategic viability. Unfortunately, in the

realm of politics, images cannot be reversed by a simple *trompe l'oeil.* Which image will best represent the underlying reality will depend in part, at least, upon the political and strategic policies that help to shape events.

The sculptor who works upon driftwood, if skilled, attempts to work with the qualities of his material, to bring out his preferred image from among the several that the characteristics of the material make potential. In a complex world of historical, political, economic, cultural, and military factors, successful policy must be adapted to general but functionally differentiated aspects of problems and to their diverse localized characteristics. Policy must avoid both a specificity detached from a more general framework of political and strategic design and a uniformity unrelated to functional differentiation or problems of localization.

Western Europe is unlike the southern half of the Mediterranean basin in two important respects. It is the immediate pressure area upon which the Soviet sphere impinges. And, fortunately, at the same time, it has sufficient cultural identification with the United States and a long and secure enough tradition of independence to be capable of serving within a common alliance in which the United States, by virtue of its size and unified political system, is the dominant partner. The major mistake of John Foster Dulles was to fail to recognize the small contribution most nations of the southern half of the basin would make to military defense, as well as the historical and cultural discontinuities that would make an alliance with the United States dysfunctional and even an apparent threat to national, political, and economic objectives.

Thus, NATO met a definite need when it was born, and it continues to meet a definite need of the northwest quadrant of the area, although in altered form, in the contemporary era. The continued credible existence of NATO is a continued reassurance not against the fear of an overt Russian attack so much as against the feeling of helplessness that would pervade Western Europe in its absence. The continued independence of Western Europe within the framework of the NATO alliance with the United States also acts as a barrier against Russian pressure on the southeast quadrant of the area.

One great mistake of the United States in its leadership of NATO has been the unconscious tendency of most American leaders to equate NATO interests in the important western sector of Eurasia with American worldwide strategic interests, and, thus, to seek to associate its allies with its independently chosen policies elsewhere in the world as the price of the American connection. We have done this in Korea and Vietnam, as well as elsewhere, when it was not necessary, and, as a consequence, we have associated ourselves with European interests in Africa and Asia that were contrary to American interests. And we have imposed upon ourselves undesirable constraints on the decisions we have made.

Thus, as the myth of Soviet military attack receded, and as the economic and political substructures of European national independence were reconstructed, strains developed within NATO that continue to this day. Moreover, in its attempt to develop a condition of détente with the Soviet Union, the United States has tended to ignore its Western European partners in the formation of policies that are of obvious and direct concern to them.

The unnecessary uniformity of posture that the United States has tended to insist upon played a clearly dysfunctional role during the Yom Kippur War in 1973. The immediate economic vulnerabilities of Western European nations might have suggested to the United States the virtue of allowing the most vulnerable Western European nations to neutralize themselves with respect to the particular controversy. Such a policy, particularly in view of the inability of the United States to reassure Western European nations with respect to their energy supplies, would have tended to reinforce feelings of solidarity and, most likely, would have enhanced joint efforts to find energy and other economic policies that would avoid such serious conflicts of interest in the future. Instead, American handling of the episode served to emphasize the conflicts of interest between the United States and Western Europe; had it not been for the perception of the current national leaders in Western Europe that this area remains highly dependent on American support, this attempt to enforce a uniformity of position that was neither necessary to American policy with respect to the war in the Middle East nor conducive to the search for ways of avoiding future conflicts of interests of the same type, might have done even more to weaken, and perhaps gravely to injure, the alliance.

Another mistake of current American policy is represented by its failure to adapt policy to conflicts of interests within the Soviet sphere, as well as to relationships between external and internal policies within Eastern Europe. With respect to the former problem, the Eastern European regimes have a distinct interest in a strong Warsaw Treaty Organization and a powerful Soviet Union, for a number of those regimes would likely fall as a result of popular discontent if these conditions did not hold. On the other hand, the current autonomy that many of the Eastern European nations have—and which they value highly—would probably not long persist in the event of Soviet hegemony in Europe. Thus, as long as Western Europe remains strong and in an alliance with the United States, the Soviet Union requires the voluntary cooperation of its Eastern European allies, for involuntary cooperation would involve both high economic and political costs for the Soviet Union, as well as military costs that Soviet generals fear.

As a result, the current situation places constraints on policies that the Soviet Union can follow, policies that might produce the kinds of threats that would undermine the political assurance of Western European countries and that might produce their self-Finlandization: a condition in which they would accept Soviet domination of European high politics while maintaining considerable internal autonomy much as Finland does today. Even this "worst case" projection may be too sanguine, however, for the "Finlandization" of Finland may be consistent with Finland's internal autonomy only because of the strength of NATO.

This problem is correctly perceived by many Western European Communists, including the powerful Italian Communist Party. Although the willingness of the Italian Communists to accept NATO is in part a response to a perceived condition for acceptability in some future leftward-leaning coalition in Italy, I believe that it probably represents as well their perception that Italian and European interests require NATO as a barrier to Soviet pressure. Although there are arguments against American initiatives with respect to a potential entry of the Italian Communists into Italian high politics—at least until their commitment to pluralistic democratic procedures assumes even greater credibility than it now has—it is inadvisable for the United States to behave in ways that appear to force choices upon Italians that may be neither in their interests nor in the United States' to constrain. Indeed, one virtue of Communist participation in cabinet politics in Italy, if the Communist Party of Italy strengthens its democratic commitment, might be the breaking of the perceived link between American interests and capitalism—a perceived link that creates resistance to common activities with the United States because it is seen as a barrier to economic reform—and the strengthening of the perceived link of America with democratic and pluralistic political developments elsewhere in the world.

In this respect, the current situation in Portugal is instructive. Although I would not agree with it, there might be an argument for a Brezhnev doctrine in reverse, in which the United States would bring down the current Portuguese regime. I utterly fail to see the virtue of a policy that views current developments with alarm, however, while taking no effective measures to prevent them. Even worse, the verbal posture of the United States, if not its official actions, serves to constrain the alternatives perceived by the current military leadership in Portugal. It may be that eventually Portugal will develop exactly as the United States fears; it may even be that this will happen regardless of the policies the United States follows. But I do not see how this can be predicted now. Wisdom would seem to indicate an effort to preserve alternatives for the more moderate of the Portuguese military and to discourage, rather than to encourage, those cries of alarm in Western Europe that encourage reactionary political tendencies as a barrier to future "Portugals," for this would produce greater divisiveness politically within at least some of the Western European states and consequently would have the effect of weakening NATO.

Strong arguments can be made for supporting authoritarian as opposed to Communist states. When Greece was authoritarian, as Spain remains today, they served as the linchpins of the Mediterranean, militarily speaking. The United States either cooperated with those regimes or it could not protect Western Europe on its southern flank. Such states were likely to be on the side of the United States, moreover, while Communist states were more likely to be on the Soviet side. And finally, authoritarian states tend to be less stable than Communist states and, therefore, constitute less of a barrier to future democratic developments.

Nonetheless, these distinctions are difficult for the average person in Western Europe to understand. From his perspective, there did seem to be certain political contradictions in the American posture. For this reason, much of the American reaction to the developments in Portugal is misperceived in Europe as opposition to socialism rather than to authoritarianism. Furthermore, however mistaken many of these developments may be from the United States' perspective, the Portuguese who hold control perceive of themselves as part of the Third World and believe that Portugal requires extreme structural economic reform—a reform they believe can be brought about only by unified political control. Without endorsing their move toward authoritarianism, as the United States should not endorse similar moves elsewhere in the world, there should have been more public American sympathy for the economic and social objectives of the Portuguese revolution, as well as for the initially apparent democratic political objectives.

As the United States extends its horizon toward the southern half of the Mediterranean basin, it comes to a number of states with strong economic and historical ties to Western Europe, and vice versa, but with strong desires to remain outside of the American defensive perimeter. Moreover, several of these states possess vast energy resources that are of essential interest to the Western European allies. Thus, the countries of the Mediterranean basin have a natural tendency to seek a solution to common economic problems in a manner that does not distinguish, immediately at least, between the consuming and the producing states. Moreover, because of the Third World perspective of the states of the southern half of the Mediterranean basin, many of these states see the current energy problem as merely replicating in milder form problems that have been faced for a long time by single-resource, export-dependent states. These southern states also sympathize with the feeling by some states that they have been excluded from the management of world monetary decisions in ways prejudicial to their interests.

From this perspective, the initial American efforts to isolate the problem of energy and to bring it before NATO were strongly counterproductive. Subsequent efforts to separate consumers from producers and to restrict consideration to problems of energy increased the strains between the nations of the southern half of the Mediterranean basin and those of the northwest quadrant. As a consequence, these efforts also increased strains between the nations of the northwest quadrant and the United States.

Furthermore, the current American posture, rather than responding to important structural problems in the developing world system, continues to treat this problem as one of crisis management—and in this case, ironically, in terms of a crisis that market forces are in the process of solving without international management, provided that oil consumption is controlled adequately. The result of this is both to defeat reformulation of programs of international cooperation within which the nations of the southern half of the Mediterranean basin might find distinct interests in common with those of the United States—thus prejudicing past feelings of goodwill toward the United States—and to emphasize discordant interests. As long as the United States does this, NATO, in many respects, will appear as a threat to the interests of the nations of the southern half of the basin, even though many of the leaders of this area may recognize it as a necessary evil, given the Russian presence. This failure of American policy to adapt to functional differentiations responsive to the conditions of the Mediterranean area serves to undermine the very important and appropriate military functions that NATO is intended to reinforce.

I referred previously to Western Europe as the thin skin—a semi-autonomous thin skin—of the Atlantic area. A second image was of Western Europe as the thin skin of Eurasia. A third image may see Western Europe as part of the central structure of the Mediterranean community. The first and third images are not necessarily in conflict, although current American policy may place them in conflict. The semi-autonomy of the thin skin with respect to the Atlantic area is the key element. National systems are sufficiently complex to be interdependent parts of separate organizations. Just as it is in the American interest, albeit with certain discordant elements, to encourage some degree of European unity, so it might be in the American interest to encourage commonality of interests within the Mediterranean basin, provided that these are not in discordance with the requirements of NATO.

One immediate function of this encouragement, provided a peace settlement is reached between Israel and the Arab states, might be the development of a Mediterranean sentiment that, although not obliterating the distinctions between European and Arabian, diminishes feelings of "foreignness" between these two cultural areas. Indeed, this might even be an inducement to such a settlement. To some extent, the hostility of Arabs toward Israel stems from a perception—neither entirely accurate nor entirely inaccurate—that Israel is a European outpost rather than an integral part of the Middle East. Distinctions change with circumstances, and a transformed American policy toward resources and monetary issues, as well as toward its alliance structure in Europe, likely will be among the factors that can transform these perceptions and identifications.

It should not be the American objective to exclude the Soviet Union from a role in the Mediterranean. The Soviet Union is part of Eurasia—a part that weighs on the Mediterranean area and that, through its allies, directly impinges upon it. Any effort to exclude the Soviet Union, apart from the fact that it has already failed, would force the nations of this area into conflicting choices that would be difficult for them and that would create resistance to American policies. The problem for American policy is to involve the Soviet Union in ways that are on the whole supportive rather than destructive of American interests. Thus, many of the area problems requiring joint solutions should be open to Soviet and Chinese participation. Although Japan is not of direct interest in a discussion of the Mediterranean area, this type of approach is of particular importance with respect to the Japanese, who require an American alliance but who, in other senses, do not wish to choose sides. The maintenance of diverse functional activities within which these states can cooperate with the Soviet Union and China would reduce their perception that they are taking sides. Thus, this would make their security policies more palatable to sections of the public who otherwise might find them distasteful.

The great failure of American policy lies in its reactive features. During the first Truman administration, a number of constructive steps were taken, such as the formation of NATO and the Marshall Plan. Even those steps, however, were formulated within the framework of an overriding concern with defense against Communist military aggression. The difficulty with this type of policy is that it attempts to maintain a static situation in a dynamic world. Historians may argue over whether Metternich delayed the collapse of the old order, but the one thing that is clear beyond doubt is that the old order collapsed.

Soviet policy is based upon the construction of a new order—one that, in my opinion, is mistaken in its fundamental assumptions as well as in its views of the alternatives facing the world. Nonetheless, that perspective provides the Soviet Union with a view of connections between domestic and external policies of the states of the world system that is of distinct value in the formulation of Soviet international policy. The Soviet Union does have a vision of a future international order that it is trying to build, and this is a vision that can be pursued within the framework of a reasonably systematic and constructive policy.

American policy, on the one hand, is too uniform in the sense that it is not functionally differentiated. On the other hand, it is reactive and responsive to techniques of crisis management, rather than to considerations of future world order.

It is far more efficient to minimize the disturbances that produce crises than to respond to successive crises in their individual terms. More than this, only an understandable constructive policy will produce the degree of public support that is required in a democratic age for the systematic pursuit of policy.

NOTES

CHAPTER I

1. It is interesting to note that General Douglas MacArthur restated this position as late as 1956.
2. Joseph P. Grew, *Turbulent Era*, edited by Walter Johnson, Houghton Mifflin, 1952, pp. 1445–1446.
3. Cf. Litvinov's statement—"We Marxists are the last who can be reproached with allowing sentiment to prevail over policy." Jane Degras, *Soviet Documents on Foreign Policy*, III (1953), p. 56.
4. Cf. W. Anders, *Hitler's Defeat in Russia*, for a contrary view. Anders, the Commander of the Polish army-in-exile, claimed that the Soviet Union is actually much more vulnerable to attack from the south than from the west because a southern attack would cut the long, but narrow, east-west belt into isolated parts.
5. A *New York Times* item of March 18, 1946, gives some indication that these strategic factors were being considered. Close to 1,000,000 Russian troops, some in the Balkans, have been in easy reach of the Turkish borders "for some months now."
6. Speech of N. Bukharin, a leading member of the Soviet Politburo, at the Fourth Congress of the Communist International, November 18, 1922.
7. O'Donnell's intemperate remarks were inserted into the Congressional Record by Senator Burton Wheeler.
8. The *Daily News* was the newspaper of Frank Knox, Roosevelt's Secretary of the Navy.
9. Contemporary press reports held that the Soviet occupation forces in Eastern Europe had been increased by 30,000 to 60,000 men in the previous week or two. They were reported to be heading toward Turkey, toward

282 THE LIFE AND DEATH OF THE COLD WAR

Iraq, and to be within twenty miles of Teheran. Within the next two weeks, however, the Soviet Union had been forced to agree to withdraw its troops, and it did so by May 6. President Truman later hinted that he had delivered an ultimatum to the Soviet Union.

10. At the Council of Foreign Ministers in New York on the subject of the peace treaties, in December. See James M. Byrnes, *Speaking Frankly,* Harper and Brothers, 1947, p. 154.

11. The tests were designed to evaluate the effects of the bomb upon a dispersed naval fleet. Whether there were also secondary political objectives is difficult to determine. However, they were viewed as a "sabre rattling" device in some quarters.

12. There is every reason to believe that Wallace's technical arguments were accepted at the highest levels in the government. Cf. Bernard Brodie, ed., *The Absolute Weapon,* Harcourt Brace, 1946, for a contemporary evaluation of the impact of the bomb for military strategy. Wallace left out of the account only the relatively easy and cheap delivery of the weapon. However, there were vast differences at the highest levels concerning the political lessons to be derived from the technical facts.

13. The reader should not read this to mean that the position was a clearly-thought-out one, with the underyling postulates unambiguously presented, or that all who accepted the position in general were agreed upon the reasons for doing so or upon the consequences that should have been derived from the position. Moreover, the position kept shifting toward Churchill's view as the prognosis of Soviet intentions became less sanguine.

14. Churchill's objective was to secure American realization of this before the British world position was destroyed. Left-wing Laborites like Richard Crossman disputed the thesis. They claimed that Britain inevitably would be destroyed in an atomic war. Therefore, the European democracies must, Crossman held, form a bloc of uncommitted nations. At first, he said, the Soviet Union would be hostile, but when it came to realize that this bloc was not directed against it, the Soviet Unon would accede and come to terms. Thus, Crossman viewed Soviet actions as the result of suspiciousness and security needs, whereas Churchill viewed them as an expression of Bolshevik policy and goals.

15. See L. B. Namier, *In the Nazi Era,* Macmillan, 1952, p. 72. The anti-Hitler Germans in the foreign office preferred "chemical dissolution" through external pressure and fifth columns to armed warfare or the open threat of force.

16. Representative Thomason, Congressional Record, *92,* 7479. Taken from John C. Sparrow, *History of Personnel Demobilization,* Department of the Army, July 1952, p. 256.

17. Sparrow, *ibid,* p. 268.

18. Sparrow, *ibid,* p. 275.

Chapter II

1. American representatives seemed to have recognized this fact only after the Soviet Union had developed the atomic bomb. At this point, it was too late to attempt to link the two classifications of weapons because the United States no longer had a bargaining counter.
2. *Forrestal Diaries,* Viking, 1951, p. 514.

Chapter III

1. That is, a party dictatorship was established in which the central organs of the party also had dictatorial control over party members.
2. Although not a member of the Communist Party, Chiang was a fellow traveler of the Communists in this period. In Moscow in 1926, Chiang declared that "the realization of the Three People's Principles means the realization of Communism . . . and one cannot deny that the Chinese revolution is part of the world revolution."
3. These events, of course, may be given a different interpretation, namely, that Chiang was a secret anti-Communist all along and only cooperated with the Communists to gain sufficient strength to destroy them. This interpretation is possible but unlikely.
4. The Comintern budget for all of Asia in 1927 was reported to have been $17,000.
5. By June 1944, the United States had taken a stronger position with regard to Korea. It was to be independent, and its people should determine the ultimate form of its government.
6. Admiral Chester Nimitz had advocated an American landing in China.
7. The career officers, not knowing of the Yalta accord, were convinced that the Soviet Union would not enter into a treaty agreement with China because of the trouble in Sinkiang and the fricton between the Kuomintang and the Chinese Communists.
8. State, War, Navy Coordinating Committee.
9. Chiang appeared downcast upon receiving this information.
10. MacArthur was not questioned on this at the 1951 Senate Far East hearings. However, when the telegram mentioned came up, he cabled Senator Knowland, in part (p. 2249) : "For anyone to read such an inference [that the proposed agreement between Chiang and the Communists] from the quotation contained in your message is almost beyond belief. . . . The Communists, but a nebulous threat at that time, constituted only one of major factions which sought to secure balance of political power." However, Wedemeyer stated (p. 2352) : "The major opposing groups were unquestionably the Kuomintang and the Communist Party." Later, the testimony continued (p. 2352) : "*Senator McMahon*: You advocated that our aid be

so used . . . to bring together and to effect a compromise between Chiang Kai-shek and the Communist forces. . . . *General Wedemeyer*: That is right, sir. *Senator McMahon*: And your objectives were to promote a unified, democratic China. *General Wedemeyer*: That is right, sir." He denied, however, that he had favored a coalition government, although he admitted (p. 2421) that the average American would read that interpretation into his telegram.

11. This became quite clear during the farce when Li was acting president and Sun Fo was premier, and neither was able to countermand the orders of the "retired" Chiang.
12. The membership was the same as the Committee of Three: Marshall, Chang Chih-chung, and Chou En-lai.
13. The embargo was lifted on May 26, 1947.
14. Marshall, in an attempt to secure agreement, was apparently giving both sides contradictory advice on the probable development of the military situation.
15. *Far East Hearings*, p. 2367. The State Department objected to the inclusion of the Soviet Union. The portion of the report naming the Soviet Union was omitted from the White Paper on China for political reasons.
16. Apparently, the Chinese Communists were supposed to "play dead" if the Soviet Union so ordered. This was most dubious.
17. This is no doubt a reference to the gold and silver that Chiang had illicitly taken from the government reserves and which he refused to release for the defense of China.
18. Wedemeyer stated that the Nationalists could have defended the Yangtze "with broomsticks" had they the will to fight.
19. Several of these officers were later dismissed because of the accuracy of their reports.
20. Joint United States Military Advisory Group.
21. General Moody, who was a member of General Barr's mission, also disagreed with Barr's conclusions.
22. The contrast with the rapid supply of equipment to Greece and Turkey in the same period was quite noticeable.
23. General Wedemeyer also thinks that American criticism may have played a role in engendering lack of morale, but the purpose of the criticism was to encourage reform.
24. Whether the actual contents of the letter Acheson sent to Connally were known by Li is conjectural. It was made clear to him, nevertheless, that the United States government had written off China.

CHAPTER IV

1. Yugoslavia claimed that, between July 16, 1946, and August 8, 1946, eighty-seven bombers, forty fighters, and forty-five transports had crossed Yugo-

slav territory without authorization. Yugoslavia had protested a score of times before the shootings.

2. Ante Pavelic, Nazi-sponsored puppet dictator of Croatia, was given sanctuary by the American army.

3. The Yugoslav commentary to the letters contended the speech was directed against the West. This is quite unlikely.

4. Gomulka supported the Yuogslavs later despite the criticism he had received at their hands. However, by mid-1948, his position in the Polish United Workers Party had been almost completely undermined, and he was under house arrest.

5. If Moscow could free the Yugoslav army from Yugoslav Communist Party supervision, it would be easier to encourage defections to the MVD.

6. The Soviet Union received an account from Sreten Zhujovic, a prominent member of the Yugoslav party.

7. The Russian reply of March 27 mentions, in addition to this letter, an earlier letter of March 18 of which there is no published record. According to Khrushchev, Stalin said he would wag his little finger and Tito would fall.

8. The Russian reply denied that access to the information had been promised.

9. The Russian release states the latter was written by the Central Committee (C.C.) of the C.P.S.U., but Yugoslav photostats show the signatures of Stalin and Molotov below the typewritten document.

10. The Yugoslavs denied this charge, but it is almost certainly correct.

11. The Yugoslavs again denied the charges and again were probably not telling the truth.

12. This was a greater concentration of formal authority in Rankovic than in his counterparts in the CPSU, but the Soviet Union was undoubtedly more disturbed by the fact that he had so effectively combated its attempts to infiltrate the Yugoslav party with its agents.

13. These last charges verged on the silly. The Communist Party controlled the situation more effectively than the parties in the other satellites. The agrarian and economic programs of the Yugoslav party compared favorably, according to Marxist standards, with the programs of the other states in the Communist bloc.

14. The Yugoslavs claimed that Bela Rakosi, the Hungarian party secretary, had criticized the Russians previously for plundering Hungary and for anti-Semitic tendencies. He had previously asked Yugoslavia for help against the USSR.

15. Adam Ulam (*Titoism and the Cominform*, Harvard, 1952) takes this fact as evidence that the Yugoslavs still had a lingering hope that the Soviet Union would see things their way. This seems farfetched to me. I rather believe that the Yugoslavs were appealing to the undecided within their own ranks who might not go along with the leadership if the final consequences were too clear at this time.

16. Gomulka "thought at first that the measures applied to deal with the CPY at the Cominform meeting were too severe. I thought one should have talked with the leadership of the CPY, sent a delegation; one should have explained, and pleaded, and perhaps conceded something." Quoted from Ulam, *ibid*, p. 142. Since this statement occurred in Gomulka's recantation, it may not express the whole truth.
17. Zhujovic recanted after the trial of Laszlo Rajk in Hungary late in 1949 and was released from prison.
18. The American Embassy claims to have notified Washington in June of the impending break.
19. Although Yugoslavia would probably have rejected any such efforts in the period immediately following the disagreement, the lack of effort was surprising.

CHAPTER V

1. "An Introduction to the Strategy of Statecraft," *World Politics*, July 1952, pp. 557–561. (Incidentally, it points out also, p. 570, "It is difficult to predict what will happen when an old and sick man [Stalin] dies.")
2. Peter Calvocoressi, *Survey of International Affairs: 1947–1948*. Oxford University Press, 1952.
3. Franz Borkenau, *European Communism*, Faber and Faber, London, 1953, p. 536.
4. According to a protocol of the Czechoslovak-Soviet treaty of November 23, 1945, the exploitation of all sources of radium and radioactive materials in Czechoslovak territory was transferred to Soviet control for twenty years.
5. In a toast during March 1945, Stailn declared: "I hate Germans. Slavs footed the bill for the first world war, and also the second world war is being solved at their expense. In the first world war the English and French fought the Germans, but the Slavs paid dearly for that. And finally the Germans were put on their feet again to form the so-called European balance of power.... The Soviet Union wants nothing else than to gain allies who will never interfere in the internal affairs of its neighbors." Eduard Taborsky, "Benes and Stalin—Moscow, 1943 and 1945," *Journal of Central European Affairs* (July 1953), XIII, p. 179. Though one need not believe everything Stalin says during a toast, the German problem evidently did preoccupy him.
6. Taborsky, *op. cit.*, p. 158. Britain protested and delayed the agreement until after the Moscow Conference of the Foreign Ministers that year. Britain was fearful that the pact might isolate the Poles. Roosevelt had approved the pact earlier. Zdenek Fierlinger claimed that Eduard Benes had opposed the alliance in the form adopted. *New York Times* (December 12, 1948). There is no evidence to sustain his statement, however.
7. Taborsky, *op. ct.*, p. 170.

8. Hubert Ripka, *Czechoslovakia Enslaved*, Gollancz, London, 1950, p. 27. The National Socialists held the important Ministry of Justice.

9. Taborsky, *op. cit.*, p. 180.

10. Jan Stransky, *East Wind Over Prague*, Hollis and Carter, London, 1950, p. 63.

11. William Diamond, *Czechoslovakia between East and West*, Stevens & Sons (1947), p. 122.

12. Diamond, *ibid*, p. 121.

13. The strike had also been used before the coup to force the nationalization of industries not otherwise eligible under official government regulations.

14. The Communst Party opposed autonomy only after it lost the Slovak elections.

15. The Slovak Labor Party was the Slovak branch of the Czech Social-Democratic Party.

16. Actually only 0.45 percent of all the votes cast were blanks. It is more difficult to estimate the effect of the disfranchisement of "collaborators."

17. The small vote of the Freedom (Catholic) Party did constitute convincing evidence that a highly organized movement succeeded in swinging most anti-Communist votes to the stronger Democratic Party; the Church organization had recommended to parishioners that they vote for the Slovak Democratic Party. The prewar strength of the Catholic Party was such that a vote of 0.85 percent could not be credited; and it became known that the Democratic Party had agreed to include among its candidates members of the outlawed Slovak People's Party. This accusation came with bad grace, however, from the Communists to whom such methods were far from unknown.

18. Diamond, *op. cit.*, p. 52.

19. Diamond, *ibid*, p. 45.

20. According to J. Stransky, *op. cit.*, pp. 45–46, a secret order of the Czech Communist Party contained the following instructions: "Never deny that the Republic is in a satellite position to the U.S.S.R. It is necessary that people should realize the position, and that our enemies should be afraid!"

21. Production in 1947 was only 96 percent of the 1929 level. However, because of deaths and expulsions, the population was 19 percent lower in 1947 than in 1929.

22. In addition, the failure of the American army to come to the aid of Prague when it rose against the Germans in 1945 had caused many citizens of Czechoslovakia to believe that their country had been assigned to the Soviet sphere of influence by the great powers.

23. *New York Times* (March 3, 1947).

24. Ripka, *op. cit.*, pp. 52–54.

25. Unlike the Polish Communists, the Czechs had been cool from the beginning.

26. Ripka, *op. cit.*, p. 56. Moscow radio announced that Poland and Rumania would not participate before the Polish cabinet reached its decision. Rumania was still denying the Moscow report on July 8.
27. Ripka, *ibid.*, p. 70. Many informed Europeans felt in this period that war was drawing close.
28. Conversation with Peter Zenkl, a leading member of the National Socialist Party.
29. Ripka, *op. cit.*, p. 91.
30. Ripka, *ibid,* p. 93.
31. Ripka, *ibid,* p. 96. Slansky apparently expressed himself more strongly than Gottwald. According to Douglas Hyde, *I Believed*, William Heinemann Ltd., 1951, p. 234, William Rust, the editor of the *London Daily Worker*, had talked to Tito several months earlier and had been informed that Gottwald was out of favor. Tito said that the Czech Communist Party had been arguing that under the special conditions prevailing in Czechoslovakia one could achieve Communism by using democratic methods of organization. At the same time the other new democracies were imposing the classical dictatorship of the proletariat. The Czechoslovak position was heretical according to Tito and was causing trouble elsewhere. He predicted that a showdown would occur soon. And though this may appear to confirm the speculation advanced by many writers of a split between Slansky and Gottwald, the evidence is very weak. Tito criticized Gottwald and the party, and Slansky was secretary-general of the party. I am not familiar with any direct evidence that in the following months any major divergence in policy occurred between Slansky and Gottwald. Slansky did support Gomulka at the first Cominform meeting. Thus, contrary to the usual interpretation, Slansky, and not Gottwald, may have been the moderate. V. Dedijer, *Tito Speaks*, Weidenfeld and Nicholson, 1953, p. 306. On the other hand, there is some indirect evidence that the Czech Communist Party was under pressure from Moscow, possibly for ideological and strategic reasons. As the international situation grew more serious, the need to secure tight control of Czechoslovak production and of the strategic *glacis* became of paramount importance to the Soviet Union.
32. *Christian Science Monitor*, August 4, 1947.
33. He claimed that only the employees who opened the packages—rather than Zenkl, Drtna, or Masaryk—would have been injured had the bombs exploded.
34. Mikoyan asked Ripka whether Fierlinger's fall did not indicate that Czechoslovakia was detaching itself from its Soviet alliance. Similar complaints came from representatives of satellite states. It is difficult to judge the extent to which these statements represented fears and the extent to which they constituted attempts to intimidate the Czechs.
35. Majer supported Lausman since he was the candidate most likely to defeat

Fierlinger. Ripka, *op. cit.*, p. 121. Lausman had received Communist support in the past, and in 1945, he had favored a merger of the Communist and Social Democratic parties. During the coup, he returned to a policy of cooperating with the Communists. Later he fled from Czechoslovakia, only to return in 1954 when he betrayed many who had participated in resistance actvities against the Communist regime.

36. Ripka, *ibid.*, p. 111.
37. Ripka, *ibid.*, p. 136.
38. According to General Wedemeyer's testimony at the *Inquiry into the Military Situation in the Far East*, p. 2329, the United States had only one division in Europe in 1948 and five understrength divisions in the United States, in addition to four divisions in the Far East. According to a statement by General Marshall, during the period of the Conference of Foreign Ministers in 1947, only one and one-third divisions in the United States were useful for transfer to combat abroad. (See Sparrow, *History of Personnel Demobilizaton in the United States Army*, Department of the Army, 1952, p. 282.) These were hardly effective military forces. They were quite unlikely to deter the Czechoslovak Communists.
39. Conversation with Zenkl. According to Pavel Korbel, a confidant of Benes, it is reliably reported that Steinhardt informed President Benes in late fall that Czechoslovakia could expect no American assistance in the event of an attempted Communist coup.
40. Ripka, *op. cit.*, pp. 138–39. The treaty was signed after the coup as the Czech democrats had specified. Ripka speculated that this was a response to American hints of trouble if the rebel Markos government in Greece were recognized. There is no evidence that the United States took so strong a stand or that a threat of this kind had any bearing on the terms of a satellite treaty. During discussions of the Yugoslav-Bulgarian treaty [February 10, 1948], which had a similar clause, Stalin referred to it as "Comsomolist" and as a "preventive war" course, and opposed it on those grounds, although the treaty specified action "linked with the United Nations." Dedijer, *Tito Speaks*, p. 329.
41. *New York Times*, November 2, 1947.
42. *New York Tmes*, November 23, 1947.
43. Ripka, *op. cit.*, p. 311.
44. *London Times*, November 29, 1947.
45. Or of Ripka, the Czech negotiator. *Christian Science Monitor*, December 17, 1947.
46. *New York Times*, December 2, 1947.
47. *London Times*, December 16, 1947.
48. *London Times*, December 16, 1947.
49. Ripka, *op. cit.*, p. 131. At the same time, the Soviet currency was deflated, rationing was ended amid great fanfare, and prices of foodstuffs and some

other goods were lowered. To fulfill the promises made to the Russians, it was necessary for the Soviet Union to step up its purchases of civilian goods. Therefore, the agreement seemed to meet internal Soviet needs that were serious and possibly of crisis proportion. See *World Dispatch,* December 23, 1947.

50. *World Dispatch,* December 23, 1947.
51. Ripka, *op. cit.,* p. 145.
52. Ripka, *op. cit.,* pp. 180–81.
53. The insane Dutchman who, unlike Dimitrov, received no assistance and was convicted of the fire plot that the Nazis themselves had staged.
54. Ripka, *ibid.,* p. 182. That meant a reduction of the Communist vote from 38 to 28 or 30 percent of the total vote. Also see the *Manchester Guardian,* April 29, 1948.
55. Ripka, *op. cit.,* p. 185.
56. i.e., of shop committees or work councils.
57. Ripka, *op. cit.,* p. 191.
58. Presumably from the Cominform and Moscow. If the decision had already been made, they would pay for blunders in carrying it out.
59. Ripka, *op. cit.,* p. 196.
60. Ripka, *ibid.,* p. 200. The formulation is peculiar. The information that the Soviet Union backed the move might have been used to intimidate the non-Communists, but why did the Communists need assurance? Was there a substantial bloc that opposed the move and had to be told that the plan was both indigenous in origin and supported in the highest Soviet Union party circles?
61. Ripka, *ibid.,* p. 215.
62. It may be questioned whether he was present to impress the Czechs with the interest of the Soviet Union in the transpiring events or whether he was also to make sure that the Czech Communist Party carried out its mission. On February 10, Zorin had attended the Moscow Conference in which Stalin had attempted to bring the Yugoslav and Bulgarian Communists into line.
63. Coincidentally, this was the same day Zorin arrived from Moscow.
64. Conversation with Zenkl.
65. Ripka, *op. cit.,* p 225.
66. Ripka, *ibid.,* p. 227.
67. Still published independently by the parties.
68. Ripka, *op. cit.,* p. 245.
69. Ripka, *ibid.,* p. 251.
70. Ripka, *ibid.,* p. 253.
71. Ripka, *ibid.,* p. 267.
72. Ripka, *ibid.,* p. 276.
73. Ripka, *ibid.,* p. 285.

74. *New York Times* (February 26, 1948). Benes said he "insist[ed] on parliamentary democracy and parliamentary government as it limited democracy." The presidium of the Communist Party said that the other parties got in touch with "hostile foreign circles" and had "aim[ed] at a *putsch.*"
75. Ripka, p. 293.
76. Particularly at a time when conditions were at last comparable to those of prewar. According to Slansky, wages (1939 = 100) were indexed at 397 in 1947 and prices at 286. *For a Lasting Peace; For a People's Democracy,* December 1947. Slansky's figures are subject to doubt, but that does not change the general picture.
77. For a distinct statement of this fear, see Zhdanov's statement to the Cominform conference, printed in *For a Lasting Peace; For a People's Democracy,* the newspaper of the Cominform, November 10, 1947.
78. Dedijer, *op. cit.,* p. 330. The conclusion, however, is mine rather than Dedijer's.
79. Dedijer, *op. cit.,* p. 306.
80. According to Douglas Hyde, *op. cit.,* Tito reported that Gottwald had got into trouble for advocating democratic methods of achieving Communism. However, Hyde's alleged source, Rust, is dead and, although Hyde seems to be an honest reporter, he lacks acuity. (Other evidence is not inconsistent, however.)
81. See *New York Times,* May 15, 1949.
82. The Soviet Union's five-year plan was designed to achieve prewar conditions by 1948. See Malenkov's statement in *For a Lasting Peace; For a People's Democracy,* December 1, 1947. The Soviet Union had nationalist economic objectives as well as nationalist strategic objectives. The satellites were being milked for the Soviet Union, particularly for the great Russians who, according to Malenkov, led all the rest.
83. *London Times,* January 10, 1948. The Polish plan was not put into outline form until late 1948, and it was not put into operation until 1950. It was a six-year plan. The other satellite powers also adopted plans emphasizing heavy industry in this period.
84. Arnost Heidrich, who was secretary-general of the Czechoslovak foreign office until he escaped just before Christmas 1948. *New York Times,* January 16, 1949.
85. Zhdanov particularly referred to the German problem and the Ruhr and the American effort to bring "under its sway the major sources of coal, iron, and steel." *For a Lasting Peace; For a People's Democracy,* December 10, 1947. James Byrnes felt the Russians would give up almost anything to get an accord on the Ruhr. Walter Millis, ed. *The Forrestal Diaries.* Viking Press, 1951, p. 347.
86. The Axis organization, Ethiopia, and the Manchurian incident were precipitating factors.

87. The Soviets feared that the Locarno Pact, which attempted to stabilize the situation in Western Europe, signified the end of their entente with Germany in Europe. The friendship pact with Germany and the statements of Gustav Stresemann, the German Chancellor, failed to reassure them.
88. 1927, 1937 and 1947 were all years in which purges were organized.
89. See *Forrestal Diaries*. See p. 15 for Clay "EYES ONLY" telegram on danger of war and p. 395 for CIA estimate of March 16 that war was not probable for next "sixty days."

CHAPTER VI

1. The State Department felt that the trusteeship recommendation might have been a little blunt for Korean feelings and contends that it did not publish the rest of the report in the White Paper on China because that report did not deal with Korea.
2. This Committee had been established in February 1946.
3. Testimony of Wedemeyer, *Hearings on the Military Situation in the Far East*, G.P.O., 1951, p. 2329.
4. *Far East Hearings*, p. 2009–10. Secretary of State Dean Acheson testified that he had not heard of this, and that he thought that heavy arms were not given because they were in short supply. The denial appears to have been a "diplomatic" one for the purpose of the hearings. Reports of South Korean threats against the North were frequently noted in the press in 1949 and obviously constituted a problem for the Department of State.
5. $212 million in the three years prior to January 1949.
6. This decision was made specifically with reference to Formosa. It was felt that Formosa could not be held by the Nationalists without military assistance that, at the time, the United States was unwilling to grant. However, it constitutes negative evidence that Korea was not part of a defensive perimeter, the weakening of which the United States was determined to prevent. *Far East Hearings*, p. 2371.
7. Aid would cease if a coalition government including one or more Communists were formed.
8. In Dulles' presence, Rhee told the assembly: "If we cannot protect democracy in the cold war, we shall win in a hot war."
9. This is inaccurate. The Department of State was informed by Ambassador Muccio that the South Korean Army had reported an invasion and that this had been "partly confirmed" by USMAG officers.
10. A skeleton draft of the resolution had been prepared by the Department of State well before the inception of hostilities.
11. The original United States draft called upon only the North Koreans to cease hostilities.

12. Secretary-General Trygve Lie had previously informed the Security Council: "The report received by me from the [UN] Commission [on Korea], as well as reports from other sources in Korea, makes it plain that military actions have been undertaken by Northern Korean forces. The present situation is a serious one and is a threat to international peace. I consider it the clear duty of the Security Council to take the steps necessary to re-establish peace in that area."

13. UNCOK was apparently a model of incompetence. South Korea had protested since May that invasion was imminent, but UNCOK chose to discount these protests. In a cable on May 29, UNCOK cited as proof of the defensive deployment of the South Korean forces their "dispos[ition] in depth." *Far East Hearings*, p. 231.

14. A Yugoslav plea that hope for negotiations should not be rejected after only two days of fighting was brushed aside.

15. JCS Communication to MacArthur on June 29 (I cannot reconcile dates, for this is obviously the Blair House decision of June 30 unless it was received in Korea on June 29) as paraphrased by Marshall.

    "... You will employ naval and air forces available to the Far East Command to provide fullest possible support for South Korean forces by attack on military targets so as to permit those forces to clear South Korea of North Korean forces.

    "Employment of Army forces will be limited to essential communications and other essential service units except that you are authorized to employ such Army combat and service forces as to insure the retention of a port and air base in the general area of Pusan-Chinhae.

    "By naval and air action you will defend Formosa against invasion or attack.

    "You are authorized to extend your operations in Northern Korea against air bases, depots, tanks, farms, troops, columns, and other purely military targets, if and when this becomes essential for the performance of your mission, as given in a preceding paragraph, or to avoid unnecessary casualties to our forces. Special care will be taken to insure that operations in North Korea stay well clear of the frontiers of Manchuria or the Soviet Union.

    "The decision to commit United States air and naval forces and limited Army forces to provide cover and support for South Korean troops does not constitute a decision to engage in war with the Soviet Union if Soviet forces intervene in Korea. Decision regarding Korea, however, is taken in full realization of the risk involved. If Soviet forces actively oppose our operations in Korea, your forces should defend themselves but should take no action to aggravate the situation, and you should report the situation to Washington."

16. The speech had gone to press before the withdrawal order.

17. It is possible, but unlikely, that a bomber would choose to fight with a group of fighter planes.

18. This transfer had been going on for two years preceding the outbreak of hostilities in Korea.

19. On October 1, Peiping Radio broadcast an ominous statement: "[The Chinese people would] not be afraid to fight aggression . . . [would not] stand aside should the imperialists wantonly invade the territory of their neighbor." On October 11, Moscow radio carried a Chinese government statement proclaiming that Peiping would "resolutely oppose the illegal extension of the war. . . . Now, when the Amercans, using large forces, are trying to cross the 38th parallel, the Chinese people cannot remain indifferent. . . ."

20. According to S. L. A. Marshall, *The River and the Gauntlet,* Eighth Army intelligence was apprehensive, and South Korean Defense Minister Sing Sung Mo opposed an advance to the Yalu for fear the Chinese would intervene.

21. See the debate on the evacuation of Korea pages 169–171 of this book. Both official Washington and General MacArthur were beginning to view the action as "hopeless" in this period.

22. In 1948, the Attlee government relinquished those provisons of the 1943 Quebec agreement giving it a veto on American use of the atomic bomb.

23. In a House of Commons debate on February 26, 1952, Prime Minister Churchill revealed that in May 1951, the Labour government had agreed that in the event of heavy air attacks from China upon United Nations forces in Korea, the United Kingdom would associate itself with action not confined to Korea. In November 1950, the use of "hot pursuit" against the Chinese returning to Manchuria was rejected after State Department consultation with America's associated states.

24. This was confirmed by General Vandenberg during the Far Eastern Hearings in 1951.

25. This statement led to a presidential directive on December 6 regarding the clearance of policy statements; the directive later figured in General MacArthur's dismissal.

26. This explanation is unlikely. The naval blockage had been approved regardless of whether the front was stabilized or evacuation became necessary. Other recommendations, as stated, were not dependent upon the military situation. It is quite possible that General MacArthur was right in believing that the Joint Chiefs had been overruled.

27. Official Washington believed at this time that United Nations forces would have to be evacuated from Korea. Under these circumstances, it would not have been deemed possible to negotiate with the victorious Communists. The United States, therefore, desired to commit the United Nations to a continuation of the struggle from a distance before the other delegations were aware of the scope of the commitment.

28. It is possible to infer that the administration took this position at the Far East Hearings to "head off" demands for attacks against Manchuria. If China took orders from the Soviet Union, a direct attack upon China would constitute an attack upon the Soviet Union. In the first place, it seems to me that this is a rather far-fetched interpretation of administration motivation. In the second place, there were simpler methods of asserting the danger of Soviet intervention if China were attacked. The Soviet Union, after all, regardless of whether or not it gave orders to China could not easily afford the defeat of the Chinese Communist regime. But, if it could afford the defeat of the regime, the Soviet Union would be unlikely to intervene even if it had given orders to China. After all, the administration assumed that the Soviet Union gave orders to North Korea. Yet the Soviet Union had not come to the aid of North Korea. Nor is there any reason to believe that the Soviet Union would have sacrificed any of its vital national interests for North Korea. If the Truman administration really employed such a strategic calculus in deciding to affirm that China took orders from the Soviet Union, it was even more incompetent than I care to believe. General MacArthur had already given the administration the perfect alternative by stating that China and the Soviet Union had parallel interests but that there was no evidence to prove that China took orders from the Soviet Union. Therefore, it was not even necessary for the administration to prove its anti-Communism by asserting that China took orders from the Soviet Union.

29. Hot pursuit technically involved the pursuit of ships violating national waters. Although pursuit of such ships could be continued in the open sea, it had to cease as soon as the ships entered the territorial waters of another nation. "Hot pursuit" of aircraft is an extension by analogy of traditional hot pursuit. But the analogy, even if considered legitimate, does not permit the extension of pursuit over the territory of another nation, for instance, Manchuria.

CHAPTER VII

1. In September 1949, a Defense Committee and five Regional Planning Groups were set up. The Northern European Group (Denmark, Norway, and the United Kingdom); the Western European Group (Belgium, France, Luxembourg, the Netherlands, and the United Kingdom—the Brussels powers); the Southern European-Western Mediterranean Group (France, Italy, and the United Kingdom); the Canadian-United States Group (Canada and the United States); and the North Atlantic Group (all members except Italy and Luxembourg). The United States had been requested to "participate actively in the defense planning, as appropriate," of all planning groups.

2. Approved by the Atlantic Council, ministerial level, in early January, 1950.

3. Secretary of State Acheson assured Congress, before NATO was approved, that the United States had made no commitments to send troops to Europe.
4. Approved by the Defense Committee of NATO on April 1, 1950.
5. Passed 361–1 by the House on July 19.
6. David K. E. Bruce, the American Ambassador to France, had informed Foreign Minister Schuman that the item would be raised at the NATO meetings in New York when he called on Schuman the night of September 4, 1950.
7. Thus, American pressure on the French was anything but subtle.
8. However, French commitments to Indochina and British commitments to Southeast Asia were often overlooked by American lawmakers.

CHAPTER VIII

1. John Kaplan of the Hudson Institute has suggested that this might be accomplished by eliminating tax credits for entirely owned foreign subsidiaries of United States corporations doing business in under-developed countries. Although this might possibly have too extensive an effect, it might well be investigated. American business ought to consider such arrangements voluntarily, as well as those in which their interests could be liquidated after a fixed period of years. Business may be deterred from such arrangements more by ideological than economic considerations.
2. When and if the modernizing elites of some of these countries discover that the attempts to modernize must fail, there may be far-reaching consequences. They may lapse into sloth and corruption. Or, in desperation, they may resort to the most radical of measures.
3. This is an exceptionally serious problem for which no clear solutions are in sight. Few ruling groups are sufficiently disinterested to reform themselves out of power, particularly if the reforms are not guaranteed to be workable. Perhaps some of these groups should be bought out or ways discovered to force others to get out or to cooperate.
4. The British were undoubtedly concerned to protect their oil interests. But the present situation is quite unstable. Too much of the Middle East is impoverished, and there are too many small oil oases disposing of immense riches. Eventually, this situation will change, and the change may be preferable if anticipated and encouraged than if opposed.
5. Unfortunately, until recently, the United States did little to support modernizing democracies, particularly when important economic interests objected to their policies. Venezuela under Betancourt was, until recently, an unfortunate example of this national myopia.
6. The strategy of using limited strategic nuclear strikes against the Communist bloc probably will be accepted in the heat of war—if there is a war. It seems unlikely to gain sufficient acceptance in time of peace, although

it would be most effective in war if adopted during peace. Thus, although the strategy has much to recommend it, discussions are likely to be confined to esoteric circles.

7. Demonstrations to the contrary do not fully take into account the massing of manpower and armor at the point of the thrust, disruption after the thrust, the response of civilians fleeing the enemy, the ability or lack of ability of defending forces to control these civilians forcibly, fifth-column activities, other political factors, and the character of the threat and promise tactics of the attacking force.

8. There are also vociferous groups opposed to American bases in England. But even larger segments of the public and leadership understand that the bases constitute a commitment that deters rather than provokes the Russians. Moreover, there is a history of alliance with the United States and some willingness to run joint risks. This is absent in Japan.

INDEX